UNDERSTANDING STATISTICS

UNDERSTANDING STATISTICS

An Introduction
for the Social Sciences

Daniel B. Wright

SAGE Publications
London • Thousand Oaks • New Delhi

© Daniel B. Wright 1997

First published 1997

All rights reserved. No part of this publication may be reproduced, stored in a retrieval system, transmitted or utilized in any form or by any means, electronic, mechanical, photocopying, recording or otherwise, without permission in writing from the Publishers.

SAGE Publications Ltd
6 Bonhill Street
London EC2A 4PU

SAGE Publications Inc
2455 Teller Road
Thousand Oaks, California 91320

SAGE Publications India Pvt Ltd
32, M-Block Market
Greater Kailash – I
New Delhi 110 048

British Library Cataloguing in Publication data

A catalogue record for this book is
available from the British Library

ISBN 0 8039 7917 7
ISBN 0 8039 7918 5 (pbk)

Library of Congress record available

Typeset in Great Britain by Alden, Oxford, Didcot and Northampton
Printed in Great Britain by The Cromwell Press Ltd,
Broughton Gifford, Melksham, Wiltshire

Contents

Acknowledgements

Many people helped to prepare this book. First, several people proofread parts, or all of it, and provided useful comments. These include (in alphabetical order) Karl Ashworth, Julie Dockrell, Andy Field, Rachel George, Paul Jackson, Martin Le Voi, Colin Mills and Soni Wright. It was also helped by teaching and talking statistics with several people over the last eight years at the London School of Economics and the City University. There are too many people to mention, but I would like to single out Colm O'Muircheartaigh who was the best at making students like statistics.

This book has also benefited throughout its production from contacts with Sage, and in particular Ziyad Marar, who besides helping out with every stage of this book, has improved my squash game. Thanks also to Richard Leigh and Rosemary Campbell for producing this final version that you see.

I use SPSS throughout this book because I feel that it is overall the best statistical package. Their support is also very good. SPSS is a registered trademark of SPSS Inc. SPSS is head-quartered at 444 North Michigan Avenue, Chicago, Illinois 60611, USA. Alternatively, you can look at SPSS web pages (http://www.spss.com) for lots of interesting details and information. I also used SYSTAT for making some of the tables. SYSTAT is owned by SPSS and can be contacted at the above address.

I would also like to thank the British Academy for awarding a fellowship to examine methodological issues across the social and behavioural sciences. This allowed me to complete this manuscript not too long past the agreed date on the contract.

Finally, enormous thanks to Rachel.

1
Statistics in Social Science Research

The aim of social science research is to understand the way in which people think and behave. In order for this to be done, information, what we call *data*, is gathered. Statistical procedures play an integral part in determining what, if any, patterns there are in the data and if the data support or discredit whichever theories are under investigation. I will use the words *science* and *scientists* throughout this book so it is important that I make clear what is meant by them. Scientists are interested in understanding and explaining various aspects of the world and use what is called the scientific approach. This approach involves *measuring* specific aspects of a situation.

The phrase *social science* covers a large range of disciplines: psychology, sociology, politics, anthropology, economics, education and others. The use of statistics varies in some ways among these. While this book offers a general introduction for all the social sciences, further specific techniques may be necessary for students to become statistically proficient in their own discipline.

As students you will use statistics for interpreting the data you collect on your own research projects, and you will also use statistics for understanding other people's research. Many chapters and articles that you will read as part of your other courses will have lengthy sections reporting the results of research. The length allocated to these sections reflects their importance in understanding the research. Unfortunately these sections are written in a dialect of English – *Statisticalese* – which can make them incomprehensible to those unfamiliar with the jargon. This book introduces you to this language and advises you on why and when you will need it. As with learning any language, it is vital that you learn the basics. After that, particular nuances can be 'picked up' with ease.

This first chapter contains by far the most important information: why statistics is used. Many new terms are introduced that are brought up throughout the rest of the book. Therefore it is essential that you understand this chapter. Before getting into the core of the chapter it is worth introducing you to two key terms: *probability* and *variable*. Chapter 2 describes in more detail the exact meaning of probability, but a few words are necessary here. Probability is the branch of mathematics that describes how likely an event is. If we toss a fair coin, the probability that it will come up heads is 0.50 or 50%. This means that we would expect if we tossed the coin 100 times that about 50 times it would come up heads and about 50 times it would come up tails. It is doubtful that it would come up heads *exactly* 50 times, but the number of heads should be close to 50. Probability values can range from 0, which means the event cannot happen, to 1, which means the event is certain to happen.

When a researcher asks people a question, such as their attitudes on capital punishment, this produces a set of responses. If 1000 people were asked about their attitudes then there would be a set of 1000 responses for this question. This set of responses is called a *variable*. Each of the responses corresponds to a particular *value*. As a group, the variables are referred to as the *data*.[1] These are very brief definitions; each will be described in more detail later.

Conducting Scientific Research

Properly conducted research usually follows a number of steps to ensure that the data gathered are adequate for the purposes of the research. The purpose is to answer some question(s) about the world. The following eight basic steps are introduced. It is important to stress, however, that these steps are overlapping; aspects of each will be in the back of your mind when making decisions at the other steps. Similar steps will appear in most introductory methodology textbooks.

1 *Literature searches*. These are conducted to find out if someone has already answered the research questions in which you are interested and to crystallise your views on the topic. They are greatly eased by the use of modern information technologies.
2 *The critical situation devised*. If the question has not been answered, you try to envisage a situation that will answer it. This is the step that requires the most ingenuity.
3 *Designing the study*. Once the situation has been devised, the technical details of how to run the study must be designed. If done well, the remaining stages should run smoothly. In order to produce a well-designed study, it is necessary to consider aspects of all the preceding and subsequent stages. This involves using some statistical knowledge in combination with common sense and experience. It is often helpful to use methodologies from previously reported research on similar topics as a guide for designing your particular study (do not reinvent the wheel!).
4 *Pilot study*. This is a dress rehearsal for the main study. Pilot studies use a small number of people (the people used are usually called *subjects*, *participants*, or *respondents*) and allow the researcher to see, for example, if the instructions given to the people are understood and to make sure all aspects of the procedure work as intended. If problems occur the researcher returns to step 3, and redesigns whichever aspects of the study are troublesome.
5 *Conducting the research*. Once all the hitches have been resolved (as far as possible), the main study can be conducted. This is where, after much work in steps 1–4, the performance begins. Often this step is difficult because problems that were not discovered in the pilot study may surface, but it is important to keep motivated.

---

1   'Data' is the plural; a datum is an individual piece of data. The word 'datum' is seldom used.

6 *Entering the data.* This step is the most boring, but it is still important. This is where the values for all the variables, the data, are organised in such a way that the appropriate questions can be asked. These days, this means they are entered into a computer (remember to save the data often to prevent electronic catastrophes). It is important to think about the data, and the statistical tests that you will conduct, before entering the data. Certain techniques will require that the data are entered in specific ways. The last thing you want to do is to enter the data twice!

7 *Statistical analysis and interpretation.* This involves estimating various characteristics about the data and determining if they are consistent with your research questions. The way scientific questions are answered is not always straightforward. You have to interpret what your results say about your original questions, and what they mean for the field as a whole. This is the focus of this book, although aspects of the other stages are mentioned.

8 *Presenting findings.* Your findings have to be presented to others in an easily understood way. This can be a difficult task because writing up statistical results is a different form of communication than most social science students are used to. Throughout this book I stress the importance of graphs and how to describe statistical relationships.

I described these as eight steps but all are interrelated in various ways and at each step a researcher may have to return to an earlier step and repeat the sequence. With particular reference to statistics, at each step of the research you should consider which statistical procedures you will use. Too often students and professionals reach step 7 (the statistical analysis and interpretation) without considering what statistics they can use to investigate their research questions. Often this means all the work done in steps 1–6 is worthless.

Levels of Measurement

The choice of which statistical test to use often depends on what is called the *level of measurement* of the data. This is a lively topic in applied statistics. Stevens (1946; 1951) argued that there are four main levels of measurement – nominal, ordinal, interval and ratio – and that certain statistical tests were only appropriate for certain levels of data.

Nominal data, or what are sometimes called categorical data, are the simplest type. Consider the following question:

If there were a general election tomorrow, for which party would you vote?	__ Conservative
	__ Labour
	__ Liberal Democrat
	__ Another party / person
	__ I would not vote
	__ Do not know / Will not say

Box 1.1   Computers and Statistics

The modern computer has revolutionised statistics. Gone are the days of performing hundreds of calculations by hand and hoping that each individual calculation was done accurately. It takes little or no statistical knowledge to get the computer to run even very complicated procedures. To make the computer run the correct procedure and to be able to understand the computer's output does, however, require statistical knowledge.

The ease with which computers can produce statistics is also their major drawback. Researchers often run complicated statistics (because computers require only simple commands) and do not explore their data with simpler techniques first. Nowadays, almost all of the main computer packages have good graphics procedures. These should be used to facilitate the exploration of the data. A simple rule in using the computer is always to start off with the simplest procedures and if necessary build up to more complex ones.

There are several different statistics programs on the market. The most common of these within academia for social scientists is SPSS (Statistical Package for the Social Sciences). It has evolved through several versions and is an excellent tool that covers almost all the procedures a social scientist would need. I will describe examples using it throughout the book. Other, what I call 'all-encompassing', packages include SAS, BMDP, MINITAB and SYSTAT. SAS and BMDP are often used after one has already learned another program. This does not necessarily mean that they are more complicated; it is just how they are used. Outside of academia, SAS in particular is often used because it has good data transformation procedures. MINITAB and SYSTAT, like SPSS, are often taught as the first statistics program.

Most of these packages have both Windows and DOS implementations (some also have Macintosh and mainframe varieties). These are the basic operating systems for common computers. If you are going to be using a computer with this course (which I strongly recommend), and if you do not already know the type of computer you will use, you will soon find out. The DOS and the mainframe versions are arguably more difficult to learn, and of these the DOS version is more likely to be used. Therefore I will describe using SPSS within its DOS version. The appropriate Windows icons and menu-driven commands are similar to the DOS code and if you learn the DOS code your knowledge will easily transfer to these.

Throughout this book I refrain from going into minute detail on the exact syntax required to run the computer programs. This is because the syntax changes as new implementations come out. If your instructor, or a book specific to the program you are using, gives a slightly different syntax, use it.

In this question there are six different options: six different possible values. A person can choose one, and only one, of these options. If comparing the responses of two people to this question, we can only say whether their responses are the same or different.

When coding responses to questions like the one above, it is usually easier, and some statistical programs require you, to put numerical values in to stand for the different options. Here, a researcher might give the code 1 to people who said they would vote for the Conservatives, 2 for Labour, and so on until 6 for the Don't know/Won't say option. The fundamental aspect of nominal data is that this coding is completely arbitrary. It will make no difference if you recode the values so that Conservative gets the value 23 and Labour gets the value −32. The values are just names, hence the description 'nominal level' (nominal literally means 'existing in name only'). You simply need to make sure that each response has one and only one code.

The *ordinal level* of measurement allows the researcher to place the response options in order as well as to name them. Most attitude scales produce ordinal data. Suppose a group of people were asked to rate how pleased they were with their life, using the following scale:

$$1 \quad 2 \quad 3 \quad 4 \quad 5 \quad 6 \quad 7$$
very unhappy   very happy

The researcher would probably code the responses according to the values shown in the scale. There is a clear ordering of the responses: if someone responds with a 7, s/he is expressing more satisfaction than if s/he responds with a 3. The statistical tests designed for ordinal data use the fact that these values are ordered.

Most of the statistics used in the social sciences are designed for *interval level* data. Besides being able to assign values to the responses and to order them, interval data tell you about the distance between pairs of points. Thus the distance between 3 and 4 is exactly the same as the distance between 4 and 5, and between 5 and 6, etc. Researchers often treat the data that are produced from attitude questions, like the one above, as interval data. Several people have pointed out that this is questionable in most circumstances, but researchers continue to use statistical tests designed for interval data. This is where the controversy among both statisticians and social scientists exists. I discuss my view, which is a 'middle of the road' view, later in this section.

The final level of measurement is the *ratio level*. While interval data allow the researcher to describe the distance between pairs of responses, ratio data allow the researcher to say one score is twice the value of another. For a variable to have ratio level data, there must be in some sense an absolute zero. An example of a variable with an absolute zero is length. An object may be zero centimetres long – that is, have no length – but it cannot have negative length. There are not as many statistical tests that are designed explicitly for ratio level data. The distinction between interval and ratio data often confuses students because each allow the researcher to quantify the relationship between the variable and some theoretical construct.

As an example, consider the data in Table 1.1. If these data are nominal, all we can say is that subjects 4 and 8, 2 and 10, and 6 and 9 are the same on this measure. If the data are ordinal we can say the lowest score is for subject 1 and the highest is for subject 5, and we can order all the remaining subjects (with some ties) between these two. We cannot say how much higher any subject's score is than another's, we can only say whether it is higher, or lower, or the same. If the data are interval we can say how much higher a subject's score is. Subject 1's score (1) is two units lower than subject 2's score (3) and this is the same difference as between subject 2's score and subject 3's score (5). If the data form a ratio scale, we can say that subject 4's score is twice as much as subject 1's (2 is twice the size of 1).

Most of the discussion about measurement level concerns differentiating between interval and ordinal data. Consider the following scale, which is typical of many attitude scales:

1	2	3	4	5
agree strongly	agree	neither agree nor disagree	disagree	disagree strongly

Most social science researchers would treat this as an interval scale. This means that they are assuming that the difference between answering 'agree strongly' and 'agree' is of the same size as between answering 'agree' and 'neither agree nor disagree'. If you are willing to assume that the differences between each of these responses are of equal distance, then you can treat the scale as interval. When pressed, most researchers will admit that the scale is probably only ordinal, that people answering with the higher-numbered responses are more opposed than those answering with the lower-numbered responses, but that the scale does not tell them how much more.

There are three reasons why researchers often do this. The first is not a good reason: interval tests are better known than ordinal tests. Ignorance does not,

Table 1.1 *Interpreting data for different levels of measurement*

Subject number	Value for a variable
1	1
2	3
3	5
4	2
5	12
6	4
7	6
8	2
9	4
10	3

however, justify their use. The second reason is that it often does not make a large difference which is used. This is a better reason, although in these cases it is probably best to try several techniques and make sure they lead to the same conclusions. The final reason is that some research questions actually stipulate some notion of distance in their theorising and often the equal spacing assumption of the interval level. However, in some cases interval techniques are improperly used. The severity of this depends greatly on the specific situation. Throughout this book I describe some techniques for dealing with ordinal data.

Distinguishing ordinal from nominal data is usually fairly easy. If you can mix up the order of the values without changing their meaning, then you have nominal data. Thus, in the example above, which asked about voting preference, the order of the values is not critical. Therefore voting preference is a nominal variable. If we consider the responses to the attitude question above, mixing up the order of the values would make a difference: 1 ('strongly agree') is nearer to 2 ('agree') than it is to 4 ('disagree').

The decision about which level of data you are working with is a difficult one and ultimately depends on how you, the researcher, view the scale. Given the same data, experienced researchers will often disagree on which level of measurement is appropriate. This subjectivity can be easily abused, but it should remain. So long as researchers can defend their decisions then they have probably made a good decision.

Sampling

One of the fundamental aspects of statistics is that information about an entire population can be inferred from data collected from a small subset of the population. This subset is called a *sample*. When you think about it, the idea that a sample of a few hundred people can be used to make statements about a population of millions is really quite startling. In order for this inference to be done well, the quality of the sampling procedures is vital.

When you investigate a research question, you have in mind a population for which your results should hold. It is often all humans or all inhabitants of a country, but sometimes the population is smaller, like all children with Down's syndrome or all multinational companies headquartered in Brussels. Normally it is not possible to contact all the members of the entire population of interest. The researcher must choose a target population from which to sample. For example, if using a telephone survey to measure people's attitudes, those without telephones will not be able to take part. With the percentage of households with telephones being quite large in many countries, the difference between the target population and the population, for this case, is fairly small. However, in some areas of the world the difference is much larger and using a telephone sample will be problematic.

In many studies the difference between the target population and the population that the researchers feel their findings should generalise to is much larger. A common example is where the researcher is testing a hypothesis that should operate in a similar manner for all humans (like some 'basic' memory process) but the target population is only second-year students from one particular university. The importance of the difference between the target population and population depends on the specific problem. I discuss this in more detail later in this chapter when contrasting experimental and non-experimental approaches.

Once a target population has been determined the researchers have to decide how to sample a subset. Sometimes they can choose all the people in the target population. This is called a *census* and occurs most often when the target population is very specific, like the students in a second-year methodology class. The more famous censuses are of entire countries. These occur about every ten years in the countries that have them and involve trying to gather information about everyone in the country. While not completely successful (see Wolter, 1991), they do gather information about most people.

Box 1.2   Qualitative and Quantitative Data

The phrase 'qualitative data' has become popular in the social sciences, but what it means is not clear. In his book, *Analyzing qualitative/categorical data*, Goodman (1978) defined 'qualitative data' as nominal and ordinal data. The subtitle of his book, *Log-linear models and latent-structure analysis*, made it clear he was describing complex statistical procedures for particular levels of data. From this perspective, the complement of qualitative data are data in which something can be said about the distance between points. These are often called quantitative data. Interval and ratio data are types of quantitative data. Nominal and ordinal data are qualitative.

Within some social science circles the phrase 'qualitative data' has a very different meaning. For many researchers, qualitative data come from some newspapers, in-depth interviews, political posters, television advertisements, etc. I prefer to call the way in which data are extracted from these sources as *content analysis*. In content analysis the researcher must devise some way to measure the appropriate attributes in order to evaluate her/his research questions. In some cases this is simply counting the use of particular words, objects or themes; in other cases it is comparing the overall structure of text using various complex procedures. The goal is to measure some aspect of the text (or picture or dialogue) thereby preparing it for statistical analysis. The resulting measurements can be any level of measurement. Therefore content analysis does not rely exclusively on any particular type of statistics. Because of the different definitions of qualitative data, I will avoid using this phrase.

In most cases a subset of the target population, a sample, has to be drawn. The researcher has to consider how to do this. There are two broad types of sample: *probability* and *non-probability*. In a probability sample each member of the target population has a chance, or a probability, of being sampled. There are several ways to do this. The best known of these is a *simple random sample* (SRS) and all the statistics presented in this book assumes that this is the sampling method used. In an SRS all members of the target population have an equal chance of being sampled. If there are 1000 people in the target population and you are sampling 100 people, each person would have a one in ten chance of being chosen. With an SRS, every possible sample has an equal probability of being chosen. In practice, SRS samples are usually only used with small target populations.

The best-known form of SRS is the lotteries. Each week in the United Kingdom, six balls are randomly chosen from a set of 49 in order to increase the wealth differential. Any possible sample of six balls is as likely as any other. The combination 9, 14, 23, 36, 42, 47 has the same chance as 1, 2, 3, 4, 5, 6. The first *looks* more random, but each is equally likely to occur from random sampling. It looks more random because it is more representative of a large set of possible samples with numbers scattered around. The reason why we doubt the randomness of the second is that a sample with six numbers in a row is highly unlikely to occur. The reason why sampling works is that not only do we know that unrepresentative samples are rare, but we can calculate exactly how rare they are. In a more typical social science application, we know an SRS could result in everyone in the sample being named Michael, but we know this is *very unlikely*.

Another type of probability sample is called a *cluster sample*. This is useful when the target population is dispersed throughout a large geographic region. In a typical face-to-face national survey the researcher first samples geographic areas or clusters. Within these clusters individuals are sampled. This is much more economical because interviewers can go to a relatively small area and interview several people rather than having to travel long distances for a single interview. Cluster samples also often occur when doing research on schools and students. Some schools are sampled and then within these students are chosen. Figure 1.1 illustrates a two-stage cluster sample for schools. First schools are sampled and then, within the chosen schools, pupils are sampled.

With probability samples, each member of the target population has a non-zero probability of being chosen. In complex survey designs, it is because we can estimate these probabilities that various statistics can be calculated. Complex sample design is well beyond the scope of this book and will not come into play in any of our examples. It is worth saying, however, that as the sampling method moves away from a simple random sample, the statistical techniques become less precise.

With probability samples researchers will have the name or address or telephone number of the person or company they are trying to contact. Some people, for a variety of reasons, either cannot be contacted or do not wish to take

Stage 1   Stage 2

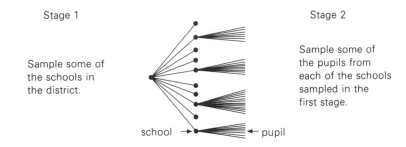

Sample some of   Sample some of
the schools in   the pupils from
the district.   each of the schools
                                                 sampled in the
                                                 first stage.

school →•◄═══◄ pupil

Figure 1.1   *A two-stage cluster sample of schools and pupils*

part. This allows researchers to calculate the percentage of non-responses. In most small research projects it is assumed that the people who do not respond are going to be similar to those who do respond. In large projects (such as those with thousands of people) researchers often try to deduce what the non-respondents are like. How this is done can become quite complex. The important methodological point is to try to have as few non-respondents as possible. This can be done by offering money to people if they participate, writing reminder letters and being friendly (and a bit aggressive) when talking to prospective participants. These issues are covered in detail in most introductory methodology books.

The second broad type of sampling is called non-probability sampling. One specific type is called the *quota sample*. This is where the interviewers or researchers choose the sample in such a way that there are specific percentages of various groups. They might be interested in comparing men and women and therefore they would want to ensure that they have approximately equal numbers of men and women in their sample. The problem with quota samples is that the choice of respondents can be biased because some people are more likely to be chosen by the interviewer. If you do not want to be chosen in a quota sample simply walk around town with your trusted Rottweiler. Quota samples are very common because they are less expensive than most probability samples.

Often it is difficult to get a list of the target population. If you were doing research, for example, on male prostitutes there is no list from which you could systematically sample. A technique that is sometimes used in these cases is called *snowball sampling*. The researcher finds one person, gathers information from that person, and then asks her/him for the names of other people s/he knows who fit into the population. There are problems with this technique – the entire sample depends on the first person interviewed, and the probability of choosing other individuals greatly depends on their social networks – but in many circumstances it is the only viable option. It is most useful when doing a small number of detailed interviews aimed at exploring issues, rather than when either testing specific hypotheses or trying to estimate population values.

The final technique produces a *convenience sample*. This means that the people chosen are the most convenient for you. This is the most common sample in psychology and I like the way the phrase sounds. There is no pretence that any systematic sampling device was used. In many cases a convenience sample is all that is necessary and, by admitting this, you make it clear to the reader that you feel a systematic sampling procedure was not needed. I describe shortly why some research works well with convenience samples.

Box 1.3   The Sampling Procedure and the Sample

The point of a good sampling procedure is to obtain a sample that is *representative* of the population. In other words, you want the characteristics of your sample to be approximately the same as the population. By definition, with a simple random sample (SRS) every possible sample has the same probability of being chosen. Thus, an SRS of all of Great Britain might produce a sample of people all with the same name. This is obviously not very representative of the population but it is a possibility. The important point, from a purely statistical standpoint, is what procedure was used to produce the sample and not what the eventual sample is. This seems odd, but it is so because we know how unlikely it is to have an SRS produce such an unrepresentative sample.

From a less statistical and more pragmatic standpoint, if you get a sample that is extremely odd, you should make sure that there is not something odd with the sampling procedure. The probability of getting extremely unrepresentative samples is very small and often occurs because of bad sampling procedures, not statistical flukes. Further, even if a good sampling procedure was used, it will be difficult to convince people that the procedure used was proper if the sample is bizarre. Imagine lottery organisers trying to explain why the set 1, 2, 3, 4, 5, 6 was chosen two weeks in a row, even though this is as likely as getting 2, 4, 16, 32, 47, 48 one week and then 14, 22, 31, 34, 38, 45 the next.

Measures of Central Tendency: the Three Ms

When most social science researchers look at a variable they are usually interested in the *central tendency*, that is to say, in the location of most people or the typical person on that scale. There are three main measures of central tendency: the *mean*, the *median* and the *mode* (the three Ms). The mean is what most people call the average and is by far the most common. A great deal of this book concentrates on the mean.

We denote the mean of a variable (remember, a variable is a set of responses) for a sample by putting a bar above the symbol used to describe the variable. Variables are usually denoted with a letter like x (this is discussed in detail in the next section). Thus, the mean of the variable x for the sample is $\bar{x}$. Providing we use good sampling procedures, this is our best guess (or inference) for the mean in the target population. We assume that this is approximately the same as the value for the population. The population values, which are what we try to estimate but seldom know, are denoted using lower-case Greek letters. I have no idea why they are denoted in this way, but it is useful to distinguish them from sample values, so I see no reason to break with tradition. The letter used for the population mean is the Greek letter μ (lower-case mu). To find the sample mean we use the following equation:

$$\bar{x} = \frac{\sum x_i}{n}$$

where the Greek letter Σ (capital sigma) means the sum of all the values and n is the number of people in the sample. The subscript i on the x is used to denote each individual response. If there are five individuals, i will range from 1 to 5 and the score for the third person will be x_3.[2] Suppose we asked five people to complete a jigsaw puzzle and measured how long it took. The times, in minutes, are listed below.

$$23,\ 14,\ 32,\ 9,\ 27$$

To find the mean we add these five numbers together and divide by five:

$$\bar{x} = \frac{\sum x_i}{n} = \frac{23 + 14 + 32 + 9 + 27}{5} = \frac{105}{5} = 21$$

Thus, our best guess or estimate for the mean time in the population is 21.

In many cases the mean is not the most appropriate statistic of central tendency. Often you are interested in the typical person. In these cases you use the median or the middle value. To find the median you have to arrange the data in order (ascending or descending) and then take the middle value. The median of the jigsaw puzzle times is 23 minutes because there are two values above it and two values below it. In this case the median and mean are about the same, but in many cases they are not.

As an example, suppose we were interested in individuals' income in the USA and drew a sample of five people. We might get something like this for a sample of five individuals' incomes (in thousands of dollars):

$$12,\ 18,\ 123,\ 6,\ 11$$

2   Sometimes the equation is written as

$$\bar{x} = \frac{\sum_{i=1}^{n} x_i}{n}$$

where the summation reads 'sum from $i = 1$ to n', meaning all the values from 1 to the total number should be summated. I do not use this notation in this book as all the summations used involve summing over all the values.

The mean of these numbers is 34, but clearly this is not the typical income. This value occurs because of one very high income of $123,000. To find the median we rewrite these numbers in ascending order:

6, 11, 12, 18, 123

and choose the middle number, 12, which in many ways describes the central tendency better. The median is good when there are a few very high or very low numbers. The mean is greatly affected by these *outliers*, but the median is not. The median would not change if the individual making $123,000 was instead making $1,000,000. The mean, however, would increase to more than $200,000.

If there is an even number of cases then the median is the midpoint of the two 'middle' values. Thus if our income data were

6, 11, 12, 14, 18, 123

the median would be 13 (the midpoint of 12 and 14).

The final measure of central tendency is the *mode*. It is the most common value. If we asked a sample of people what their occupations were, the mode would be the most frequent answer. When you have nominal data, like job occupation, only the mode makes sense. When the data are ordinal the mode and the median each make sense. When the data are interval all three of the measures can be used.

All statistics packages, including SPSS, have some way of calculating these three statistics. In the example below, 105 British people, 40 years old or more, were asked their age when they left full-time education. In SPSS (there is a brief introduction to SPSS in Box 1.5) we first tell the computer which procedure is to be used.[3] In this case it is the FREQUENCY procedure. You need to tell the computer which variable(s) you want investigated. In this case it is called left which stands for the age of the person on leaving full-time education. The /STATISTICS part of the command tells the computer that you want it to tell you the mean, median and mode of the variable.

I have also included the command /BARCHART which tells the computer to make a barchart. A *barchart* shows the number of times each of the options was chosen. It can be used with any kind of data, but can become very long when there are many options. *Histograms*, shown in the next example, are better when there are many options and could also have been used here.

From the table (in the 'Percent' column) we see that 36.4% of the people left education when they were 14. This is more than any other value and therefore is the mode. Looking at the barchart, this value has the longest bar. The mean is 15.5 and the median is 15.

---

3 When I print computer output, I have changed the font (the style of the lettering) so that all the columns remain lined up. This is important to do when you are printing output. I have placed the commands in bold and the SPSS keywords in capitals. Also, in most cases throughout this book, only partial output is printed. Finally, I add comments about the output to the right.

FREQUENCY /VARIABLES left /STATISTICS MEAN MEDIAN MODE
   /BARCHART .

LEFT   Age left full education

Value	Frequency	Percent	Valid Percent	Cum Percent
13	1	1.0	1.0	1.0
14	38	36.4	36.4	37.3
15	34	32.5	32.5	69.9
16	14	12.9	12.9	82.8
17	5	4.8	4.8	87.6
18	4	3.8	3.8	91.4
19	1	1.0	1.0	92.3
20	3	2.4	2.4	94.7
21	4	3.3	3.3	98.1
24	1	1.0	1.0	99.0
29	1	1.0	1.0	100.0
TOTAL	105	100.0	100.0	

Cum percentage is the total percentage up to that value. Thus, the 82.8 for 16 means 83% left by the time they were 16.

LEFT   Age left full education

```
13 ■ 1
14 ████████████████████████ 38
15 ██████████████████ 34
16 ████████ 14
17 ███ 5
18 ██ 4
19 ■ 1
20 ██ 3
21 ██ 4
24 ■ 1
29 ■ 1
I
I  ........I........I........I........I........I
0        8       16       24       32       40
Mean  15.536  Median  15.000  Mode  14.000
```

Another concept that arises in statistics is a variable's *distribution*.[4] The main difference between the barchart above and a distribution (or histogram) is that when a distribution is drawn the spacing on the axes is equal. In the above graph, the ages go from 20 to 21 to 24 and then to 29. For the distribution, the spacing is equal. There would have been spaces for 22, 23, 25, 26, 27 and 28. Examples of distributions are shown throughout the remainder of this book.

Sometimes a variable's distribution is *skewed*. The concept of skewness is probably best explained through an example of a skewed distribution. A

4   In some statistics courses this is referred to as the variable's density function. However, in most social statistics it is called the distribution and this sounds less intimidating.

histogram shows how many occurrences there are for each band of values. It differs from a barchart, in which each value has a bar. Below is the histogram of the population of states of the USA (including the District of Columbia). This example comes from a data set on the US states (see Appendix A) from which examples will be taken throughout this book. In this case the mean is about 4.9 million people and the median is about 3.3 million. When the mean is much larger than the median this indicates that the distribution is positively skewed. Visually, the positive tail of distribution – its end on either the bottom or right, depending on how it is drawn – is stretched out. Here this is due to a couple of populous states. I have listed the names of these on the graph. SPSS does not do this but the words can be typed in afterwards. We will talk more about skewness later in the book.

```
FREQUENCIES /VARIABLES POPULA /HISTOGRAM /STATISTICS MEAN
MEDIAN.
```

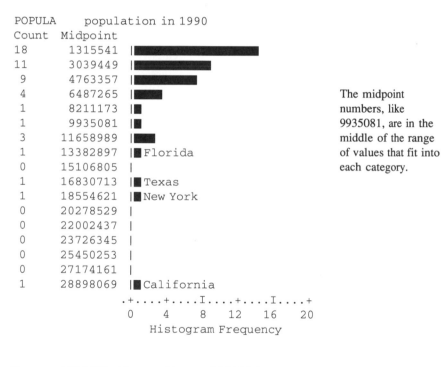

POPULA   population in 1990

Count	Midpoint		
18	1315541	████████████	
11	3039449	█████████	
9	4763357	███████	
4	6487265	██	The midpoint
1	8211173	█	numbers, like
1	9935081	█	9935081, are in the
3	11658989	██	middle of the range
1	13382897	█ Florida	of values that fit into
0	15106805		each category.
1	16830713	█ Texas	
1	18554621	█ New York	
0	20278529		
0	22002437		
0	23726345		
0	25450253		
0	27174161		
1	28898069	█ California	

```
          .+....+....I....+....I....+
          0    4    8   12   16   20
             Histogram Frequency
```

Mean   4876664.18   Median   3294394.00

In Figure 1.2 a positively skewed distribution, a symmetrical or non-skewed distribution and a negatively skewed distribution are shown. In the first the mean is larger than the median, in the second they are about the same and in the third the mean is smaller than the median. Unlike the output from the SPSS example, these distributions have been drawn as smooth lines. They are mathematical distributions.

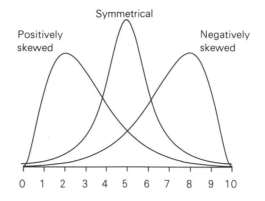

Figure 1.2   *A positively skewed, a symmetrical and a negatively skewed distribution*

Constants, Variables and Equations

There are two types of number in which social scientists are interested: constants and variables. Constants, which are sometimes called *parameters*, are what we try to estimate. In many cases we are interested in testing whether a constant is equal to zero. A typical example in psychology would be if we wanted to see if giving a group of ten depressed people a certain drug made them less depressed. A researcher might give the subjects a standard test of depression, give them the drug treatment, and then retest them with the same test (see Table 1.2). There are some problems with this design, which are discussed in the next section, but it will suffice for the present purposes. The scores from most tests of this sort are treated as interval data. The statistical technique that would usually be used is called a *paired t test* (discussed in Chapter 3) and these days it is usually run on a computer. In a paired *t* test the score on the second test is subtracted from the score on the first test for each subject.

Most researchers would be interested in whether the drug treatment made an appreciable difference or whether the two sets of scores were approximately the same. To see if the treatment made a difference, the researcher would statistically test the hypothesis that the difference is equal to zero (this is called the *null* hypothesis). We would not expect the drug to have the same effect on everybody. We would expect some people's scores to go up and other people's scores to go down. The purpose of this research would be to see if the average effect was beneficial. The statistical procedures discussed throughout this book

Table 1.2   *Subjects' depression scores before and after drug treatment.*

Pre-test	32	43	23	60	29	33	32	65	57	28
Post-test	26	48	16	40	42	33	35	49	53	20
Difference (x_i)	+6	−5	+7	+20	−13	0	−3	+16	+4	+8
Residual (e_i)	+2	−9	+3	+16	−17	−4	−7	+12	0	+4

describe how large a difference there has to be before you can say it did not occur by chance.

If we add up all the differences in Table 1.2, taking into account their signs (so $6 + -5 = +1$), we get 40. If we divide by the number of subjects (10) we find that the mean difference between the two scores is $\bar{x} = 4$. Thus, if we wanted to estimate the effect of the drug treatment on people's scores on the depression scale we would say, on average, they decreased by about 4. For those who do not mind equations (if you do mind them please see Box 1.4, and then continue reading this), we could write this as:

$$x_i = \bar{x} + e_i$$

This equation says that the difference between the two tests for each individual, each x_i, is equal to the mean difference for the whole group, $\bar{x}$, plus what is called its *residual*, denoted e_i. This is simply the difference between the mean of the group and the individual's observed score (it will get a bit more complicated in future chapters). Figure 1.3 shows the data and the residuals for each subject. Each vertical line represents the residual for one individual. Ideally the residuals will be as small as possible. In this case small residuals would allow you to be fairly precise when asked how the drug should affect individual patients. With these data, although on average people improve by four points, some deteriorate quite a lot while others improve considerably.

Suppose we were interested in children's mathematical ability (I use this example in the next few chapters also so it is worth getting used to). We might compare how well one group of children did on 20 addition problems when presented in symbolic form ($4 + 6 = \_\_$) with another group of children who were given similar problems presented in verbal form (Paul has four pennies. Helen has six pennies. How many pennies do they have together? Answer: __). The researcher would be interested in differences in the way children answered these two types of question and in particular if one of the forms appeared to elicit a higher number of correct responses.

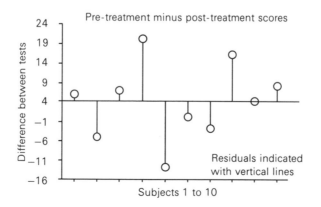

Figure 1.3   *Exploring residuals for a single group with one variable*

Box 1.4   The Anatomy of an Equation

Most sciences rely on mathematical equations to help describe their theories and their data. It is therefore vital to understand what the elements of an equation are. A very simple equation is:

$$\text{Temp}\,°F = 1.8 \times \text{Temp}\,°C + 32°$$

This is the equation used to translate temperature in degrees Celsius into degrees Fahrenheit. Consider putting 0°C into the equation. First we multiply it by 1.8. Anything multiplied by zero is equal to zero so this product (product meaning the result of the numbers being multiplied together) is zero. We then add 32° to zero and get 32°F (32°F and 0°C are the same temperature, the freezing point of water). If we enter 100°C, the boiling point of water, we get $180° + 32° = 212°$. The equation can be represented as a line, as shown in Figure 1.4.

   The temperature conversion equation is an exactly determined equation; each temperature in degrees Celsius has one and only one value in Fahrenheit. A more typical statistics equation is something like:

$$Maths_i = 0.8 \times Verbal_i + 14 + e_i$$

Here we are comparing scores on a mathematics test with scores on a verbal test. There are two big differences between this equation and the last. The first is each of the variable names, *Maths* and *Verbal*, has a subscript i next to it. These are used to represent the scores for each individual. If there are 25 individuals, i will range from 1 to 25. The scores for the 8th individual are denoted $Maths_8$ and $Verbal_8$. The second difference is the e_i at the end. These are called the residuals. The e_i is added to the end to make the equation work. Individuals have their own residual, their own e_i. The residuals are what is not being explained by the equation, what is left over. Sometimes this is called the error or the variance term. Most of the statistical techniques discussed in this book, either explicitly or implicitly, are designed to make the residuals as small as possible.

   If a subject scored 50 on the verbal test, it does not necessarily mean s/he will score exactly 54 ($0.8 \times 50 + 14$) on the mathematics tests. Suppose s/he scored 64 on the mathematics test. The value for her/his residual would be +10 (the difference between the observed value (64) and the value predicted from the equation (54)). Table 1.4 provides a further example of this kind. It is worth noting that the multiplication sign, $\times$, is usually not used. The above equation is usually written as:

$$Maths_i = (0.8)Verbal_i + 14 + e_i$$

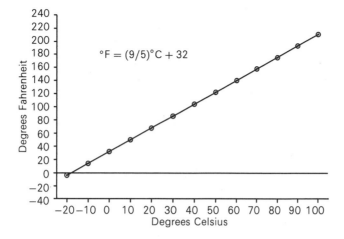

Figure 1.4   *Measures of temperature: the relationship between degrees Celsius and degrees Fahrenheit*

When trying to predict a variable, here the number of correct responses out of 20, the normal notation for the variable is y. The score for any child would be denoted y_i for the ith subject. If there were ten children, there would be ten ys $(y_1, y_2, y_3, y_4, y_5, y_6, y_7, y_8, y_9, y_{10})$. In statistical terms this is what we are trying to *model*.

The purpose of the research is to see if the question form makes a difference. This can be done in a variety of ways. In practice a researcher would usually use what is called a group t test and would probably let a computer to do all the calculations. The details of this test are described in Chapter 4, but for convenience, it will be explained here as two simple lines and one equation. Table 1.3 gives the data for this example plus an additional variable representing the type of question the child was given. I have arbitrarily coded this as 0 for symbol form and 1 for word form (this is a nominal variable). Later in this book I describe different types of coding, but this is the simplest for this problem.

The mean for the symbol group is 8, $\bar{x}_s = 8$. The mean for the word problem group is 13, $\bar{x}_w = 13$. The subscripts s and w denote which group the mean is for. Another convention in statistics is to use Greek letter β (lower-case beta) to represent constants. Subscripts are added to each β when there is more than one.

Table 1.3   *Comparing two groups of children for the number of mathematics problems solved correctly*

Form	Symbol group					Word group				
Form	0	0	0	0	0	1	1	1	1	1
Number correct	14	2	3	4	17	15	13	11	10	16

The final constant is usually denoted β_0 (pronounced 'beta nought'). The equation we solve is

$$y_i = \beta_1 Form_i + \beta_0 + e_i$$

We are interested primarily in the value of β_1. If it is equal to zero then the question form does not make a difference. To solve the equation we first solve for β_0. For each child in the symbol group the variable $Form_i$ has the value zero. Thus, regardless of the value of β_1, we know the product of it and $Form_i$ will be zero. We estimate the value for β_0 in the same may as we did for the drug treatment example. It is simply the mean for the symbol group: $\beta_0 = \bar{x}_s = 8$. The value for β_1 will be the difference between the two means $(\beta_1 = \bar{x}_w - \bar{x}_s = 13 - 8 = 5)$. The solution is

$$y_i = 5 Form_i + 8 + e_i$$

Table 1.4 shows how this works for the ten subjects. Note that if we add together all the e_i, taking into account their signs (that is, $+6 + -6 = 0$), we get zero.

As with the last example, it is useful to graph the data to see what is going on. In Figure 1.5 the scores are shown with the means for the two groups shown by the horizontal lines. For the symbol group, there are two scores that are much higher than the others in the group. These large residuals are sometimes called *outliers*. One explanation for this might be that the children are all fairly good at solving word problems but only some of the children can solve the symbol problems.

Experimental and Non-experimental Research

There are two basic methods of conducting scientific research: experimental and non-experimental methods. Each is equally valid but for different purposes.

Experimental methods involve *randomly* allocating subjects into *experimental conditions*. The experimental conditions are treated differently. The critical

Table 1.4 *Calculating the scores of individuals from the equation*

β_1		Value for $Form_i$		β_0		e_i	Number correct
5	×	0	+	8	+	+6	14
5	×	0	+	8	+	−6	2
5	×	0	+	8	+	−5	3
5	×	0	+	8	+	−4	4
5	×	0	+	8	+	+9	17
5	×	1	+	8	+	+2	15
5	×	1	+	8	+	0	13
5	×	1	+	8	+	−2	11
5	×	1	+	8	+	−3	10
5	×	1	+	8	+	+3	16

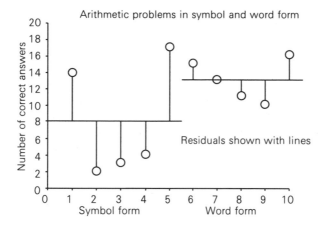

Figure 1.5 *Exploring residuals for a single variable and two groups*

methodological factor in experimental studies is to ensure that the subjects are randomly allocated to the conditions. This does not mean that the two groups will be exactly the same, but it does mean that they are likely to be similar.

Consider the simple drug treatment example from above. There exists a population (P) of depressed people, and it is these people in whom the researcher is interested. The target population (TP) might be all the depressed patients living in the same city as the researcher. From these a group of 20 is chosen to be in the sample (S). In the example above, the patients were given a test that measures depression, then they received a drug treatment, and then they are retested. The scores of the second test are lower, indicating that the drug treatment appears to help. However, there are several explanations for the difference that do not rely on the drug itself being beneficial. The most obvious alternative explanation is that the patients may have improved anyway. After all, in order to be sampled they probably went to a clinic to seek help and believed their treatment would help.

To help alleviate this problem researchers use control groups. The important aspect is how these people are allocated into conditions. This is more important than how these patients are chosen to take part in the study. The critical part of an experiment is ensuring that the sample is randomly allocated to different experimental conditions. This means that each person is equally likely to be in either group. In this example one of the groups should have been allocated to an experimental group (E) which have the drug treatment and the other group should be allocated to what is called a *control group* (C) which do not have the drug treatment. The control group should be treated in exactly the same way as the experimental group except for the variable that the researcher wants to isolate.

In this case researchers would presumably be interested in isolating the effects of the drug. They would give the control group the exact same treatment as the experimental group except they would give them a *placebo*, a pill that does nothing, instead of the drug being tested. The subjects should think they are receiving a drug treatment. When the subject does not know which group s/he is in we have what is called a *single blind* experiment. Because the people conducting the experiment might inadvertently treat people differently if they knew which group they were in, it is also common practice, when feasible, for the people administering the treatments not to know which subjects are in which groups. This is called a *double blind* experiment.

The experimental design for this example is shown in Figure 1.6. In order to establish that the drug itself is the cause of the lower depression scores, we compare whether the decrease found in the experimental group is larger than any decrease found in the control group. Statistics allows us to determine how big that difference must be for us to accept that there is a difference that cannot simply be attributed to chance. There are several other experimental designs, and what are called quasi-experimental designs, that are described in detail in all introductory methodology books. For statistical purposes I will keep with relatively simple cases. The assumption for experiments is that the sample is *randomly* assigned to a condition.

The second type of basic methodology is non-experimental research. Often people confuse the word 'non-experimental' with 'non-empirical'. 'Non-experimental' simply means that the subjects or respondents are not randomly allocated to different experimental conditions. 'Non-empirical' means that there was no 'study' *per se*; nothing was measured.

I will begin with what seems like a simple example. Suppose we were interested in the amount of coffee students at a particular university drink. The researcher must decide how to sample students. If students were sampled in the cafeteria and asked something like 'how many cups of coffee do you drink on a typical weekday?', it is likely the estimate would be too high since many people who go to cafeterias are actually getting coffee. Students could also be sampled outside the library, but my guess is this would also overestimate the percentage. There are several possible samples and most have problems associated with them. The problems occur because the proposed target populations (cafeteria users, library users, etc.) do not represent the whole population of students. For this problem, that at first seemed relatively simple, the researcher would probably need to get a list of all the students and systematically sample them.

Now consider a slightly more complex example. Most researchers are interested in comparing groups of people. Suppose we wanted to see if students

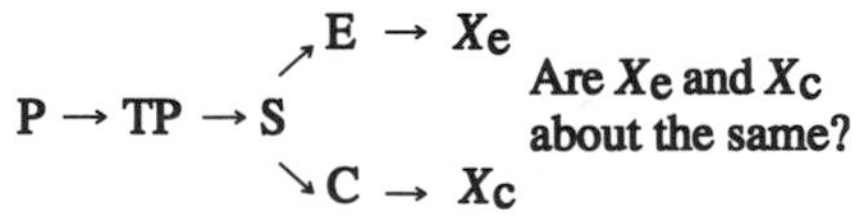

$$P \to TP \to S \nearrow^{E \to X_e}_{\searrow C \to X_c} \quad \text{Are } X_e \text{ and } X_c \text{ about the same?}$$

Figure 1.6   *An experimental design. From the population (P) first a target population (TP) is chosen and then a sample (S) taken. This sample is split into an experimental (E) and a control (C) group and the variable X is measured for each. The critical part of this design is how the sample is split into conditions.*

from one university had more liberal attitudes than students from another university. First we would either construct some scale for liberalism or find an existing scale. Then we would measure the liberalism of students from the two universities. The important aspect of non-experimental research is the sampling. If the attitudes of students from these two universities are to be compared then it is vital that the students are sampled in exactly the same way. If, for example, students from the first university are sampled from outside a physics lecture theatre and students from the second university are sampled from outside a history lecture theatre, any observed difference in attitudes could as easily be attributed to differences between students who attend these types of lectures instead of differences between the universities. Figure 1.7 illustrates this design. The critical point is that the way in which the target population is chosen from the respective populations is identical and the way in which the individuals are sampled from the target populations are identical.

Suppose the study was carried out, comparable sampling procedures were used and the difference between the attitudes was very large. The researcher would conclude that liberalism differed between the two universities, but could s/he say why the attitudes differed? The pragmatic answer is that s/he probably will report some possible explanations. The reason for designing the study and carrying it out was presumably because the researcher had some ideas about why the two might differ. From the actual data, however, the researcher can only claim that there is a difference. It might be that the reasons why the students chose to go to each of these universities were based on their political ideologies and/or that once they entered the university this environment influenced their attitudes. This is the main difference between experimental and non-experimental studies; non-experimental research cannot unequivocally determine causal relationships.

Summary

This is by far the most important chapter of the book and I strongly recommend that you look it over again just to make sure you understand the basic concepts. The remainder of the book assumes that you are comfortable with the concepts introduced here. The main issues discussed were:

$$P_1 \rightarrow TP_1 \rightarrow S_1 \rightarrow X_1 \quad \text{Are } X_1 \text{ and } X_2$$
$$P_2 \rightarrow TP_2 \rightarrow S_2 \rightarrow X_2 \quad \text{about the same?}$$

Figure 1.7 *A non-experimental design. Populations P_1 and P_2 are compared on variable X. The important consideration is that the target populations and samples are selected from P_1 and P_2 in identical ways*

- the stages of conducting research and the role of statistics in them,
- the use of computers as an aid to statistics,
- the debate about the levels of measurement of data,
- different kinds of sampling,
- the mean, the median and the mode (measures of central tendency),
- what variables and constants are,
- what an equation is and what each part of it means,
- calculating values from an equation,
- experimental methods and the importance of random allocation into conditions,
- non-experimental methods and the importance of sampling.

You should understand what each of these mean before progressing. If you do not, reread the appropriate section. As an aside, make sure you ask questions in your statistics classes!

Before going on to the next chapter it is necessary to get used to using statistical packages on the computer. I refrain from giving any details about how to start on the computer because each system is different. You should be able to do Exercises 6 and 7 on the computer. In Box 1.5 I have listed the code necessary to run Exercise 6 on SPSS-PC. SPSS continues improving and each new version has slight differences. Your instructor should inform you if this is incompatible with your version.

Box 1.5   Brief Introduction to SPSS

SPSS is a powerful tool for analysing data. It comes in a variety of different forms: for Windows, Macintosh, DOS and for mainframe computers. The system that you will use is bound to have some particular idiosyncratic features. Here I simply describe some of the overall structure of the program, though a more customised introduction may be necessary.

For SPSS to run statistics, there must be data somewhere. It is advisable to keep your data in their own file. The first thing to do within SPSS is to tell the program where the data are. This can be done with the DATA LIST command. Suppose we wanted to work on the file c:\staff.dat (data from a study exploring the staff of various companies) and this file had three variables: an identification number for each company, the number of employees in that company, and the number of sites the company has. Then the command

```
DATA LIST FILE = 'c:\staff.dat' FREE /compnumb staff
    sites.
```

correctly identifies the data's location and names the three variables (the slashes, single quotation marks and full stop are all important). The **FREE** tells the computer that the variables are arranged with a space between

---

them. You can also use the **FIXED** method in which you name the columns that each variable is in (this method is described in Chapter 2).

There is a proper style for running statistics on a computer that makes things easier in the long run. First, choose variable names that describe the variable. There are a couple of limitations on what you can use as variable names (not more than eight characters, not beginning with a number, etc.). It is also important to add longer variable names and value labels if these are not obvious from the short name. This is done in the example below. (Note: in the computer examples throughout this book I use a different font. If you use a scalable font, which may look better for text, the spacing gets misaligned. Use something like Courier.)

Using any sort of text editor, put these data into a text (ASCII) file called c:\staff.dat:

```
 1    32   3
 2   164   2
 3    68   7
 4    37   3
 5    19   1
 6   105   0
 7    54   6
 8    38   2
 9    27   3
10    69   5
11   211   3
12    22   4
13   135   3
14    46   3
15    27   7
16    31   3
17    76   5
18    81   2
19   142   1
20    18   5
```

The SPSS commands which you will need to run are:

```
DATA LIST FILE = 'c:\staff.dat' FREE/compnumb staff sites.
VARIABLE LABELS
    compnumb 'the identification number'/
    staff 'the number of staff'/
    sites 'the number of sites'.
FREQUENCY /VARIABLES STAFF
    /STATISTICS MEAN MEDIAN MODE /HISTOGRAM.
FREQUENCY VARIABLES SITES
    /STATISTICS MEAN MEDIAN MODE /BARCHART.
```

Each procedure has the following form (computer syntax): first, the procedure name, which has to be in the first column; then the names of the variables the procedure will use; and then a series of slashes (/) followed by particular options. If you are using the Windows or a menu-driven version of SPSS, finding these commands should be relatively straightforward.

Assignment

There are brief answers for some of the exercises in the back of this book.

1   What do you think the levels of measurement of the following variables are: gender, age (in years), religion, height (in inches), shoe size and IQ? Give your reasons.

2   A sample of ten medical doctors were asked how many hours they had worked in the previous week. The results were:

83, 45, 28, 72, 21, 32, 68, 42, 87, 18

What are the mean and the median of this group? There are large differences among these responses. Can you think of any other questions you would have liked to ask to help explain these differences?

3   A researcher was interested in children's ability to match pictures of animals with the animals' names. The children were shown 20 pictures. The number of correct responses are shown below for 15 children. What are the mean, the median and the mode of these data?

20, 18, 13, 16, 9, 11, 17, 20, 14, 13, 20, 8, 17, 20, 14

Which of these measures best summarises the data? Why?

4   Two hundred people tried four different colas and were asked which one they enjoyed most. Of the mean, median and mode, which measure would be the most appropriate statistic to report and why?

5   The following data compare the effectiveness of a new reading programme. Twenty pupils took part in the study. Each pupil was given a standardised reading test. They were then randomly allocated to one of two groups. The first group was not given any special instruction. The second group was given the new reading programme. Afterwards, the pupils were retested. The data for this are shown below.

(a)   Write out a diagram, like Figure 1.6, to show the experimental design.
(b)   Find the means of the differences for each group.
(c)   Find the values for the equation that describes this study in the same way as was done with the children and mathematics study described in the text.
(d)   Draw a graph like Figure 1.5 to represent this equation.
(e)   Describe, in words, your interpretation of this graph.

					Control group					
First test	83	56	76	41	78	69	57	64	32	70
Second test	76	46	82	50	60	74	58	77	28	70
Difference	−7	−10	6	9	−18	5	1	13	−4	0

					Experimental group					
First test	42	76	54	64	40	37	35	80	72	65
Second test	55	82	49	73	38	41	53	82	75	62
Difference	13	6	−5	9	−2	4	18	2	3	−3

6 Using the computer, find the mean, median and mode of the number of staff in the companies described in Box 1.5. Follow the instructions and make sure you get 70.1 for the mean, 50 for the median and 27 for the mode. Which of these measures best summarises the data? Repeat this with the days in training variable. For the number of staff, a histogram was produced. For the number of sites, a barchart was produced. Comment on these figures.

7 A researcher asked a sample of ten people how happy they had been as children. The responses ranged from 1 ('I had a really lousy childhood') to 7 ('I had a great childhood'). Calculate by hand the mean, median and mode of the following data:

$$1, 5, 6, 1, 4, 7, 1, 6, 7, 4$$

Comment on the usefulness of these measures.

8 Briefly describe, in one paragraph, the difference between probability and non-probability samples.

9 Why is it often all right to use a convenience sample when conducting experiments? Keep your answer to approximately four or five lines. (Throughout this book diagrams might be helpful when answering 'discuss' questions.)

10 Briefly say what the following symbols mean: e_i, $\bar{x}$, x_i, μ and Σ.

Further Reading

Most methodology textbooks cover many of the issues described here. Two recent books which I recommend are:

Breakwell, G.M., Hammond, S. and Fife-Schaw, C. (eds) (1995) *Research Methods in Psychology*. London: Sage.
Oppenheim, A.N. (1992) *Questionnaire Design, Interviewing and Attitude Measurement*. London: Pinter Publishers.

The following two books give an introduction and describe in detail the way to run statistical analyses with the Windows and the DOS versions of SPSS. There are several other books, including the official SPSS manuals, that also do this. All of the ones that I have read seem fine. Also, the help facilities on these programs are good.

Kinnear, P. R. and Gray, C. D. (1992) *SPSS/PC+ Made Simple*. Hove: Lawrence Erlbaum Associates.

Kinnear, P. R. and Gray, C. D. (1994) *SPSS for Windows Made Simple*. Hove: Lawrence Erlbaum Associates.

This textbook goes through some of the concepts of statistics rather quickly. There are several more basic books. My personal favourite (not surprisingly) is:

Wright, D. B. (forthcoming) *Ten Steps for Learning Statistics*. London: Sage.

It has the advantage that it uses similar notation to this book and the author obviously has the same basic underlying philosophy and approach to statistics.

2
Introduction to Hypothesis Testing

Chapter 1 introduced the way in which statistics fits into a research programme and how to construct models of the data that are intended to mirror the real world. This is the essence of any scientific endeavour, and statistics allows you to assess how well the data fit the models. When assessing these models, it is necessary to know how accurate the estimates are.

In this chapter measures of dispersion are discussed, and it is shown how these relate to the accuracy of the estimates of the mean. These notions are then extended to statistical tests of particular models. The notion of probability, as it is used in statistics, is introduced as well as how this concept is used (often technically incorrectly) by many social scientists. Having read (and understood) the first two chapters, you will have mastered the conceptual underpinnings of statistics. The remaining chapters apply these concepts to specific problem types. In this chapter only interval data will be considered.

Measures of Dispersion

The three Ms (the mean, median and mode, discussed in Chapter 1) are measures of central tendency. They tell us where the centre of the distribution lies, but they do not tell us how spread out the distribution is. Figure 2.1 shows the income (in thousands of dollars) of 50 people from two hypothetical societies. The means for these samples are the same ($\bar{x} = 10$) but in the first sample the differences in people's income are not as great as in the second sample. The incomes in the sample from society 2 are more spread out or dispersed than are those drawn from society 1. If someone asked us to compare the incomes of people from these two societies, saying they have the same mean is only part of the story.

There are several possible ways to measure the spread of a distribution. We will consider only the most common measures: the *range*, the *standard deviation* and the *variance*.

The range is the difference between the highest and the lowest value (sometimes called the maximum and the minimum). The range for the first group is $14 - 7 = 7$ thousand dollars. When writing the range of a set of scores you should always include the highest and the lowest scores to help the reader understand more of the data. Thus, if asked to calculate the range for the two samples, you should write (including the proper units):

The range for the first sample is $14 - 7 = 7$ thousand dollars.
The range for the second sample is $18 - 2 = 16$ thousand dollars.

The range only tells you about the extreme scores of a variable's distribution. It is greatly affected by these values and is not affected by the bulk of the scores. This means that most of the information is being ignored, which can lead to important differences being missed. The most common measure for dispersion that uses information from all the scores is called the *standard deviation* (or the closely related *variance*). It is a measure of the distance of the scores from the mean of the sample. Box 2.1 describes the standard deviation in more detail.

Recall the sample mean, denoted $\bar{x}$, was used to give our best estimate for the population mean μ. In order to estimate the population standard deviation, which is denoted with the lower-case Greek letter σ (lower-case sigma), the following equation is used (s stands for standard deviation):

$$s = \sqrt{\frac{(x_i - \bar{x})^2}{n - 1}}$$

The larger the standard deviation, the more spread out is the distribution. As the value of $x_i - \bar{x}$ increases in magnitude, the standard deviation increases. The effect of extreme scores, whether higher or lower than the mean, is the same. Thus, an income \$2000 below the mean has the same effect as an income \$2000 above the mean. An important characteristic of this measure is that, like the mean, it does not increase just because a larger sample is used.

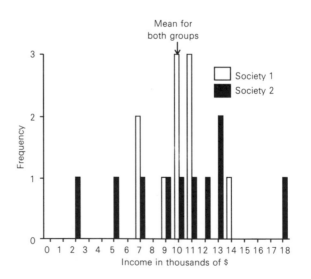

Figure 2.1   *The distribution of incomes from samples of two societies. The incomes in society 2 are more spread out than those in society 1*

Consider the following data on the arithmetic problem-solving from Chapter 1 (Table 1.4). Suppose we were interested in estimating the standard deviations for each of these groups. In Table 2.1, the scores for each group, the deviation from the mean of the group for each individual, and the squares of the deviations are shown. The sum of the squared deviations (sometimes denoted *SS* for sum of squares) is shown at the bottom of the table. To estimate the standard deviations this sum is divided by 4 (the number of people in the group minus one). The standard deviation is higher for the first group; the scores for the symbol group are more spread out than the scores for the word group. The units of the standard deviation are the same as for the variable. Thus, the standard deviation for the symbol group is approximately seven correct responses.

There is an equivalent formula, shown here for the symbol group, that is sometimes easier to compute because it does not require first finding the mean $\bar{x}$.

$$s = \sqrt{\frac{\sum x_i^2 - \frac{\left(\sum x_i\right)^2}{n}}{n-1}} = \sqrt{\frac{514 - 320}{4}} = \sqrt{48.5} = 6.96$$

Many textbooks suggest that this formula should be used. However, the other has the advantage that it is a much better conceptual representation of what the standard deviation is. While this one may be easier if you have not calculated the mean, in most cases you should calculate the mean before calculating the standard deviation. Further, as most statistics are now calculated by computer, computational ease is no longer a real issue. For these reasons I suggest you keep with the original formula, but be aware that the other form exists.

The final measure of dispersion that I discuss is the *variance*. The variance is the square of the standard deviation. It is often used in statistical tests and will be discussed in more detail in later chapters. However, it is not as easily interpreted

Table 2.1 *Calculating the standard deviations for the mathematics problem-solving data*

Symbol group mean = 8			Word group mean = 13		
Score x_i	Score−8 $x_i - \bar{x}$	Squared $\left(\bar{x} - x_i\right)^2$	Score x_i	Score−13 $\bar{x} - x_i$	Squared $\left(x_i - \bar{x}\right)^2$
14	6	36	15	2	4
2	−6	36	13	0	0
3	−5	25	11	−2	4
4	−4	16	10	−3	9
17	9	81	16	3	9
Sum of squares =		194	Sum of squares =		26
$s = \sqrt{\dfrac{194}{4}} = 6.96$			$s = \sqrt{\dfrac{26}{4}} = 2.55$		

as the standard deviation because it is in squared units (the variance for the symbol group is 48.5 answers^2). The variance for the population is denoted σ^2 (sigma squared).

Box 2.1   The Standard Deviation

Intuitively, a plausible way of measuring a distribution's spread is the average distance of the individual scores from the mean of the whole sample. This is called the *mean absolute deviation* and is calculated as follows:

$$mad = \frac{\sum |x_i - \bar{x}|}{n}$$

where the vertical bars (| |) surrounding $\bar{x} - x_i$ mean the absolute value of these differences. The absolute value of a number is the distance the number is away from zero, regardless of whether it is positive or negative. All absolute values are positive: $|-4| = |4| = 4$. This is important because it makes sure that values below the mean have the same effect as values above the mean.

Another way to make sure differences on both sides of the mean affect the measure equally is to square all the differences (that is, multiply each one by itself; this is denoted by the superscript 2: $4^2 = 4 \times 4 = 16$). This has other advantages for many statistical tests. If we take the average of the squared deviations we get the *mean squared difference* or the *variance*:

$$variance = \frac{\sum (x_i - \bar{x})^2}{n}$$

The square root (the opposite of squaring and denoted by $\sqrt{\ }$: $\sqrt{16} = 4$) of this is called the *standard deviation*:

$$standard\ deviation = \sqrt{\frac{\sum (x_i - \bar{x})^2}{n}}$$

This is the value that we use to describe how spread out the data in a sample are. Recall from Chapter 1 that while we measured the sample mean, $\bar{x}$, we were interested in using it to estimate the population mean, μ. Similarly, we measure the standard deviation of a sample in order to estimate the standard deviation of the whole population from which that sample is drawn. This population parameter is denoted with the lower-case Greek letter σ (sigma). Unfortunately the best estimate for σ is not exactly equal to the standard deviation of the sample. Because of this we use a slight modification, in which the n in the denominator of our estimate of σ

is replaced by $n - 1$. Except when n is small (less than 50), the two equations produce nearly identical results. Therefore, people usually just write

$$s = \sqrt{\frac{\sum(x_i - \bar{x})^2}{n - 1}}$$

and this will suffice throughout this book. There is also a slight modification when the sample size is a considerable percentage of the whole population. This does not occur very often and therefore is also not necessary for this book.

The Normal Distribution and z Scores

We have been discussing the characteristics of a variable's distribution. In this section I describe one particular type of distribution and how it is often used. The distribution is called the *Normal distribution* and it has many useful properties for statistics. The distribution is shown in Figure 2.2. It is symmetric around its mean (meaning it looks the same on both sides) and it tails off at the ends. It is sometimes referred to as 'bell-shaped', like the old-fashioned bells.

There are certain variables that are known to be Normally distributed, because they are constructed specifically to be this way, but most variables are not. This makes the word 'Normal' somewhat misleading. Sometimes this distribution is referred to as the Gaussian or Laplace distribution, but Normal is much more common in the English-speaking world. To distinguish between the two meanings of the word 'Normal', I will capitalise it when referring to the distribution and use lower case when referring to its English meaning. Intelligence quotient

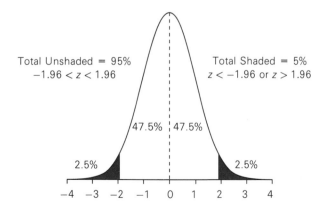

Figure 2.2 *The Normal or z distribution*

(IQ) scores are an example of a Normally distributed variable. IQ tests are constructed so that their mean (for a particular culture) is 100, their standard deviation is 20 (the standard deviation varies between the particular form of IQ test used) and their distribution is shaped like the one in Figure 2.2.

Given this information, we can calculate the percentage of people that have IQs above or below a certain percentage. To do this we calculate what is called a *z score*. This is a measure of the distance from the population mean but instead of saying a person is a certain number of IQ points above the mean it allows us to say how many standard deviations above the mean that person is. We use the following equation:

$$z = \frac{x - \mu}{\sigma}$$

In words, the numerator of the equation is the distance between any individual's score x and the population mean μ. The units of $x - \mu$ depend on the scale (miles, pounds, degrees, inches, etc.). By dividing this difference by the standard deviation (σ), which is also in units corresponding to the scale, the values are no longer dependent on the original units. The z scores measure the number of standard deviations a person is above or below the mean.

Suppose you wanted to know how exceptional a person with a 130 IQ is (where the IQ test has a mean of 100 and a standard deviation of 20). There are a number of ways of thinking about this. First, we could say the person's IQ is 30 points above the mean $(x - \mu)$. On its own this is rather meaningless because most people do not know how much this is. We divide this difference by the standard deviation in order to convert the difference to units of standard deviation.

$$z = \frac{130 - 100 \text{ points}}{20 \text{ points}} = 1.5 \text{ standard deviations}$$

Thus, we can say the person with a 130 IQ is 1.5 standard deviations above the mean. Again, this is not particularly informative to most people. The next step is to see how many people would score higher than this person. The percentage of the area underneath the Normal distribution curve beyond any particular z value is equal to the percentage of people who would be beyond this point, assuming IQ is Normally distributed.

To find out this percentage we go to the z table (in Appendix B) and look up the value 1.5 in the z column. There are several other columns in this table. The number in the 'one-tailed' column represents the area under the curve to the right of the person's score. This number, 0.0668, refers to the proportion of people (6.7%) who score higher than this person. Thus, we can say s/he has a fairly high score on the IQ test. The value in the 'two-tailed' column refers to the proportion in both tails whose score is as 'extreme' as that of the person. In this example, it refers to the proportion of people whose IQ is more than 30 points above or below the mean. It is twice the value of the probability listed in the one-tailed column. The two-tailed value is useful in many statistical tests and is described more fully in Box 2.2.

Figure 2.3 illustrates this example. In calculating these percentages it is extremely useful to draw a little diagram like the one in Figure 2.3 and to mark off the areas you wish to include.

The Standard Error of the Mean

> The next step is the most important in statistics, so read carefully!

When calculating a z score for a single person on an IQ test we were saying how many standard deviations away from the mean that individual's score was. We chose one particular individual. In a similar manner, when we sample a group of individuals we are choosing one of a large number of possible groups (recall the discussion on sampling in Chapter 1). When we test a hypothesis we are seeing how extreme the value produced by the chosen sample is compared to all the possible samples that could have been chosen.

While the units used for our z score in the last example were in standard deviations of the distribution of individuals, the units we use to compare a sample mean to the distribution of possible means are in *standard errors of the mean* (or just standard errors for short). This is the standard deviation of the means you would get if you tested all the possible samples. Instead of comparing one individual to a lot of other individuals, we are comparing one sample, or one mean, with a lot of other means. This is the basis of what is called the *frequentist* philosophy of statistics, which is dominant in most of the social sciences (see Box 2.3).

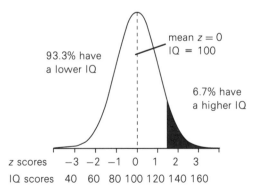

Figure 2.3 *Locating an IQ score of 130 on the distribution of IQ scores (with a standard deviation of 20)*

This is a major conceptual leap. It allows us to see how extreme a sample's mean is compared to the distribution of means for all possible samples. If our model hypothesises a particular population mean, then we can calculate how likely we are to get a sample mean fairly near it and fairly far away from it. Getting a sample mean that is many standard errors away from the hypothesised value is unlikely if the hypothesised value is true. Therefore, if the percentage of possible means that are more extreme than our sample's mean is low, then we reject the hypothesised value. This is the basis of hypothesis testing in statistics! (It is worth pausing at this point and going over the past three paragraphs again.)

In order to find out by how much the mean of a sample differs from a hypothesised mean value we need to measure the distance from the sample mean to the hypothesised mean in units of standard error of the mean. When this is based on the known population standard deviation it is called a *z test*. In the next chapter I discuss what to do in the more common situation where the population standard deviation σ is not known. We interpret this distance, using the *z* tables, as the likelihood of getting a sample mean as extreme as was found if the null hypothesis were true (that is, the sample having the same mean as the population). We use the following equation:

$$z = \frac{\bar{x} - \mu}{SEM} = \frac{\bar{x} - \mu}{\sqrt{\sigma^2/n}} = \frac{\bar{x} - \mu}{\sigma/\sqrt{n}}$$

where *SEM* denotes the standard error of the mean. As the sample size, *n*, increases, *SEM* decreases, the precision of our test increases and *z* is likely to increase.

I will use the IQ example again to illustrate how a *z* test works. IQ scores are often used as examples in these situations because we know that the variable is Normally distributed, that the population mean $\mu = 100$ and we can assume a known standard deviation. Suppose the test we used has a standard deviation of $\sigma = 30$. If we randomly sample 16 people from the population we can calculate the distribution of all possible samples of this size in the same way as we did with the *z* scores. We are able to calculate what percentage of samples with $n = 16$ would be more than a certain distance away from the mean. The standard error of the mean is $30/\sqrt{16} = 7.5$ IQ points. This allows us to compare specific samples with all possible samples.

Suppose a researcher wanted to see if children who ate certain types of vitamins had higher IQs than other children. The researcher would locate children who used these vitamins (this is the target population) and then s/he would sample some of these children and administer an IQ test. The researcher would be interested in whether the sample mean, $\bar{x}$, is equal to the population mean, μ. The null hypothesis, denoted H_0 (pronounced *H* nought), would be that the mean in the vitamin-taking population is 100. It is unlikely that the sample mean would be exactly 100. The researcher would be interested in whether the observed difference is far enough away from zero to be confident that the population from which this sample is drawn (vitamin-eating children) is different from the entire population with respect to this characteristic.

Suppose the researcher tested 16 children and found their mean IQ was 110. The difference between the sample mean and the population mean is 10 points $(\bar{x} - \mu = 10)$. We want to know how likely we would be to get a mean this high (or higher) if the children had been chosen at random from the whole population instead of being chosen because they had taken the vitamins. To do this we find the z value:

$$z = \frac{\bar{x} - \mu}{\sigma/\sqrt{n}} = \frac{110 - 100}{30/\sqrt{16}} = \frac{10}{7.5} = 1.33$$

When we look up 1.33 in the z table, we see that the one-tailed value is 0.092. This is called the p value (for probability). This means that if we had sampled 16 children from the whole population several times, in about 9% of these tests we would get a mean of 110 or more. This is a fairly large percentage, and we would probably not want to reject the possibility that children who ate these vitamins had the same IQ scores as others. This does not mean that the vitamins did not make a difference, only that these data do not provide enough evidence to convince us that the vitamins make a difference. The researcher should say something like: 'from these data I was unable to reject the possibility that the vitamins make no difference'. This may sound a little awkward, but it is important to be correct. Often when researchers obtain a value like this they say something like: 'the vitamins made no difference'. This is wrong! Do not say this. If you do marks will be subtracted from work and your friends will tease you (well, maybe just marks will be taken off).

Suppose the company making these vitamins was discouraged by this finding because it felt that its vitamins were making a difference. It had 100 children tested who had been taking vitamins and also found a mean of 110. Putting these numbers into the formula gives $z = 3.33$. This z value is much larger because the sample size is larger. Looking this up in the z table we find that the probability of obtaining a mean this high is less than (the symbol $<$) 0.001 or less than one in a thousand. Thus, we are very unlikely, if the null hypothesis is true (that is, that the mean IQ for children who take these vitamins is 100), to observe a sample mean this high, and the company would proclaim that these children did have higher IQs.

When we get a small p value then we usually say that the finding is *statistically significant*. This is another one of those phrases that has a different meaning in statistics than in English. In statistics, significant does not mean the effect is large or important, only that the data provide enough evidence to allow us to reject the null hypothesis. A better word would have been *detected*; a low p value means an effect has been detected.

There are two observations worth making about this example. The first is that the observed mean was the same for both the first researcher and the company and yet they reached different conclusions. The problem for the first researcher was s/he had not collected enough data to reach any conclusions. This demonstrates the importance of sample size. The second observation is that the company cannot unequivocally claim that its vitamins are enhancing IQ, only that people who happen to use these vitamins have higher IQs. It may be that people who have higher IQs choose to take vitamins (see Chapter 1 on non-experimental designs and causality).

I will work through one more example. In many places fluoride is put into the drinking water. Suppose a researcher was interested in the effects of this on IQ. S/he would probably be interested in shifts in either direction (fluoride increasing or decreasing IQ) and therefore would do what is called a two-tailed test. This is much the more common type of test (see Box 2.2).

Suppose the researcher gave an IQ test (with $\mu = 100$ and $\sigma = 20$) to 25 people who drank fluoridated water and that their mean IQ was $\bar{x} = 96$. Putting these values into the z equation produces a z of -1.0. Because the Normal distribution is symmetrical we can test negative z values just as we tested positive values (see Figure 2.4). When we look up 1.0 in the z table, the two-tailed probability is 0.317. Thus, there is about a 30% chance of getting a score this extreme even if the fluoride makes no difference. This is a large enough percentage that the researcher would say that these data do not provide sufficient evidence that fluoride makes a difference (failure to reject the null hypothesis). The finding is said to be *non-significant*.

Testing Hypotheses: What to Do with *p*

After the data have been analysed, either you look up a probability value in a table or the computer provides one. The question is what you do with it. There are three schools of thought (see Box 2.3); here I present the one most widely accepted within the social sciences.

When conducting research you are investigating a model about the state of the world (see Table 2.2). From this model a null hypothesis is created. Usually this is something like there is no difference between two groups. When the

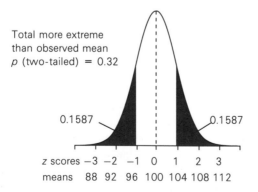

Figure 2.4   *A two-tailed z test: exploring the effects of fluoride on IQ test scores*

statistical package or table you use gives you a p value you have to decide whether to reject this null hypothesis (H_0) or not. There are two possible states of the world: either H_0 is true or it is false. For example, if you are comparing the IQ of two groups, they are either the same or different.

Box 2.2   One- versus Two-tailed Tests

One question that often comes up is when to use a one-tailed test and when to use a two-tailed test. This is one of those areas about which statisticians disagree because it depends on the specific problem. When you do a one-tailed test you are saying that you are interested only in differences in one particular direction. With a two-tailed test you are interested in shifts in either direction.

Consider the study by the drug company on the relationship between vitamins and IQ scores. I presented that as a one-tailed test; the drug company was only interested in whether the vitamins increased IQ, not whether the vitamins caused a difference in either direction. In that example, the sample mean was 110 and the company rejected the hypothesis that there was no difference. It therefore concluded that people who took these vitamins had higher IQs. But suppose its sample mean had been 90 or even 70. Because it was only investigating shifts in one direction, it would conclude that there was no evidence in the data that people who took the vitamins had higher IQs than other people (full stop). If the company did this (and somebody found its data), clearly there would be claims that their interpretation was fraudulent.

One reason why researchers often use one-tailed tests is that they produce lower probability values. Suppose the company was planning on rejecting the null hypothesis if it got a probability, or p value, of 5% or smaller. To be in the top 5% (one direction, so one-tailed) the mean IQ for the 100 children would need to be 105.8 or above. If, however, you need to be in the most extreme 5% (two directions, so two-tailed; corresponding to the lowest 2.5% and the highest 2.5%) then the mean would need to be either less than 95.1 or greater than 104.1. While the probability of either of these is the same if the null hypothesis is true, if the observed mean was 105, the company might be tempted to use a one-tailed test. This temptation is due to the researchers being overly concerned with probability values (see the summary of this chapter).

In most situations a two-tailed test is correct, but there are some situations in which one-tailed tests are probably appropriate. An example is a replication of an existing and accepted finding. Still, it is often easier always to do a two-tailed test as a matter of course and say, if appropriate, that the effect was in the predicted direction. If you do a one-tailed test you must justify why you are interested only in a shift in one direction, and this often produces a slight suspicion in the reader.

Table 2.2 *Rejecting and not rejecting the null hypothesis (H_0): when Type I and II errors can occur*

		State of the world	
		No effect – H_0 true	Effect exists – H_0 false
Decision based on observed p	Reject H_0	Type I Error	Correctly rejected
	Not reject H_0	Correctly not rejected	Type II Error

In practice, if pressed, most researchers would say that the null hypothesis is not that there is absolutely no difference but that the difference is tiny. There are problems with this (see Serlin and Lapsley, 1993; Cohen, 1994) and the resulting p values are not exactly appropriate. However, the difficulties are eased as long as researchers do not treat p values as being handed down from God and use a little common sense.

If the p value is very small, you should reject H_0 on the grounds that if it was true, obtaining data as extreme as those observed is unlikely. However, there is always the possibility that the data are extreme by chance and that it was a mistake to have rejected H_0. This is called a Type I error. If H_0 is true, the probability of a Type I error is equal to the highest p value at which you still would be willing to reject H_0. This is called the α (the first letter of the Greek alphabet, lower-case alpha) level. p is the observed probability of obtaining a score this extreme assuming H_0; α is the highest acceptable p for which you would reject H_0. These are called conditional probabilities because they depend on things being true. The p value is not the probability of a Type I error, it is the probability of a Type I error if the null hypothesis is true. The distinction between these is often confused but it is important when considering what is called the *power* of a test (described below and in more detail throughout this book).

It is necessary to set your α level before you collect your data or begin your analysis. Most textbooks, journals, supervisors, etc., feel that 5% is about the maximum allowable α level. This means that when H_0 is true, you will reject the null hypothesis, on average, on one occasion in every 20. When a statistic gives a p value less than 5% we say it is significant; when the value is above 5% we say it is non-significant.

There are two difficulties with this. The first is that significant and non-significant, as used in statistics, have a different meaning than when used in other dialects of English. Sometimes statistically significant effects occur when the sample is very large but the size of the effect is too small to be of concern. You should not assume just because a statistic is significant that it is important, and you should not assume that there is not something interesting in a study just because the statistical tests did not yield significant results. The phrases 'effect detected' and 'effect not detected' are more accurate, but I will keep with the traditional terms as their use is too widespread to combat.

The other difficulty is that an over-reliance on 5% as an absolute criterion creates several problems. One such problem is that in many cases making a Type I error would have serious consequences and therefore a lower α level is required (and in some cases a higher α level is appropriate). Another is that the 5% threshold differentiates a p value of 0.045 from one of 0.055 when the two are essentially the same. The 5% level is a convention. While it should not always be used, there is something useful in having a convention. It means researchers are discouraged from making up their own α levels after seeing their data.

The second option the researcher has is not to reject H_0. This occurs when the p value is above the α level (that is, p is fairly high). This does not mean that you accept H_0. You have only failed to reject it. The vitamins and IQ example illustrates this. The researcher who measured only 16 children would not want to have accepted that the vitamin consumers had the same IQ as everyone else. After all, there was a 10 point difference, which is rather large. It was just that with only 16 children the researcher was unable to say that this difference could not have occurred by chance.

When researchers fail to reject H_0, when it is false, they are making another type of error called a Type II error. There are several reasons why Type II errors occur. First, while there may be some difference between the groups, this difference may be very small. The researcher must decide the smallest size of error that s/he feels would be important enough to detect. Another common problem is using a small sample, like the researcher asking only 16 children, or using unreliable measuring devices (which would occur if the IQ test used was poorly designed). Both of these lead to large standard errors. Type II errors are also more likely when you are using a small α level, for example $\alpha = 0.001$. As you lower your α level, and therefore decrease your chances of making a Type I error, you increase your chances of making a Type II error. This is because by lowering the α level, you will not be rejecting as many null hypotheses and some of these will be false.

The probability of failing to reject the null hypothesis when it is false is the *power* of the test. To improve the power the researcher may increase the sample size, improve the measuring device, alter the α level (but with care since this increases the chance of a Type I error) and/or choose a different way of studying the phenomenon in which the expected effect size is larger. From Chapter 4 the power of the various statistical tests will be described. Ideally the probability of a Type I error and a Type II error will each be as low as possible.

Summary

In these first two chapters I have presented the core principles of statistics. Neither chapter is very long so I recommend you reread the relevant parts if any of the concepts seem confusing. In this chapter I described in some detail the main technique for measuring the dispersion or spread of a sample: the standard deviation (and the closely related variance). This plays an integral part in many statistical tests because the more spread out a sample is, the less precise the estimates are.

Box 2.3   Philosophies about *p*

Throughout this century there has been much discussion within statistical circles about what probability values, or *p* values, are. Three schools of thought are usually discussed: the Bayesian school and two varieties of the frequentist approach. The Bayesian school is named after the eighteenth-century cleric Thomas Bayes. This notion of probability, which has become known as inverse probability, is the likelihood of a hypothesis given some data. In an entertaining and readable (that is, non-technical) chapter, Gigerenzer (1993) argues that this definition of probability is the one that many social science researchers want to believe and often errantly use.

However, while the Bayesian statistical approach is common in some academic disciplines (economics, decision analysis, etc.), throughout most of the social sciences the frequentist approach is used. For the frequentist statistician (this book will take you some way down the road to becoming a frequentist statistician), the probability value that you look up in a table or that the computer generates for you is the probability of obtaining *data* as extreme as in your sample *if* the null hypothesis is true. It is *not* the probability that the null hypothesis is either true or false, and it is not a direct measure of the belief you have in H_0. While the Bayesian probability is about a hypothesis conditional on some data, the frequentist probability is about data conditional on a specific hypothesis. Both approaches are valid. Within statistical circles, whether you are a Bayesian or frequentist can be critical, and many will argue at length on the advantages of their approach (trust me). Within the disciplines that use statistics, researchers usually take on the perspective that is dominant in their field as a convention.

The two frequentist approaches are primarily credited to three statisticians working in the early and middle part of this century: Ronald Fisher for the first and the combined efforts of Jerzy Neyman and Egon Pearson for the second. Gigerenzer describes how Fisher's theory was actually incompatible with the Neyman–Pearson theory, and that the resulting frequentist perspective that is taught is often a confused hybrid of these approaches. Others have argued that the two approaches are more similar (Lehmann, 1993). There are two overriding differences that the typical social scientist believes differentiates the Fisher and Neyman–Pearson brands of frequentist statistics.

Fisher is often labelled as the one who *forced* social scientists to use a *p* value of 0.05 as an absolute cutoff for all studies. This is an unfair criticism. While in his earlier works (in the 1920s and 1930s) he did say it would be useful to have some cutoff (and he did suggest 5% for convenience), in his later works he states that adopting a fixed standard is ill advised. According to Fisher's later writings (in the 1950s) researchers should report their exact *p* values and let the reader judge their worth. In the pre-computer era, this was difficult because for many statistical tests the tables only list the probability values for a handful of critical levels. Now that the computer prints precise *p* values Fisher's advice can be heeded.

The main point that is usually attributed to Neyman and Pearson is that they argued researchers should adjust the probability of rejecting a true hypothesis (a Type I error) and the probability of failing to reject a false hypothesis (a Type II error) rather than trying to minimise one or the other. This has developed into the area of *power analysis*. While Fisher did not like their terminology, Lehmann points out that in a number of ways he accepted the substance of their arguments. They also seemed to appreciate many of his contributions. The differences between their statistical philosophies seem by most accounts to have been magnified by personality conflicts.

Today, there remain disagreements among Bayesians, Fisherians and Neyman–Pearsonians and various unresolved problems for each. It is important to stress that contemporary statistics is a lively field both in the development of new statistical procedures and in debating more philosophical and foundational concepts. The formulation presented in this text is frequentist. In some ways I bypass many of the issues involved in the Fisher versus Neyman–Pearson debate by stressing that researchers should be more concerned with their models (the forms of the equations they use to represent their data) than with the specific resulting *p* values.

The critical conceptual leap was thinking of the sample as one of many possible samples. Mathematical statistics provided information about the distribution of samples for different hypothesised values. This allows us to construct the distribution of the possible samples if the null hypothesis is correct. We can then compare the value we observe with this distribution and see how unlikely we would be to obtain a value as extreme as observed if the null hypothesis were true.

The computer (or a table) produces a probability (*p*) value that refers to how unlikely we are to observe a value as extreme as the observed value if H_0 were true. There is a convention in the social sciences that if this value is less than 5% (0.05) then we reject the null hypothesis. If it is above 5% than we 'fail to reject the null hypothesis'. If you only remember two points from this chapter remember the following:

1   There is nothing magical about 5%. It is a convention. Some findings that are significant at this level may be of little importance. Some findings that are not significant may be worthy of much interest.
2   There are several reasons why you might fail to reject a hypothesis even when the hypothesis is false.

People who use statistics often worry too much about a particular *p* value. The values that you obtain are often only approximations and sometimes not even very good ones. As scientists you should be more concerned with the model you have proposed and the size of any effects than with the precise *p* value. Statistical tests are not simply for rejecting or failing to reject hypotheses, but form an integral part of a larger scientific programme in which models of the world are constructed.

Assignment

1   A media researcher was interested in the number of advertisements shown during major sports events. She sampled, at random, 25 different sports programmes for one month and watched the final hour of each. She recorded the number of minutes (to the nearest half) of advertisements. The data are

5, 6½, 16, 5, 8½, 6½, 8½, 12, 8, 9, 3, 4½, 13,
8½, 10, 2, 8, 8½, 21, 7½, 5½, 6, 11, 8½, 2

(a)   What is the standard deviation of this sample?
(b)   Suppose the researcher was told that, on average, for all shows, there are 5 minutes of commercials for each hour of air time and that the standard deviation of this is 5. Assume that the number of minutes is Normally distributed. From these data, do sports programmes appear to have more commercials than other programmes?

2   Content analysis is sometimes used in order to examine whether a manuscript should be attributed to a certain author. One technique involves counting the percentage of certain words used in a manuscript and comparing this to works known to have been written by the author. Methods like this have been used to help attribute authorship of parts of the Bible, the Federalist Papers and some manuscripts allegedly by Shakespeare. Suppose that for all the known manuscripts of an author, the word 'the' was used about seven times in every hundred words. Further, assume there is a standard deviation of 3 for the known manuscripts. A new anonymous manuscript was discovered that several people thought may have been written by this author. In this manuscript, the word 'the' was used five times in every hundred words.
(a)   If we assume that the author's use of 'the' is Normally distributed across the author's works, what percentage of the works use the word 'the' less often than the new manuscript?
(b)   What percentage use it more often?
(c)   From this information, would you say that the manuscript was written by this author?

3   The average number (that is, the mean) of people at a particular restaurant during a weekday lunch period is 13 with a standard deviation of 5. One Friday the owner counted 17 people.

(a)   If we assume that the number of customers is Normally distributed, on what percentage of days would there be this many or more people?

(b)   The owner thought that Friday might be different from the other weekdays. S/he recorded the number of tables on five different Fridays. The numbers of customers were

13, 15, 14, 18, 15

Should the owner reject the hypothesis that Fridays are different in terms of the number of customers?

(c)   Suppose s/he repeated this study but on 100 different Fridays and found the mean ($\bar{x}$) to be 14 customers. Should s/he reject H_0?

4   Researchers investigating how happy people feel about their lives developed a questionnaire to measure this. Each individual scored between 0 (extremely unhappy) and 40 (extremely happy). The standard deviation of these scores was 10 with a mean of 25. Suppose you were interested in whether twins were happier than other people (because they have someone their own age to play with). You sampled 100 people who had twin siblings and gave them this questionnaire. The mean you found was 29.

(a)   What would you conclude from this research?

(b)   Why did you choose a one- or a two-tailed test? Do not just say 'because I was interested only in increases' or 'because I was interested in shifts in either direction'. Say why you were interested.

5   I have been careful to capitalise the N in 'Normal distribution'. Why (in about two lines)?

6   Put yourself in the following student's shoes. A student completes a study on the relationship between political attitudes on a left–right dimension and whether the respondents voted in the last election. It was a well-designed study and he questioned 100 people. When the two groups (voters and non-voters) were compared using a technique to be discussed in Chapter 4, the computer produced a p value of 0.64.

(a)   Should you:

  (i)   say this probability is fairly high and therefore the finding is non-significant;

  (ii)   or say this probability is fairly high and therefore the finding is significant?

If you answered (ii), reread the section on testing hypotheses and try again.

(b)   Once you are convinced that the finding is non-significant, should you:

  (i)   say that the data did not provide evidence that there was a difference;

  (ii)   or say that voters and non-voters have the same mean on the left–right political dimension?

If you answered (ii), reread the section on testing hypotheses and try again.

7   In each of the following three scenarios the researcher found the difference was non-significant. For each of these, the null hypothesis (H_0) was in fact false. In other words, the researcher made a Type II error. Assume for all the

following that an α level of 5% was used. Match the following three explanations for why s/he may have found no significant effects: the sample size was too small, the size of shift was small, and the measurement device was poor.

(a) It is well known that chess masters win more often when they go first (that is, use the white pieces). A researcher was curious if this effect also exists at lower levels. S/he tested a computer playing against itself when set to a 'novice' level. S/he had the computer play against itself for 200 games, ignoring draws. The white side won 97 of these. S/he failed to reject the hypothesis that playing white makes no difference on the outcome.

(b) A classroom teacher wanted to compare the intelligence of children who sat in the front of the room with those who sat in the back. Instead of using an IQ test or looking at pupils' grades over the previous months, s/he asked each a single question: what is the largest mammal? About the same percentage of pupils in the front of the classroom got the question right as did pupils in the back. The p value was non-significant.

(c) Being curious about the relative ability of men and women to eat lots of food, a researcher contacted, at random, two men and two women and took them to all-you-can-eat restaurants for every meal in a week (I always had to fill out boring questionnaires). The amount of food consumed was accurately recorded. The researcher was surprised to discover that the amount of food eaten was about the same by the two men and the two women.

8 There exist clubs that only admit people with high IQs. While it is common knowledge that the mean of IQ tests is 100, most people do not think about the standard deviation of the test. Suppose one IQ test had a standard deviation of 20, and another had a standard deviation of 30. Suppose also that the society only admitted people with an IQ above 150.

(a) What percentage of the population could be admitted if they used the first test?

(b) What percentage could be admitted if they used the second test?

9 Redo Exercise 1 but by computer. Use the following commands, commenting briefly on the results.

```
DATA LIST FIXED /  advert 1-4 (2).
BEGIN DATA
  5.0
  6.5
 16.0
  5.0
  8.5
  6.5
  8.5
 12.0
  8.0
  9.0
  3.0
  4.5
```

```
13.0
 8.5
10.0
 2.0
 8.0
 8.5
21.0
 7.5
 5.5
 6.0
11.0
 8.5
 2.0
```

END DATA.
VARIABLE LABELS ADVERT 'Advertisements per hour'.
DESCRIPTIVES /VARIABLES advert.

A few words are needed about how these data were read. First, these data are in 'fixed' format. This means the computer has to be told the columns in which each variable is stored. Here the computer is told the variable advert is stored in columns 1–4. The (2) tells the computer that the last two columns refer to the decimal point and one place after the decimal point. The method for telling a computer where the variables are located varies between different implementations so follow your instructor's directions if they are different from these.

10 Using the states.sps file in Appendix A, find the means and standard deviations of the variable dropout (the high school dropout rate) and lowtemp (the record low temperature in each state). The DESCRIPTIVES or the FREQUENCIES command may be used.

11 Besides being able to do this problem on a computer, I strongly recommend that you practise with other problems so that you feel comfortable with the basic operations of your statistics package. It is also advisable that you practise writing in a statistical form with your word processor. Most of the word processing packages that people use allow you to make nice tables and to write out equations. It would be good to get used to doing this.

Further Reading

A great deal of conceptual information has been presented in this chapter. It will be helpful if you reread any sections you did not understand. I also recommend the following papers:

Cohen, J. (1990) Things I have learned (so far). *American Psychologist*, *45*, 1304–1312.

Cohen, J. (1994) The Earth is round ($p < .05$). *American Psychologist*, *49*, 997–1003.

These are excellent papers describing some of the uses and misuses of statistics and how the situation might be improved. I recommend looking at them now, but reading them in more detail when you finish this book.

Also cited in this chapter are two interesting papers of the Fisher versus Neyman–Pearson debate. The Gigerenzer paper is less technical (and more amusing) but it may not be in your library. Lehmann's paper includes some more complicated sections, but these can be skipped without losing much of the gist of his paper.

Gigerenzer, G. (1993) The superego, the ego and the id in statistical reasoning. In G. Keren and C. Lewis (eds), *A Handbook for Data Analysis in the Behavioral Sciences: Methodological Issues*. Hillsdale, NJ: Lawrence Erlbaum Associates, pp. 311–339.

Lehmann, E. L. (1993) The Fisher, Neyman–Pearson theories of testing hypotheses: one theory or two? *Journal of the American Statistical Association, 88*, 1242–1249.

The following book provides a more detailed discussion of the rationale of hypothesis testing.

Chow, S. L. (1996) *Statistical Significance: Rationale, Validity and Utility*. London: Sage.

3
Comparing the Means of Paired Data

You have now overcome the main conceptual obstacles to learning statistics. The remaining chapters will introduce you to particular techniques. Each of these chapters will have a similar structure. A problem type will be described and examples will be given. There will be some description of how the techniques can be done by computer. In many cases, there will be alternatives to the techniques and these will also be discussed, but much more briefly. Each chapter will also introduce a new conceptual issue.

In this chapter the paired t test is introduced. The paired t test is used to compare two sets of scores when the scores are matched or paired. This occurs when you are comparing two responses for the same person, when you are doing a before–after study or when you have *matched* the people in some way.

The additional conceptual issue raised is the use of so-called distribution-free or robust methods as an alternative to the standard procedures. There are certain assumptions that have to be made for many statistical tests. For example, to conduct many tests you have to assume that the data have a certain distribution. I discuss this in detail in this chapter. Sometimes when these assumptions are not satisfied the p values are incorrect, but the general conclusions that are made from the data are fairly valid. On other occasions the consequences are much more severe, and you miss out on interesting aspects of the data and/or misinterpret them.

Student's Paired t Test

I have a long-held romantic notion about how this test came about (this probably says more about me than about the test or its creator). The person who devised it was named William Gossett. He worked at the beginning of this century for the Guinness brewery, which would not allow him to publish using his real name; he therefore published several articles (mainly in a fairly technical journal called *Biometrika*) using the pseudonym 'Student'. I always imagine him relaxing on a Sunday afternoon in a lush green valley on the outskirts of Dublin, sipping the fruits of his labour, and having wise statistical thoughts. I have not investigated the accuracy of this image so as not to ruin the romance of it (ignorance is often bliss).

Anyway, the statistical tests that 'Student' is credited with are very common in the social sciences. The technique that is described in this chapter, the paired *t* test, is used when you want to see if there is a difference between the means of two variables either for different questions or for the same question at two points in time. In the next chapter I describe how to compare the mean of a single variable for two different groups using another test credited to 'Student'.

The paired *t* test is used to examine the likelihood of observing a difference between two variables as large as is observed if the null hypothesis (that the means are the same) is true. This situation is very similar to the *z* test presented in Chapter 2. The difference between the *z* test and the *t* test is that a *t* test is done when we do not know the population standard deviation (σ). Because we seldom know population parameters like the standard deviation, *t* tests are much more common than *z* tests.

When doing a *t* test we estimate the population standard deviation with the standard deviation of the sample. Although this is our best guess, it is not perfect and the resulting scores are not exactly Normally distributed. The reason for this, and some of the implications, are described in Box 3.1. The result is that instead of using the *z* table we use the *t* table (Appendix C). The most important difference between the *z* table and the *t* table is that the *p* values for the *t* table depend on the number of people in the sample. As the sample grows larger, the distribution of *t* values becomes more and more like the Normal distribution.

Instead of just using the number of people, the table lists the *degrees of freedom* (df). This is an important concept in statistics. For a paired *t* test, the number of degrees of freedom is equal to the number of cases minus one ($n - 1$). When this number is large, say above 100, the *t* distribution is for most purposes the same as the Normal distribution (see the final row of the *t* table in Appendix C). When there are fewer degrees of freedom (that is, fewer observations), the *t* distribution is more spread out than the Normal distribution (see Figure 3.2).

Example: Political Attitudes

Suppose a political science researcher was interested in whether people's political attitudes were different before and after an election. S/he sampled 20 people and asked them a series of political questions designed to measure people on the left–right continuum from zero (very left wing) to 100 (very right wing). Respondents were given these questions before the election and then again after the election. Table 3.1 shows the results of this, and, as was done with the drug treatment example in Chapter 1, the differences and residuals are also calculated. The mean or average difference is positive, indicating that the mean shift was for more right-wing responses after the election. The mean shift is only two points on the scale, which does not seem like much. To see how likely we would be to observe a difference this large or larger if there was no difference in the population we use the following equation:[1]

$$t = \frac{\overline{(x_{2i} - x_{1i})} - \mu}{s/\sqrt{n}} = \frac{\bar{d} - \mu}{s/\sqrt{n}}$$

For this example, the x_{2i} are the attitude scores after the election and x_{1i} are the scores before the election. These are subtracted to create a difference score, d_i, and the mean of these differences is found, here denoted $\bar{d}$ (see Table 3.1). s is the estimated standard deviation of the population and n is the number of people questioned. μ stands for the hypothesised mean, which in this case is zero (the null hypothesis is that there is no difference between the mean before and after the election, or that $\mu = 0$). To find the standard deviation of the sample we use the equation presented in Chapter 2 and input the differences:

$$s = \sqrt{\frac{\sum(d_i - \bar{d})^2}{n-1}} = \sqrt{\frac{\sum(d_i - 2)^2}{19}} = \sqrt{\frac{1040}{19}} = 7.40$$

We then enter this value into the t equation:

$$t = \frac{2}{7.40/\sqrt{20}} = \frac{2}{7.40/4.47} = 1.21$$

We use the t table (Appendix C) to determine how likely we would be to get a t this large if the null hypothesis was true. The first step in using this table is to decide whether we are doing a one- or a two-tailed test (see Box 2.2). Usually we will do a two-tailed test, and this example is no exception because we are interested in a difference in either direction. Next, we figure out the degrees of freedom; here 19 because there are 20 people. We go down the 'df' column until we come to 19. Then we look in the column corresponding to our α level. In this case, if we were using $\alpha = 0.05$, the observed value of 1.21 is less than the critical value of 2.09. This means we fail to reject the null hypothesis. Looking at the table, we could not have rejected the hypothesis even if we had used $\alpha = 0.20$. The proper way to write this result is $t(19) = 1.21$; $p > 0.20$. The 19 refers to the degrees of freedom $(20 - 1)$. If the computer does the test for you, it will give a precise p value. In this case you would write $t(19) = 1.21$;

1 In some textbooks you will see this equation with $\sqrt{n-1}$ rather than $\sqrt{n}$. The difference is because the standard deviation presented here is the unbiased estimate of the population standard deviation (σ). If when calculating the standard deviation you divide by $\sqrt{n}$ rather than $\sqrt{n-1}$, then you would divide by $\sqrt{n-1}$ here. Unless you have a small sample, the difference between $\sqrt{n}$ and $\sqrt{n-1}$ is negligible.

Table 3.1   *Left–right political attitudes before and after an election*

Before score x_{1i}	After score x_{2i}	After−Before $x_{2i} - x_{1i} = d_i$	Residual e_i
34	29	−5	−7
31	26	−5	−7
22	14	−8	−10
21	24	+3	+1
67	74	+7	+5
51	54	+3	+1
78	93	+15	+13
19	21	+2	0
55	63	+8	+6
62	74	+12	+10
41	37	−4	−6
32	27	−5	−7
72	86	+14	+12
43	47	+4	+2
7	10	+3	+1
62	71	+9	+7
58	59	+1	−1
31	21	−10	−12
68	61	−7	−9
31	34	+3	+1
Mean $x_1 = 44.25$	Mean $x_2 = 46.25$	Mean $d = 2.0$	Mean $e = 0$

$p = 0.24$. When the probability is very low, the computer says the p value is 0.000. In these cases write $p < 0.001$, rather than $p = 0.000$.

A p value of 0.24 would often result even when H_0 is true. This is a large percentage. Therefore, we would say the result is non-significant, and we would fail to reject the null hypothesis. We would not be claiming that there was no difference, only that our data do not provide evidence to the contrary. However, with only 20 people asked, unless there was a very large shift, it is unlikely that a statistically significant finding would have occurred. In this case there is a high probability of a Type II error. The researcher would ideally want to question more people.

A couple of characteristics of the t table are worth noting. First, I have only listed the most often reported probability levels. I have also only listed a limited number of degrees of freedom: all of them up to 25, then in steps of five to 50 and ten to 100. If the precise number of degrees of freedom that you have for your problem is not listed, if you are worried about a Type I error you should round down. If you are more worried about a Type II error you should round up. Most textbooks argue you should always round down. While this is often the case, it is not always. Fortunately, these days your computer will give you a precise probability for most tests. Also, many of the computer packages have functions built in so that you can calculate a *p* value from the *t* value and the degrees of freedom. This is how I produced the *t* table in Appendix C.

Another Example: a Very Satisfying Day

Consider another example. O'Muircheartaigh *et al.*, (1993) asked people on how many days in the previous week they felt satisfied with life and then, immediately afterwards, asked on how many days they were very satisfied. We wanted to see if adding the word *very* made a difference. I sampled 50 respondents from this study: the mean for the first question was 2.9 (the scale ranged from zero to seven days) and the mean for the second was 2.2, a difference of −0.7. The standard deviation of the difference was 2.1. To get the standard error of the mean we divide this by the square root of the number of observations ($\sqrt{50}$ which is approximately 7). Putting the numbers into the equation for the *t* test yields:

$$t = \frac{\bar{d} - \mu}{s/\sqrt{n}} = \frac{-0.7}{0.3} = -2.34$$

As with the *z* values for the fluoride example in Chapter 2, a negative *t* value simply reflects the fact that the first mean is larger than the second; we treat it as if it were +2.34. Because there were 50 people, there are 49 degrees of freedom (df = 50 − 1). When we go to the table we find that in order to achieve a significant result with $\alpha = 0.05$ with a two-tailed test, we need a *t* larger in magnitude than about 2. Figure 3.1 illustrates that the observed *t* is larger in magnitude than the critical value (2.01) and therefore the result is statistically significant at the $\alpha = 0.05$ level. It is important to stress that all this means is that an effect was detected; it does not mean the effect is large.

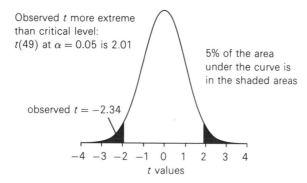

Figure 3.1   *Testing for the effects of the word 'very' in survey questions (the same people were asked questions with and without 'very')*

Box 3.1   Why Do I Have to Use the *t* Table?

It would be much easier if we could always just use the *z* table and not bother with the *t* table. Therefore it is worth going into some depth as to why it is important to use the *t* table. There are two related reasons. The first is statistical: if we use the *z* table our *p* values will be too low. The second reason is why this statistical problem matters: it is usually better to be conservative when rejecting hypotheses (Type I errors are usually thought of as being worse than Type II errors). I will begin with the statistical reason.

When we are doing a *z* test, we divide the mean of the differences by the standard error of the mean. For the *z* test, the standard error of the mean is based on the *known* population standard deviation and therefore it has no sampling error. However, when we conduct a *t* test, we estimate the population standard deviation using the sample standard deviation and therefore this estimate is subject to sampling error; it depends on who in the population happens to be sampled. Since the standard error of the mean is based on this, it too will have sampling error. The distribution of possible sample standard deviations usually provides a good estimate of the population standard deviation (it is unbiased, see Box 2.1), but it is positively skewed. More often than not, the sample standard deviation will be less than the population standard deviation. This increases the value of *t*. To control for this, the *t* distribution is more spread out than the *z* distribution.

How much more spread out the distribution is depends on the degrees of freedom. When there are only a few subjects, the *t* distribution is much more spread out. When the number of subjects increases the two distributions are much more similar (see Figure 3.2). When the number of subjects is above about 100, the two distributions are extremely close. With an infinite number of subjects, the distributions are the same.

One characteristic of the *p* values you get from the *t* table is that they are always larger than those you would get from the *z* table. Therefore, if the null hypothesis is true you are less likely to get a statistically significant result using the *t* tables than using the *z* tables. If you mistakenly use the *z* tables when you should have used the *t* tables, your chance of making a Type I error is increased. Although the probability of a Type I error is usually arbitrarily set at $\alpha = 0.05$, social scientists tend to be very concerned about the probability levels, and they like to be conservative when rejecting hypotheses. Thus if we decide to reject a hypothesis if the *p* value is less than 5% we usually want to make sure that the observed probability was in fact below this level. Suppose you ran a *t* test with 25 people and got a *t* value of 2. This value is not significant with a two-tailed *t* test at $\alpha = 0.05$. You need a value of 2.06 for it to be significant. However, it would be significant with a *z* test because you would need a value of only 1.96. The *t* value is more correct.

The insistence by many lecturers on using a *t* test is because of this difference. As I say throughout this book, however, researchers should be more concerned with their models and less with the precise *p* values, so perhaps this insistence is misplaced. On the other hand, it is important that researchers realise that they are doing a *t* test so that they know they are estimating the standard deviation as part of the procedure. Twenty years ago, when people were doing more work by hand and *t* tables were not always available, it could have been argued that unless you had a small sample then the *z* tables would suffice. Nowadays with computers doing almost all of the calculations, a *t* test should always be used when it is appropriate. When given two options for producing *p* values, it is obviously better to use the more accurate one.

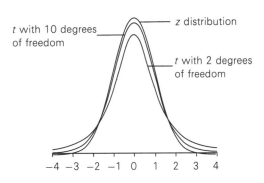

Figure 3.2   *The difference between the Normal (z) and the t distributions*

Confidence Intervals of the Mean

In Chapter 1 I distinguished between two types of statistics: one in which the researchers test particular hypotheses about the world, and the other where researchers try to describe or estimate particular aspects of the world. These two are related and it is often difficult to distinguish them. In this section I describe how to estimate the value of a population mean. This is often called *parameter estimation*.

Because these estimates are based on information from a sample rather than everyone in the population, they are liable to have some sampling error. The exact mean we observe from a sample is likely to be close to the true mean of the population, but is unlikely to be exactly the same as the population. To denote this uncertainty we construct a *confidence interval* around the observed value. Most people encounter confidence interval techniques when they read the reports of, for example, a survey that says 45 ± 2% of the population would vote for a particular party or that the house prices in the United Kingdom have increased by $2.1 \pm 0.2\%$ this year. These refer to the intervals 43% to 47% and 1.9% to 2.3%, respectively.

The $\pm$ (plus or minus) sign gives the likely range for the true value. Usually people use 95% confidence intervals (which are similar to the 5% level). This means that if researchers repeated their procedure hundreds of times, about 95% of the time the true population value would lie within the reported interval.

The way in which confidence intervals are found is fairly similar to conducting a t test. First you find the sample mean. Recall that the sample mean is an unbiased estimate of the population mean (discussed in Chapter 1). Next, you estimate the standard deviation for the population. This allows you to calculate the standard error of the mean. You then go to the t table and find what t value corresponds to the number of degrees of freedom in the sample and the level of confidence. If you want the 95% confidence interval, you look in the 0.05 column (two-tailed). If you want the 99% confidence interval, you look in the 0.01 column. Although the precise values vary according to the degrees of freedom, a 95% confidence interval should be about two standard errors on each side of the observed mean, and a 99% confidence interval should be closer to three standard errors on each side of the mean. The 95% confidence interval is the more common.

Suppose we were interested in estimating the population mean of left–right attitudes after the election (column 2 of Table 3.1). First, we would find the mean of these (46.25). Then, we would estimate the population standard deviation. In this case our estimate is 25.21. The standard error of the mean is this value divided by the square root of the number of cases (here 20), which gives 5.64. If we wanted to find the 95% confidence interval, we would look up the 5% two-tailed (confidence intervals are always two-tailed) level for 19 degrees of freedom and find the value 2.09. The general equation for confidence intervals is

$$CI = \bar{x} \pm t(\mathrm{df}, \alpha)SEM = \bar{x} \pm t(\mathrm{df}, \alpha)\frac{s}{\sqrt{n}}$$

When inserting the appropriate mean (46.25), critical value with 19 degrees of freedom and $\alpha = 0.05$ ($t = 2.09$), standard deviation (25.21) and sample size (20) we obtain

$$CI = 46.25 \pm (2.09)\frac{25.21}{\sqrt{20}} = 46.25 \pm 11.79$$

which can be written either as 46.25 ± 11.79 or as the interval (34.46, 58.04). If we had decided to use a 99% confidence interval the critical t value would be 2.86. The confidence interval would be 46.25 ± 16.13 or (30.12, 62.38). This is much wider than the 95% confidence interval. The reasons for choosing a particular confidence interval parallel the discussion about Type I and Type II errors. If it would be catastrophic for the researcher to report a confidence interval and have the true value outside of it, then s/he would want to choose the wider interval associated with the 99% confidence interval. Of course, this means that the reported interval is less precise. If you want to get a relatively precise confidence interval *and* still be confident that the true mean is within that interval, you usually need to increase the size of your sample and/or improve your measurement instrument.

Assumptions of the *t* Test

When either doing a paired *t* test or estimating the confidence interval for the mean of a variable, you are making various assumptions about the data. First, you are assuming that each pair of data, or each person questioned, is independent of the others. This assumption is made for almost all statistical tests. Lack of independence can occur, for example, when you sample all the people in each household and do not take into account that their attitudes, behaviours and circumstances will tend to be similar, or when you sample pupils and do not take into account that pupils from the same school tend to have similar backgrounds. You should try to make sure that each case you use is in fact independent of others, though there are some advanced (that is, beyond the scope of this book) techniques to help circumvent this problem (for example, Goldstein, 1995; Kreft and de Leeuw, forthcoming).

Another assumption for the paired *t* test is that the variables being measured are supposed to be interval. Strictly speaking, this assumption is required whenever you are talking about means. If the mean is meaningful (no pun intended) for your purposes, then this assumption is satisfied. It is always important to ask if the test you are doing makes sense. This is one problem with the computer packages; they do not ask. Because computers perform so many tests so simply, it is easy to run lots of different tests without examining what the data are really like. Fortunately, most statistics packages now have facilities to help you explore your data.

The assumption that researchers are most worried about is whether the distribution of the differences is Normally distributed. This means it should look similar to Figure 2.2. There are several statistical tests to judge whether a distribution is fairly Normal, but most researchers just *eyeball* it. If you make a histogram and its mode (its highest point) is near the centre and the distribution slopes away fairly evenly on each side, then most researchers are willing to assume that it comes from a Normally distributed population. Otherwise, some of the techniques described in the next section are necessary.

Related to this assumption is a mathematical theorem called the *central limit theorem*, which Stewart (1995: 3) describes as 'a very beautiful theorem' (I wonder if he has any beliefs about how Gossett developed the *t* test?). The central limit theorem states that as the size of the sample gets larger and larger, regardless of the variable's distribution, the distribution of means gets closer and closer to the Normal distribution. If it starts out fairly similar to the Normal distribution, this convergence is rapid. If it does not, it takes a larger sample for the sample of means to be approximately Normally distributed. Because it is the distribution of means rather than individual cases that is actually being tested when doing a *t* test, as your sample size increases you can become less concerned about the distribution of cases for testing differences in means (this does not mean you should not still be interested in it for its own sake; see the example below).

The final assumption (and for this technique it is actually the same as the previous one, but this is usually not the case) is that the residuals are Normally distributed. In addition, ideally they should not be related to other variables. This means that there should be no pattern in the residuals. Recall in Chapter 1 we presented this type of problem using the following equation:

$$d_i = \bar{d} + \mu + e_i$$

where d_i is the difference between the two scores for the ith individual $(d_i = x_{2i} - x_{1i})$, $\bar{d}$ is the mean of this difference, μ is the hypothesised difference (usually zero) and e_i is the residual for the ith individual. Conceptually, the t value is based on the magnitude of the observed mean of the differences $(\bar{d})$ divided by a measure of the spread of the residuals (e_i). When the magnitude of $\bar{d}$ is large compared with the magnitude of the residuals, then the t value will be large. To illustrate how to do a t test and some simple graphs using SPSS, we return to the left–right attitude example.

Computer Example

On p. 60 are the SPSS commands used to analyse these data. The first line (DATA LIST FREE /before after.) tells the computer that there are two variables and that they are arranged with a space or a comma between each value (they are in 'free form'). The data are then input (they are not printed here out of space considerations), and then a *t* test is conducted (T-TEST /PAIRS after before.). This single line produces the means, standard deviations and standard errors for both variables (x_{2i} and x_{1i}), and for the difference (d_i). It also gives what is called the correlation, a technique described in Chapter 5. This is a measure of how related the two variables are. It is high (it can range between -1 and $+1$, so 0.970 is very high), indicating that people who had positive views before the election also tended to have positive views after the election. The *t* test, degrees of freedom and probability are then printed.

The final command (PLOT /PLOT. . .), including the title and naming the axes, produces the accompanying graph (the different versions of SPSS have different graphical capabilities and syntax). This relatively simple graph shows that there is a pattern in the residuals (1 stands for one case, 2 stands for two cases, and so on if there were more cases). People who began as right wing tended to have positive residuals and those who began as left wing tend to have negative residuals. Returning to the data in Table 3.1, we see that right-wing people tended to be more right wing after the election and left-wing people tended to be more left wing. Thus, while the overall shift of the mean is not significant, there certainly were systematic differences. This illustrates the importance of graphing your data. If you had simply run the *t* test and reported that there was no significant difference between the means, then you would have missed this facet of the data. It appears as if people's political attitudes have been polarised by the election.

Alternatives When the Variable is Not Normally Distributed

When the assumptions of a statistical test are not met, there are three basic options that researchers usually choose from: ignoring the problem; using tests which do not require the assumptions; and transforming the variable. The first is just to do the test anyway. Strictly speaking this is wrong, but because it is usually the simplest alternative it is often done. The problem is that the conclusions made can be wrong. Statistical techniques like the *t* test weight extreme values, or outliers, very heavily, allowing these few cases to distort the overall picture. Consider the following example. A researcher wanted to see whether people tended to have more or less money after some tax changes were instigated. Ten people were sampled at random and their before and after incomes are shown in Table 3.2.

Table 3.2 *Take-home income with and without tax changes (in £ thousands)*

	1	2	3	4	5	6	7	8	9	10	$\bar{x}$	Median
Without	7.5	10.2	4.2	8.8	173.9	12.3	3.5	11.0	10.8	7.8	25.0	9.5
With	6.9	9.1	3.8	8.0	221.5	10.7	3.5	9.9	9.6	7.0	29.0	8.55
Difference	−0.6	−1.1	−0.4	−0.8	+47.6	−1.6	0.0	−1.1	−1.2	−0.8	+4	−0.8

Using the *t* test equation we get $t(9) = 0.83$; $p = 0.43$ with the mean increasing a considerable amount (£4000). The question is, if the government said that there was no evidence that people were doing worse, would these data support their claim? Even though the mean increases, clearly the typical person is doing worse. The median income is lower after the tax change. In fact, only one person gets richer, it is just that this person gets a lot richer. The government's claim that the average income goes up can be criticised in two ways. The first, and the more obvious, is that to say that people's income increases when eight out of ten incomes go down seems scandalous. The problem here is that the mean income is not the ideal measure for this situation. If you are concerned with the typical person, then the median is a better measure. The mean is highly influenced by the extremely high income, and this distorts the true picture.

```
DATA LIST FREE /before after.
BEGIN DATA
      Place data in here
END DATA.
T-TEST /PAIRS after before.
```
Paired samples t-test: after
                        before

Variable	Number of Cases	Mean	Standard Deviation	Standard Error
AFTER	20	46.2500	25.213	5.638
BEFORE	20	44.2500	20.295	4.538

	(Difference)						
Mean	Standard Deviation	Standard Error	2-Tail Corr.	Prob.	t Value	Degrees of Freedom	2-Tail Prob.
2.0000	7.398	1.654	.970	.000	1.21	19	.242

```
COMPUTE resid = (after – before) – 2.
PLOT /PLOT resid WITH before
     /TITLE 'Examining Residuals'
     /VERTICAL 'Residuals'
     /HORIZONTAL 'Before attitude (mean 44.25)'.
```

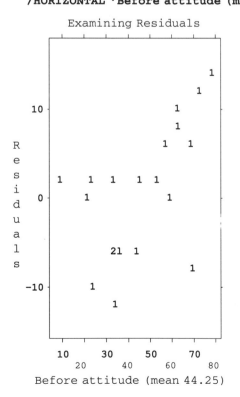

Before attitude (mean 44.25)

A government spokesperson could retort that the government is interested in the mean income because it still believes in the trickle-down theory of economics, where the rich people invest their income in industry, leading to greater wealth for everyone (and not just the heads of those industries who often set their own salaries). In this case, the data still do not strongly support its view. The problem is the probability values for a *t* test assume that the variable is Normally distributed. While small deviations from this are usually acceptable, large ones are not. This example illustrates one of the reasons why. The entire result is based on one person in the sample. If this person had not been sampled, then an entirely different conclusion would have been reached.

One method of minimising the influence of outliers is to discard the lowest and highest values (if the sample is large more could be discarded but it is important that the same number of low values as high values are discarded).[2] When case 6 (the largest decrease) and case 5 (the largest increase) are discarded the result is significant $t(7) = -5.21$; $p < 0.001$ in the direction of a decrease in funds.

Distribution-free Techniques

When the value of a statistic can be changed dramatically by a single case, we say that the test is not *robust* in that situation. There is a group of statistical tests called *distribution-free* that do not make assumptions about the distribution of the variable and they are more robust when there are a few outliers.[3] There are several robust statistics that can be used as alternatives when comparing two sets of matched data. The two main ones are the sign test and the Wilcoxon matched-pairs signed-ranks test (hereinafter referred to as the Wilcoxon pairs test).

For the sign test you are investigating whether about the same proportion of people are changing in each direction. In this case you would be testing whether the tax changes caused about the same number of people to have less money as to have more money. The typical scenario is when you have two scores for the same person, as with the tax example. This test makes no assumptions about the distribution of the variable(s) under consideration and can be used when the data are ratio, interval or ordinal.

When run on a computer, the number of cases whose second score is higher is compared with those whose first score is higher. For the above data, one person made more money, one person made the same amount of money and eight people made less. The person who made the same amount is excluded. Cases

2   If you are removing several points then the standard error also needs to be adjusted. Readers are encouraged to read Wilcox (1995) for details.

3   These are sometimes referred to as non-parametric tests. This is a confusing misnomer because many of these tests still test/estimate the values of parameters and still assume the variables are based on some metric (that is, scale). For this reason I will use the phrase distribution-free rather than non-parametric.

that do not change are excluded because they provide no information about whether there is an increase or a decrease. Excluding the single case leaves nine people whose income has changed. This statistic calculates the probability of an eight to one split if a person was equally likely to make more or less. In SPSS, the following command is used:

NPAR TESTS SIGN /VARIABLES after before.

The result is $p = 0.04$ in the direction of a decrease in income.

An alternative that is often used is the Wilcoxon pairs test. This is used when you assume interval data, but you do not require the variable to be Normally distributed. Like the sign test, all cases where there was no difference are excluded. Conceptually, this test takes all the differences (the d_is) and ranks them according to their magnitude (that is, ignoring their sign). Then, all the negative change scores are added together and all the positive change scores are added together. Those who did not change are excluded. The sums of the negative change and positive change cases are compared. When run on a computer various corrections take place (for the number of tied ranks, etc.). These corrections should be used. The following command is used in SPSS and produces a z value of -1.60. This could be looked up in the z table, but fortunately the computer calculates the p value (here, $p = 0.11$).

NPAR TEST WILCOXON /VARIABLES after before.

When comparing the paired t test, the sign test and the Wilcoxon pairs test it is worth considering two factors. The first is the impact that single outliers may have on these statistics. The t test is the most affected, followed by the Wilcoxon and then the sign test. Outliers have a very small effect on the sign test; many researchers feel too small an effect. Another aspect is what is called the *power* of the test. Recall from Chapter 2 that the power of a test is the likelihood of rejecting the null hypothesis when it is false. When the difference between the two scores is Normally distributed, the t test is more powerful than the Wilcoxon test which is in turn more powerful than the sign test. These differences, however, are not that large. When the variable is not Normally distributed, the distribution-free alternatives can be more powerful (see Blair and Higgins, 1985).[4]

---

4 In many courses people are taught that the t test is usually, or even always, more powerful than its distribution-free alternatives. This myth is probably due to the fact that it is more powerful when all the assumptions are satisfied, and researchers often take this for granted. More often than not the distributions have several outliers and in these cases the distribution-free alternatives can be substantially more powerful. As Cliff (1993; 494–495) has noted, the distribution-free tests only 'sacrifice a little power when circumstances are optimum for the normal-based ones, but often have greater power, sometimes substantially greater, when classical assumptions are violated'. Interested readers may wish to consult Wilcox (1995) for details of other alternatives.

Transforming the Variable

The final option a researcher has when the variable of interest is not Normally distributed is to transform it into one that is. This is often done, for example, when comparing either individual incomes or when using reaction time data. It is well known that these variables are highly positively skewed (they stretch far to the right). Researchers use transformations in order to get them to be more like the Normal distribution. One popular transformation is taking what is called the natural logarithm of the variable. It makes the variable less positively skewed.

Consider the following histogram of the natural logarithm of the population of the states of the USA. In Chapter 1 the histogram of the untransformed variable was shown and we noted it was highly positively skewed. Now it is considerably less skewed and the new mean (14.9) and median (15.0) are about the same. I have also printed the skewness. When a distribution has no skewness, its value is 0. When it has a long tail to the left, the skewness is negative, and when it has a long tail to the right it is positive. Here the skewness is 0.002. Therefore the distribution is essentially symmetric. The skewness of the untransformed variable was 2.56 which indicates that it is highly positively skewed.

```
COMPUTE lnpop = LN (popula).
FREQUENCIES /VARIABLES lnpop /HISTOGRAM /STATISTICS MEAN
MEDIAN SKEWNESS.
```

```
LNPOP natural log – transformed – population
Count  Midpoint
   2    13.10   |■
   5    13.35   |■■■■■
   1    13.60   |■
   4    13.85   |■■■■
   2    14.10   |■■
   4    14.35   |■■■■
   2    14.60   |■■
   4    14.85   |■■■■
   6    15.10   |■■■■■■
   7    15.35   |■■■■■■■
   5    15.60   |■■■■■
   1    15.85   |■
   2    16.10   |■■
   3    16.35   |■■■
   2    16.60   |■■
   0    16.85   |
   1    17.10   |■ California
            I...............
            0 2 4 6 810
            Histogram Frequency

Mean  14.903   Median  15.008   Skewness  .002
```

Another common transformation involves truncating the data. This means you simply count all values beyond a certain value as being equal to that value. For example, in Wright *et al.* (1994) people were asked how much television they watched on a typical weekday. The responses ranged from zero to 20 hours, but most of the people said they watched less than five hours a day. In order to do the necessary analyses, we counted all amounts above nine hours as equal to nine hours. If this had not been done the '20-hour couch potatoes' would have had an extreme influence on the analysis.

Summary

Three main concepts should have been learned in this chapter. The first is a general understanding of 'Student's' paired *t* test; when, why and how to use it. Briefly, it is appropriate when you have two values for each case or pair, and want to see if the means are different. The second is that while statistical tests can be done much more quickly using a computer, doing so without 'getting a feel' for the data can lead to wrong conclusions. The example of left–right attitudes illustrated this, as do several others throughout the remainder of this book. Finally, alternatives were introduced when the assumptions of the paired *t* test are not satisfied. These procedures can be extremely useful.

Assignment

1   Half of my time in the library used to be spent waiting to photocopy various materials. That was until I applied statistics to this problem. I randomly sampled ten days and went into the photocopying area of my library at 10 a.m. and 4 p.m. on these days. I counted the number of people and the data are shown below.

Day	1	2	3	4	5	6	7	8	9	10
10 a.m.	4	7	4	8	3	11	4	2	6	2
4 p.m.	8	5	10	8	12	6	15	8	6	7

What conclusions would I make from these data and how would it have affected my behaviour?

2   The effect of caffeine on problem-solving ability is of interest both to scientists working on the relationships between drugs and cognition and to many students. A researcher asked 100 students to take a standardised test on two subsequent days. For the first day, they were given a pill without any chemical additives, a so-called placebo. On the second day they were

given the same test but with a caffeine pill. The means for these tests were 112 and 132, respectively. The standard deviation of the difference was 25. Is the difference between these scores statistically significant? Is the conclusion that caffeine improves scores necessarily valid?

3   The students described in Exercise 2 had their heart rate measured before both tests. When tested after taking the caffeine pill, the students' heart rates were, on average, 2.4 beats per minute faster. This difference had a standard deviation of 16. Is there evidence from these data that caffeine affects heart rate?

4   In the states.sps data set there are variables for the number of prisoners per state for 1989 and for 1990 (in Appendix A). Is the increase in prisoners in 1990 beyond what might be expected from chance if there was no underlying cause for the difference?

5   Many surveys ask the same respondents questions at several points in time. In these longitudinal or panel surveys, responses to various questions often change. Usually this is due to the person's circumstances changing, but sometimes it is due to a mistake, or a data entry error. Consider the following data taken from five people three months apart. The question asked 'How many children, of your own, do you have living in your house?'

Number of children January 1994	1	3	2	0	4
Number of children April 1994	1	3	22	0	4

A *t* test on these data results in a *t* of 1.0 which with 4 degrees of freedom has a *p* value of 0.374. Comment on this result.

6   This is a trick problem. A researcher wanted to see the effect on reading achievement of letting children progress at their own pace while the instructor walked around offering help. The researcher compared this to more formal teaching methods. Fifty pupils were sampled. They were grouped into pairs based on their present reading skills, parents' socio-economic status and gender. Thus, there were 25 pairs of pupils. One member of each pair was put into the formal classroom setting and the other into the new-style setting. After two months, they were given a standard reading test scored from 0 to 100. The data are shown below. Each pair has three numbers: a pair number (to help identify each pair), the score for the pupil put into the formal class and the score for the pupil put into the new-style class.

    Complete the necessary statistical (and possibly graphical) analysis. Note also that the variable labels and the slashes are important for SPSS. If you are using another package, or another implementation of SPSS, there will be similar commands. (You should put these data and commands in a file because they will be used again for Exercise 7).

```
DATA LIST FREE /pairno formal newst.
BEGIN DATA
   1  57  55
   2  28  30
   3  83  92
   4  58  55
   5  42  34
   6  18  30
   7  55  51
   8  74  81
   9  42  33
  10   6  22
  11  36  28
  12  12  27
  13  40  34
  14  79  88
  15  32  29
  16  74  85
  17  19  27
  18  22  29
  19  13  24
  20  49  43
  21  78  84
  22  62  64
  23  64  61
  24   5  22
  25  52  47
END DATA.
VARIABLE LABELS pairno 'pair number'/
   formal 'score for formal'/
   newst 'score for new style'.
```

7 Conduct a sign test and a Wilcoxon pairs test on the data in Exercise 6. Comment on these results. Which of these tests do you feel is the more appropriate?

8 Thirty married couples were asked to talk about a recent movie they had seen together. The interviewer recorded the number of words said by each husband and wife. The null hypothesis was that husbands and wives would each talk about the same amount. The output from SPSS is shown below. What conclusions, if any, would you make?

```
T-TEST PAIRS wife husband.
Paired samples t-test: WIFE
                      HUSBAND
```

Variable	Number of Cases	Mean	Standard Deviation	Standard Error
WIFE	30	26.6333	9.915	1.810
HUSBAND	30	34.0667	18.396	3.359

(Difference)

Mean	Standard Deviation	Standard Error	2-Tail Corr.	Prob.	t Value	Degrees of Freedom	2-Tail Prob.
-7.4333	16.654	3.041	.437	.016	-2.44	29	.021

9   For both the sign test and the Wilcoxon test, when there is no difference between the measurements on the two occasions, these cases are discarded. Briefly, why is this justified?

10   It is no secret that meteorology, the prediction of weather, is not an exact science. When weather reporters say it is going to be 19 °C today, they would not bet their lives on it being exactly 19 °C. What they mean is that it is likely that the temperature will be about 19 °C. Suppose their estimates were based on 25 observations and that the mean of these measurements was 19 but with a standard deviation of 5. What is the 95% confidence interval for the temperature? What is the 99% confidence interval?

11   Look through the numerical figures that a newspaper reports without confidence intervals. Write some of these down which you feel are not exact figures, but are actually estimates that should include some form of confidence intervals.

4

Comparing the Means of Two Groups

In the previous chapter I described how to compare the means of two variables for one group of people. Another common situation is when you want to compare the mean of one variable for two groups of people. This often occurs when you are interested in differences between naturally occurring groups, such as men and women or employed and unemployed, or when you use an experimental and a control (or alternative) group.

The most common statistical technique for this situation is called the group t test. According to my romanticised image, this test also was conceived in the lush green valleys of Ireland, pouring forth from the quill of William Gossett as he evaded the authorship constraints of his employer (see the start of Chapter 3 if you have no idea what I am talking about). Like the paired t test, this technique is also attributed to 'Student' and in many ways it is similar to the paired t test. Towards the end of this chapter I will compare these two tests in detail. This comparison allows the concept of power to be discussed in more depth and also opens up many methodological questions that are intertwined with the statistical techniques.

The Group t Test: Formal Definitions

The group t test is used to compare the means of two groups for a single variable. It is similar to the paired t test in that the difference between the means is divided by the estimated standard error of this difference. Calculating this standard error is fairly tricky, and is described in Box 4.1. The difference between the two t tests is that here we are interested in the difference between the two means, rather than the mean of the differences. Suppose we measure the attitudes of people from two different countries towards further European integration. The group t test is used to tell us if the people in one country are more (or less) in favour of European integration than the other.

The group t test equation is shown below. In this equation the overbars (the ⁻) are above the variable for each group individually. $\overline{x_1}$ and $\overline{x_2}$ are the means of the variable x for the first and second groups, respectively. The sample sizes of these groups are n_1 and n_2, and s_1 and s_2 are the estimated standard deviations for each group. In this equation it is assumed that the standard deviations of the two groups are approximately the same. This is known as the pooled estimate because the two standard deviations are *pooled* together. It is evaluated with the t table for $n_1 + n_2 - 2$ degrees of freedom.

$$t = \frac{\overline{x_1} - \overline{x_2}}{s_{\overline{x_1} - \overline{x_2}}} = \frac{\overline{x_1} - \overline{x_2}}{\sqrt{\dfrac{n_1 s_1^2 + n_2 s_2^2}{n_1 + n_2}} \sqrt{\dfrac{1}{n_1} + \dfrac{1}{n_2}}}$$

This equation is slightly simpler than the one produced in some textbooks. The difference stems from the *s* used here being the estimated population standard deviation (σ), while some textbooks continue to use *s* as the sample standard deviation.

The derivation of this equation is described in Box 4.1. Here it is simply important to understand how the value of *t* varies with the other factors. If we are interested in showing a difference between the two groups we want a *t* value that *is as large* as possible (as *t* goes up, *p* goes down). Clearly as the difference between $\overline{x_1}$ and $\overline{x_2}$ increases, the *t* value goes up (for all these comparisons I am assuming everything else stays the same). If the standard deviation of s_1 and/or s_2 goes up, which could occur if a less reliable measurement scale is used, the *t* value will go down. The opposite is true if a more reliable scale is used. If more people are questioned (resulting in an increase in n_1 and/or n_2), then the *t* value will go up.

As with the paired *t* test, when we look up the *t* value we need to know the degrees of freedom. For the group *t* test, the degrees of freedom are $n_1 + n_2 - 2$, or the total number of people minus two. The reason for this will be explained when showing the equation-based model for this test.

Two Examples

Consider the following example adapted from a paper by Bornstein (1994). Bornstein was interested in how potential jurors attribute blame in civil liability cases, depending on whether the defendant is a large corporation or a small independent company. He asked 64 people to rate, on a scale from -100 to 100, the sympathy they felt for the defendant in a liability case. Suppose that for 30 people the defendant was the large corporation and for 34 the defendant was the small company, but except for that the case descriptions were identical.[1] The mean for people told it was a corporate defendant was -12 (slightly negative) with a standard deviation of 38.4, and the mean for those told it was a small company was $+12.5$ with a standard deviation of 34.4. The resulting *t* value is -2.69:

$$t = \frac{-12 - 12.5}{\sqrt{\dfrac{30 \times 38.4^2 + 34 \times 34.4^2}{30 + 34}} \sqrt{\dfrac{1}{30} + \dfrac{1}{34}}} = \frac{-24.5}{9.10} = -2.69$$

---

1 Bornstein (1994) actually used a within-subject design, which, as discussed later in this chapter, is more powerful.

Because there are 64 people in total, there are 62 degrees of freedom. This is close enough to 60 to look at this row, and we see that 2.69 is larger (just) than the value in the 0.01 column (2.66). Thus, even if we had set the rather stringent target of $\alpha = 0.01$, we would still be able to report a significant difference. We would write this result either as $t(62) = -2.69; p < 0.01$ or as $t(62) = 2.69; p < 0.01$. Since the ordering of the two groups is arbitrary, we can choose either the positive or negative t value.

Let us reconsider the arithmetic problem from the first two chapters. In those chapters, we saw that the mean number (out of a maximum of 20) of correctly answered problems when presented with symbols (that is, $4 + 7 = \_\_$) was 8 with a standard deviation of 6.96. When the problem was presented as a word problem (Dan has 4 cookies, Rachel gave him 7 more. Now how many does Dan have? $\_\_$)[2] there was a mean of 13 with a standard deviation of 2.55. In both groups there were only five pupils. When these numbers are entered into the equation for t we obtain a value of -1.51. With only 8 degrees of freedom $(5 + 5 - 2)$ it is significant only at $\alpha = 0.20$. Although the actual difference between the means is fairly high (and if you recall from Chapters 1 and 2 there was a good explanation for this difference) because the sample sizes are so small we cannot conclude that the difference was not simply due to chance. We 'fail to reject the null hypothesis that there is a difference between the groups'.

$$ t = \frac{8 - 13}{\sqrt{\frac{5 \times 6.96^2 + 5 \times 2.55^2}{5 + 5}} \sqrt{\frac{1}{5} + \frac{1}{5}}} = -1.51 $$

This equation assumes that the standard deviations of the two groups are approximately the same. Because of the large difference between the two standard deviations we would want to use what is called the separate variance estimate. This is described in Box 4.1 and most of the main computer packages, including SPSS, print this out for you.

Comparing Group Standard Deviations

It is often of substantive importance to compare the standard deviations (or the variances) of two groups. To do this we use what is called an F test. The F statistic is simply the ratio of the larger variance to the smaller variance. To test the null hypothesis of equal variances or, equivalently, equal standard deviations $(H_0 : \sigma_1 = \sigma_2)$ we use F tables (see Appendix D). Like the t test, the F test also depends on the degrees of freedom, but this time two different degrees of freedom have to be taken into account. The estimate of σ for group 1 (s_1) has $n_1 - 1$ degrees of freedom. Likewise, the estimate of σ for group 2 (s_2) has $n_2 - 1$ degrees of freedom. These must both be used.

2   Dan's wife is named Rachel. This is a particularly enjoyable example.

Box 4.1   Estimating the Standard Error

There are two basic cases that arise when estimating the standard error for a group t test. The first is where you are assuming that, in the populations from which the samples are drawn, the two standard deviations are equal. In this case you *pool* the group standard deviations together to estimate a single standard deviation. Deriving the equation for this requires some algebra, but it is not that difficult (the derivation is carried out below). In the second case, you do not assume that the standard deviations are equal. Differences in standard deviations may be interesting in themselves, but present a more difficult statistical problem. Some suggested solutions are described at the end of this box. Fortunately your statistical package will solve for both and allow you to choose which one is more appropriate.

We saw in Chapter 3 that the best estimate for the standard error of the mean, here denoted $se_{\bar{x}}$ (denoted $\hat{\sigma}_\mu$ in some books), is

$$se_{\bar{x}} = \frac{s_x}{\sqrt{n}} = \sqrt{\frac{s_x^2}{n}} \quad \text{or} \quad se_{\bar{x}}^2 = \frac{s_x^2}{n}$$

When doing a group t test, we want to find the standard deviation of the difference between the two means. In general, the standard deviation of a difference of two variables is

$$\sigma_{x-y} = \sqrt{\sigma_x^2 + \sigma_y^2 - 2\mathrm{Cov}(x,y)}$$

where $\mathrm{Cov}(x,y)$ is called the *covariance* of the variables x and y. This is a measure of how related the two variables are and will be discussed in detail in Chapter 5. In a group t test, the people in the groups are different. In statistical terms they are independent, which means that the covariance of x_1 and x_2 is 0 and therefore the $2\mathrm{Cov}(x,y)$ term is equal to zero and can be dropped. In this case, the equation is

$$se_{\bar{x_1}-\bar{x_2}} = \sqrt{se_{\bar{x_1}}^2 + se_{\bar{x_2}}^2} = \sqrt{\frac{s_1^2}{n_1} + \frac{s_2^2}{n_2}}$$

It is at this point that our assumption about equal population standard deviations comes into play. We combine s_1 and s_2 to estimate a single (pooled) standard deviation, which we call s_p. We could simply take the average of the two group values. This works when both groups are large or if they are of the same size. In some cases one group has a much larger sample size; therefore, you would trust the estimate from this sample more. To account for this we weight the standard deviations according to their sample sizes. Each standard deviation is multiplied by the percentage of the total number of cases in its group.

$$s_p = \sqrt{\frac{n_1}{n_1 + n_2}s_1^2 + \frac{n_2}{n_1 + n_2}s_2^2} = \sqrt{\frac{n_1 s_1^2 + n_2 s_2^2}{n_1 + n_2}}$$

When the group sample sizes are equal, this simply is the average. Now, we use this pooled standard deviation term for both standard deviations when estimating the standard error:

$$se_{\bar{x}_1 - \bar{x}_2} = \sqrt{\frac{s_p^2}{n_1} + \frac{s_p^2}{n_2}} = s_p \sqrt{\frac{1}{n_1} + \frac{1}{n_2}}$$

$$= \sqrt{\frac{n_1 s_1^2 + n_2 s_2^2}{n_1 + n_2}} \sqrt{\frac{1}{n_1} + \frac{1}{n_2}}$$

Although this equation may seem a bit cumbersome, you will be pleased to know that your computer can solve it with ease.

When the standard deviations are not approximately the same then the above procedure is not appropriate. Instead, when doing a t test by hand the earlier equation is usually used:

$$se_{\bar{x}_1 - \bar{x}_2} = \sqrt{se_{\bar{x}_1}^2 + se_{\bar{x}_2}^2} = \sqrt{\frac{s_1^2}{n_1} + \frac{s_2^2}{n_2}}$$

Since a larger standard error for either of these groups will increase the standard error of the difference, the degrees of freedom used should be the smaller of $n_1 - 1$ and $n_2 - 1$. This makes it more difficult to get a statistically significant result. There are more complex ways to solve this problem and most computer packages will use these methods. When the computer shows the 'separate variance' or 'unequal variance' estimates, it will usually give a different number of degrees of freedom (see example below). This uses a much more complicated procedure and is a better estimate than the simple 'smaller of $n_1 - 1$ and $n_2 - 1$' rule. In practice, however, the two estimates are usually fairly similar.

As an example, consider the following. In survey and questionnaire research there is much interest in how strongly worded the verbal anchors of a response scale should be. When asking people how pleased they are with some situation, some researchers feel the scale should run from 'unhappy' to 'happy' while others feel it should run from 'very unhappy' to 'very happy'. With various assumptions, the prediction is that adding the word 'very' to the anchors should force people's responses towards the middle, thereby lowering the variance. Suppose two versions of a question were used, asking people to rate how happy they thought they were. The first group ($n_1 = 62$) had the unmodified anchors and the second group ($n_2 = 63$) had the intensifier 'very' added to each anchor.

The standard deviation for the first group was 1.24, while the standard deviation for the second group was 1.12. We divide the larger of these by the smaller so that the F value is larger than 1.

$$F(n_1 - 1, n_2 - 1) = \frac{s_1^2}{s_2^2} = \frac{1.24^2}{1.12^2} = 1.23$$

To assess whether this value is significantly different from 1, which would mean the two standard deviations were significantly different from each other, we use the F table. Unlike the z and t tables, the values in the F table refer only to one side of the distribution. This is most useful for tests discussed in Chapter 6 where we compare means amongst groups. When comparing standard deviations, however, we have to double the probability; the reasons for this will become clearer in Chapter 6. It has to do with this being a two-tailed test. Because the F table only gives the values for $\alpha = 0.05$ and $\alpha = 0.01$, using the table we can only test at $\alpha = 0.10$ and $\alpha = 0.02$. Also, the F table does not list all possible degrees of freedom. However, $F(50, 50)$ is close enough to $F(61, 62)$ for present purposes. The critical values for $\alpha = 0.10$ and $\alpha = 0.02$ are 1.60 and 1.95, respectively, therefore we fail to reject the null hypothesis. If you use a computer program to find the precise probability of $F(61, 62) = 1.23$ you get $p = 0.42$. If we had been doing a one-tailed test then we would not have had to double the probabilities, but do consider the warnings about this from Box 2.2. For this example, we would still fail to reject the null hypothesis.

The arithmetic problem-solving example produced different standard deviations. To test whether this difference is significant, we square each standard deviation and put the larger (corresponding to the symbol group) variance over the smaller. The resulting value of 7.46 can be evaluated with the F tables for 4 and 4 degrees of freedom. Because the number of cases is so small, this also fails to reach statistical significance at the conventional $\alpha = 0.05$ level. However, if we were trying to decide whether to treat the standard deviations as being equal, we would be more concerned with the value of F rather than its significance. Because it is much larger than 1, we would probably not want to assume that the standard deviations in the populations from which these samples were drawn are the same. In general anything above about 3 is high enough that you would not want to assume that the population variances were equal even if the statistic is not significant.

An Equation Form of the Group t Test

The group t test can also be represented as a simple equation and with a graph, as was done in Chapter 1. In the equation below, x_i stands for the variable of interest, and g_i is the variable denoting the group. It is common practice to have this variable equal to 0 for all the people in one group and 1 for all the people in the other. This variable is called a *dummy* variable. In some cases it is better to use slightly different coding (for example, -1 for one group and $+1$ for the other, which is sometimes called *effects coding* or *deviation coding*), but this 0/1 variable will suffice here. Other coding techniques are discussed in Chapter 6. The parameters that we are trying to estimate are denoted with the Greek letter β (beta) and with subscripts. In this equation β_0 is the intercept which in this case measures the mean for the first group (since g_i equals zero for this group) and β_1 measures the difference in the means between groups. The e_i are the residuals. When we do a group t test we are testing the null hypothesis that $\beta_1 = 0$ (that is, there is no difference between the groups).

$$x_i = \beta_1 g_i + \beta_0 + e_i$$

Suppose a sample of ten men and ten women were asked about their attitudes towards nuclear disarmament on a scale of 1 ('the world is safe because we can blow it up') to 7 ('we should dispense with weapons of mass destruction that cannot rationally be used'). The data are shown in Figure 4.1. If we let g_i equal 0 for males and 1 for females then β_0 is the mean score for males and β_1 is the difference between males and females. A positive β_1 means that women were more in favour of nuclear disarmament than men. The observed values for β_0 and β_1 are 4.5 and 0.5 respectively. In doing a t test we are testing whether β_1 is significantly different from zero (H_0: the means are the same). The significance will depend on the size of the residuals and the overall sample size. Here the difference is not large enough to be significant at $\alpha = 0.05$.

Assumptions of the Group t Test

The assumptions for the group t test are similar to those for the paired t test. The two that researchers are most concerned with are that the variable is Normally distributed and the groups have approximately the same standard deviation.

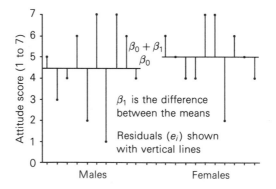

Figure 4.1   *Attitude towards nuclear weapons by gender*

When these assumptions are not satisfied, the probability of the resulting t value is inappropriate.

When the sample sizes are large and there is approximately the same number of people in each group, the Normality assumption is less critical. It is important, however, to inspect the distribution. If it has a peculiar shape, then this may be of some interest itself. As I mentioned before, when the standard deviations (or variances) are not equal, this is also an important observation. Too often researchers see examining the distributions and the standard deviations as methodological chores, rather than as something interesting in its own right.

When these assumptions cannot be satisfied, you have three choices: go ahead and do the group t test anyway; perform one of the distribution-free alternatives; or transform the data. The first of these is the lazy way and will often lead to wrong conclusions. To illustrate these alternatives consider the following problem Anne McDaid and I faced a few years ago (Wright and McDaid, 1996). We were investigating differences between police line-ups (where the eyewitnesses try to identify the culprit) conducted at specialist line-up suites and those conducted at ordinary police stations. The outcomes at the suites were different from those at the ordinary stations. This worried the police, but the cases sent to the suites were different from those conducted at the ordinary stations and, therefore, this could have been the reason for the difference in outcomes. One difference appeared to be the time between the crime and the line-up.

We looked at the difference between the suites and the ordinary police stations with regard to the elapsed time between the crime and the line-up. I have taken a sample of 720 line-ups from the original data set for explanatory purposes. The distribution of elapsed time of this sample was positively skewed. While most (over 70%) occurred within the first two months, there were some that took place over a year after the crime. A t test resulted in a non-significant result $(t(718) = -0.40; p = 0.687)$. The negative t value indicates that the elapsed time at the suites was longer than at the ordinary police stations. If we had stopped there, we would have reported failure to reject the hypothesis that the elapsed time was the same for these groups. However, because the distribution was highly skewed the cases that had long elapsed time had an unduly high impact on the t test. One method to minimise this problem is to conduct what is called the Mann–Whitney U test (sometimes called the Wilcoxon rank-sum W test, but to avoid confusion with the Wilcoxon pairs test introduced in the previous chapter, I will refer to this as the Mann–Whitney U test). In this test, all the times (for both groups) are ranked. Then, these ranks are added together *within* each of the groups. As with the Wilcoxon pairs test, the computer deals with ties in a specific way. When this test is run, the result is significant: $z = -2.91; p = 0.004$.

The final method (and the one used in our analysis) is to transform the variable. The two most common transformations are to rank all the values of time and to take the natural logarithm of the time (the square root transformation is also often used). Both of these help correct for the skewness. With both of these highly significant t values are obtained. For the natural logarithm $t(628.60) = -3.46$, and for the ranked data $t(699.5) = -2.92$ (ranking procedures will produce approximately the same value as the Mann–Whitney test).

If we had just run a t test on the untransformed data, we would have reported a non-significant result. This demonstrates what is often found: when the assumptions of a t test are not met, the distribution-free and transformed methods are more powerful. The code and output for these tests are listed below. My comments appear on the right. (Note: I have removed some of the output, such as the lines that tell you how long it took the computer to run the test.)

```
DATA LIST FILE='lineup.dat' FREE /suite time.
VALUE LABELS suite 0 'station' 1 'suite'.
VARIABLE LABELS time 'elapsed time in weeks'.
```

These lines tell the computer where the data are and what the variables are called.

```
T-TEST /GROUP=suite (0,1) /VARIABLE time.
```

A group t test.

	Number of Cases	Mean	Standard Deviation	Standard Error
Group 1	359	8.3185	9.824	.518
Group 2	361	8.6134	9.827	.517

		Pooled Variance Estimate			Separate Variance Estimate		
F Value	2-Tail Prob.	t Value	Degrees of Freedom	2-Tail Prob.	t Value	Degrees of Freedom	2-Tail Prob.
1.00	.995	-.40	718	.687	-.40	717.98	.687

Note that the two standard deviations are very similar. The F value tests whether these are significantly different. They are not (p is large), therefore the pooled t is used. The result is non-significant (large p), therefore we fail to reject H_0.

```
NPAR TEST MANN-WHITNEY time BY suite (0,1).
- - - - - Mann-Whitney U - Wilcoxon Rank Sum W Test
  Mean Rank  Cases
    337.97    359    SUITE =   .00  station
    382.90    361    SUITE = 1.00  suite
              720    Total
                     Corrected for Ties
       U        W         Z     2-tailed P
   56711.5  121331.5  -2.9102     .0036
```

According to the Mann–Whitney test there is a significant difference: there are longer elapsed times at suites.

```
COMPUTE lntime = LN (time).
RANK time.
```

These create two new variables.

```
From       New
variable   variable  Label
TIME       RTIME     RANK of TIME
```

To denote the ranked variable, the computer adds an r to the front: time becomes rtime

```
T TEST /GROUPS suite (0,1) /VARIABLES rtime lntime.
t test for: rtime
```

In SPSS, you can run t tests on several variables from the same command. Here two are run.

	Number of Cases	Mean	Standard Deviation	Standard Error
Group 1	359	337.9708	221.721	11.702
Group 2	361	382.9044	189.220	9.959

	Pooled Variance Estimate				Separate Variance Estimate		
F Value	2-Tail Prob.	t Value	Degrees of Freedom	2-Tail Prob.	t Value	Degrees of Freedom	2-Tail Prob.
1.37	.003	-2.93	718	.004	-2.92	699.49	.004

For the ranked data, the result is highly significant.

The negative *t* value means the second group has the higher mean.

t test for: LNTIME

	Number of Cases	Mean	Standard Deviation	Standard Error
Group 1	359	1.5108	1.243	.066
Group 2	361	1.7847	.841	.044

	Pooled Variance Estimate				Separate Variance Estimate		
F Value	2-Tail Prob.	t Value	Degrees of Freedom	2-Tail Prob.	t Value	Degrees of Freedom	2-Tail Prob.
2.18	.000	-3.46	718	.001	-3.46	628.60	.001

It is also highly significant for the natural logarithm of the elapsed time.

Power Analysis[3]

The field of power analysis, while really beginning with Neyman and Pearson in the 1920s and 1930s, was not introduced into mainstream social sciences until the late 1960s. The most influential book has been Cohen's (1988) handbook of power. There is a short paper by him (Cohen, 1992) that explains the concept in more detail and is worth reading. Essentially, the way most people use power analysis is, before conducting the research, to calculate how many subjects or respondents they need to have a reasonable chance of rejecting the null hypothesis. It is also sometimes used after conducting the research to estimate the probability of a Type II error for the observed effect size. Strictly speaking, the first of these is more what power analysis was designed for, but both are used. I will concentrate on the first usage here.

The power of a test is one minus the probability of a Type II error (failing to reject a false null hypothesis) if there is an effect. Cohen (and others) point out that if a null hypothesis states that some parameter is equal to an exact value (which is what we hypothesise when H_0 is that there is *no* difference between two groups) then it is always false. This is because it is just a single point along a continuous line. If we collect a million responses, even the most trivial difference will be *statistically significant*. There is always some effect, however minuscule, that is present in the population. Cohen stresses that researchers should be concerned with the size of this effect rather than with whether one

---

3 The calculations involved in this section are slightly more advanced than in most of the rest of the book. Try to work through these, however, because they introduce the conceptual basis of power analyses, which is the most important part. Cohen (1988; 1992) has provided tables so that the calculations are usually not necessary.

exists. The size of the effect for a difference in population means, denoted by a bold lower-case **d**, is defined as follows:[4]

$$\mathbf{d} = \frac{\mu_1 - \mu_2}{\sigma}$$

If we know the expected differences in population means and the standard deviation, we can calculate the effect size. Using this value and the number of subjects we can then calculate the expected value of t and the distribution of observed t values for this effect size (in the same way as I described for calculating the distribution of sample means for H_0). Using the appropriate tables we can calculate how often we would expect to reject the null hypothesis if the effect size is as large as **d**.

Unfortunately, we usually do not know either the expected effect size or the standard deviation before an experiment and therefore we cannot estimate the effect size. Cohen defined for several statistical tests what he considered small, medium and large effect sizes. While these are just guidelines, they are frequently used in research. For the paired and group t tests, he said a small effect was 0.20 standard deviations (that is, **d** = 0.20), a medium effect 0.50 standard deviations and a large effect 0.80 standard deviations. The expected value of t is (if the sample sizes are equal and the standard deviations of the groups are the same; Cohen (1988, eqn. 2.5.5) describes what to do when they are not):

$$t = \mathbf{d}\sqrt{\frac{n}{4}}$$

where n refers to the total number of subjects in both groups. We then use the t table to find out how often we would expect to observe a value large enough so that we can reject the null hypothesis of no difference between the means if this was our expected t value.

This is best explained through an example. Suppose you were commissioned by the transport ministry/department to compare the speed of traffic along two stretches of motorway. On one, the police had put video surveillance equipment to deter speeders. The hypothesis is that installing the surveillance equipment makes people drive more slowly (one-tailed test). You have to decide how many observations to make on each of these stretches of road. You decide to measure the speed of 50 cars on each stretch (thus 100 in total). It is likely that the transport ministry does not know the expected effect size, but it might say that it would be interested in even a small difference because this could save lives. You decide that Cohen's small effect, **d** = 0.2, will suffice. (The English word

---

4 There are many different ways people denote effect sizes. Often Greek letters are used, but these could be confused with population parameters. In Cohen's original handbooks he used lower-case **bold** letters. I will stick to this convention.

'small' as uttered by the transport minister need not be the same as used by Cohen. It is best to get clients to be as precise as possible about what they want.) Inserting this and $n = 100$ into the above equation gives us an expected t of 1.0.

Figure 4.2 illustrates the next step (drawing figures is necessary for doing power analysis). The two curves are t distributions, each with 98 degrees of freedom $(50 + 50 - 2)$. One is centred on the null hypothesis, where the mean t value is zero. The other is centred on the expected value of $t = 1.0$. First, we find the critical value for rejecting H_0 using the curve centred at zero. For $\alpha = 0.05$, one-tailed, this is $t(98) = 1.66$. Now, we see what percentage of the area under the other curve is beyond this point. The distance along the x axis is $1.66 - 1.00 = 0.66$ away from the centre of this distribution. We need to find the probability of observing a case that far away (that is, the one-tailed probability of $t(98) = 0.66$). This equates with a one-tailed p value (the shaded area under the curve on the right side of Figure 4.2) of about 25%. This means there is only a one in four chance of correctly rejecting the null hypothesis. If you have a computer program that calculates p values (and most packages allow this) you may use this, and it will show that the area under the curve for a t distribution with 98 df is 0.2554. If you do not have a program to do this, the z table will suffice. This gives you a probability of 0.2546. In almost all cases the z table will give accurate enough estimates.

Because there is not much cost involved in measuring car speed, you would probably want to increase the number of cars observed. If you recorded the speed of 300 cars on each stretch (600 in total) this would increase the expected t to 2.45 and increase the power to 0.79. You would expect to fail to reject the null hypothesis only 21% of the time (assuming there is a 'small' effect). This is a much more satisfactory percentage. A power of 0.80 is the basic standard and this is fairly close to that. It equates with a Type II probability of 0.20 if the effect size is as hypothesised. The power analysis for this problem is illustrated in Figure 4.3.

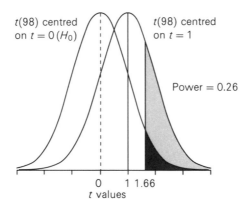

Figure 4.2   *The power calculations for a one-tailed ($\alpha = 0.05$) group t test with a 'small' effect size and 100 cases in total.*

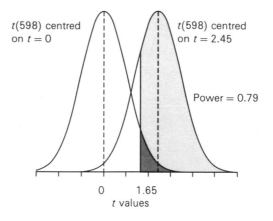

$t(598)$ centred on $t = 0$

$t(598)$ centred on $t = 2.45$

Power = 0.79

0   1.65

t values

Figure 4.3   *Power analysis for a one-tailed test ($\alpha = 0.05$) with 'small' effect and 600 cases in total*

Often, however, there is a much higher cost associated with observing each case. Suppose you were interested whether the heart rate during workouts was higher for professional tennis players or for professional basketball players. In this case it is much more difficult to make each observation. It would require obtaining each person's consent, having her/him exercise and then measuring her/his heart rate again. We would not want to have a larger sample than is necessary.

Suppose we are interested only in detecting a large effect size (0.8 standard deviations) and did not know which group's heart rate would be higher (two-tailed). If we had 25 athletes in each group (50 in total) this would produce an expected t of 2.83. If we were using an α of 0.05, then the critical value to reject H_0 is either below -2.06 or above 2.06. Because this is a two-tailed test, strictly speaking we should also include the chance of rejecting the null hypothesis when the observed mean is below -2.06. However, with this effect size, we would expect this to happen only about six times in every million. This is small enough to be disregarded. Figure 4.4 illustrates this. The area under the curve to the right of the critical value is about 0.78. This is a fairly good power level and we would probably be happy with it. As a reminder, it is vital that you draw diagrams when calculating power, otherwise mistakes can be very easily made.

In the previous example if we had wanted to be extremely careful not to make a Type I error we might have wanted to use the more stringent α of 0.01. The critical value for the t test is now 2.68, nearly the expected value. Therefore we would expect to reject the null hypothesis correctly only slightly more often than half the time. The new power level is 0.56. This is a fundamental characteristic of the relationship between the α level and power: if you lower the α level, the power drops.

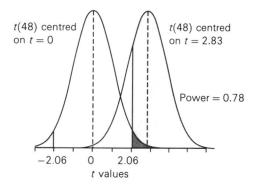

$t(48)$ centred on $t = 0$

$t(48)$ centred on $t = 2.83$

Power = 0.78

−2.06   0   2.06

t values

Figure 4.4   *Power analysis for a two-tailed test* $(\alpha = 0.05)$ *with 'large' effect and 50 cases in total*

Suppose that other researchers felt you should have done a one-tailed test. Because the critical *t* is lowered to 2.41, the power is raised to 0.66. This is another characteristic of power: one-tailed tests are always more powerful.

Cohen (1992) shows that the necessary sample sizes to achieve a power of 0.80 for *t* tests when using an α of 0.05 (two-tailed) for small, medium and large effects are 393, 64 and 26, respectively. Remember, however, that these effect sizes are just guidelines. Also, these figures were calculated assuming equal group sizes and equal standard deviations. Cohen (1988) goes into much more detail and I encourage you to look at it if you have a more complicated problem.

Power calculations can also be done for the paired *t* test. Consider the political attitudes example discussed in Chapter 3 in which 20 people were asked their attitudes before and after an election. Suppose we were interested in observing a medium shift $(\mathbf{d} = 0.5)$.[5] The equation to calculate the expected *t* is:

$$t = \mathbf{d}\sqrt{n}$$

With 20 people this produces an expected *t* of 2.24. Using a two-tailed test with 24 degrees of freedom at $\alpha = 0.05$, the critical value to reject $t = 0$ is 2.06. Because the expected *t* is larger than the critical value, the power will be greater than 0.50. However, the difference between this and the expected *t* is only 0.18 and therefore the power will not be much higher than 0.50. When we look up the probability, using either the *z* table or a package that produces exact *t* probabilities, we find that 0.43 of the time we would fail to reject the hypothesis (that is, 43% of the time we would make a Type II error). This equates with a power of 0.57, which is probably not high enough for most researchers. Suppose

5   It is important to realise that this medium effect has a different meaning because the standard deviation here is of the differences between the two variables. Cohen (1988) goes into some detail on the difference. In general, the medium effect reported here is more of a medium to large effect.

we decided to ask 40 people. The analysis for this is depicted in Figure 4.5. The critical value for 39 degrees of freedom is +2.02. The expected size of the *t* is 3.16 for a medium effect when *n* = 40. The resulting power is now 0.87, which is much more satisfactory.

The power of a test is affected by many things. Most obviously, it increases when you are expecting a larger effect. Often this is beyond your control, but sometimes carefully designing a study and using good measurement instruments will substantially improve power. You do, however, have control over the power using other characteristics. If you increase the size of your sample then the power increases. This is why it is important to have as large a sample as possible. It also goes up if you use a less stringent α level, but you should be careful doing this because it increases the chances of making a Type I error. You can decide to do a one-tailed test rather than a two-tailed test, but in general I advise against this (see Box 2.2). Finally, the particular statistical test that you use can affect the power of a comparison. This is discussed throughout this book in relation to distribution-free tests and in more detail in the next section comparing the paired and group *t* tests.

Comparing the Paired and the Group *t* Tests

In Chapter 1 I discussed how statistics fits into an overall methodology for conducting scientific research and how, along with other methodological factors, it must be considered in every stage of research. If you are interested in the difference between two variables, you have two basic choices. After sampling a group of people, you can either split them up into two groups and measure one of the variables for the first group and the other variable for the second group and then compare the values for these two groups (a group *t* test), or you can measure both variables for the entire group, subtract the values, and examine the

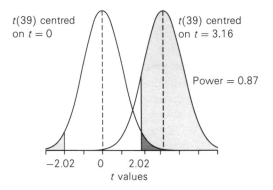

Figure 4.5   *Power analysis for a paired t test (two-tailed; α = 0.05) with 'medium' effect and 40 cases*

mean of these differences (a paired *t* test). In this section, I discuss what factors should be considered when deciding which of these methods to use.

To do this we will go through two of the examples from earlier chapters. First, consider the arithmetic learning study. Children were given arithmetic problems to solve that were either in the standard symbolic form or presented as word problems. There were two separate groups and therefore the group *t* test was the appropriate procedure. The researcher could have considered testing all the children with both methods, but children may learn from these problems. This learning effect could create a methodological problem because whichever set was presented second could be solved more easily. There could also be detrimental effects due to exhaustion if several problems were used. The biggest problem with these so-called *carryover effects* is that they are often difficult to predict. One solution is to randomise (or systematically allocate) the order of the different conditions. However, sometimes this is not possible or not advisable (if the measure is fundamentally different depending on when it is asked, then you should be cautious interpreting such results).

However, there are many advantages to using the same people in both conditions. Consider the political attitude example from Chapter 3. There was no overall difference in means but there was a difference: political attitudes were polarised. The people who tended to be left wing before the election were even more left wing afterwards, and vice versa with the right-wing people. If we had asked different people at the two points in time we would not have been able to identify how people changed. This is even more evident from the 'trick' problem of Exercise 6 in Chapter 3.

There is also a purely statistical advantage in using a paired *t* test: the power of the paired *t* test tends to be higher. If people who score high on one measure tend to score high on the other, then you are far more likely to have a statistically significant result with the paired test. The exact reason for this is described in the next chapter. Briefly it is because the paired *t* test is testing the difference between the scores for each individual. The purpose of most statistical tests is to minimise the unexplained proportion of the data. Usually, much of this unexplained proportion can be explained by aspects of the individual. In a paired *t* test we are controlling for these individual differences by comparing the same person. In the group *t* test we are not.

The decision whether to devise a situation requiring a group or a paired *t* test depends on many factors. In more general terms, these are described as between-subject and within-subject designs, respectively. The relevant issues are discussed in detail in most methodology books.

Summary

The main purpose of this chapter was to describe the group *t* test and the appropriate alternatives (the Mann–Whitney *U*, the sign test and the different transformations). In devising the *t* test equation, I noted that researchers often assume that the standard deviations (or variances) for the two groups are equal. I stressed that it is vital to look at this, not just to make sure that a *t* test is valid, but because differences in the spread of distributions are important in their own right.

I also described how to calculate the power of a statistical test and, by working backwards, the necessary sample to achieve certain power levels. These require that you have an estimate of the effect size and the standard deviation. Because these are often not known, researchers tend to use Cohen's guidelines, where a small effect is 0.2 standard deviations, a medium effect is 0.5 and a large effect is 0.8. The most important thing to stress about doing power analysis is to draw diagrams. Power analysis is an example of a statistical technique that is necessary before data are collected. In terms of the stages of research presented in Chapter 1, estimating the necessary sample size should be done at stage 3 (designing the study).

Finally, I looked at another aspect of stage 3 from Chapter 1. When designing a study the researcher often has the choice of whether to measure some variable twice on the same people or once on two sets of people. This decision, between using a within-subject or a between-subjects design, is vital for many methodological and statistical reasons. I discussed how the paired *t* test is usually more powerful. The technical details are discussed further in the next chapter.

Assignment

1   There has been some discussion in the UK parliament and newspapers about the difference in price of compact discs in the UK and the USA. To investigate this, most people would telephone randomly sampled record shops in each country and ask what the cost of a just released top ten CD is. Hypothetical data are shown below, converted to US dollars and rounded to the nearest dollar for prices at 20 music shops. What would you conclude from these data?

United Kingdom	United States
17	14
18	16
21	16
19	14
18	15
21	18
19	21
20	16
21	20
18	17

2   Researchers gave 100 12-year-old boys a questionnaire designed to measure
    attitudes towards violence (0 being against violence, 100 being for violence).
    They also asked these children whether they watch any of the so-called video
    nasties (videos depicting lots of violence). The means, sample sizes and
    standard deviations are listed below.

Children who watch video nasties	$\bar{x} = 45.0$	$n = 60$	$s = 5$
Children who do not watch video nasties	$\bar{x} = 35.0$	$n = 40$	$s = 6$

Is there a significant difference on the violence scale for the two groups?
Suppose a politician used these data to claim that watching video nasties
causes violent attitudes. Is the politician's conclusion valid or are there other
explanations?

3   There is a great concern about how to teach the public about science. In
    order to target resources efficiently, it is best to know which groups in the
    population know the least about science. Suppose a series of ten true/false
    knowledge questions were asked, and the mean number of correct responses
    for 18 men was 8.2 with a standard deviation of 3.6 and the mean number
    correct for 22 women was 7.7 with a standard deviation of 4.3. Is there
    evidence of a gender difference?

4   Using the US states data set (Appendix A), compare the rate of violent crime
    in states where the governor is a Republican with those states where the
    governor is a Democrat. Because Washington, D.C. has no governor it has
    been given the code -9 and treated as a missing value. The MISSING
    VALUE command tells the computer to treat this as missing and therefore the
    T-TEST command will ignore this case. There are also a couple of states
    that have a governor without party allegiance. Here you should exclude these
    states. When running a *t* test, if there are more than two categories, you must
    tell the computer which groups you wish to compare (here the values are 0
    and 1). This ensures that the computer will exclude the 'independent' states.

5   Exercise 4 can also be represented as an equation:

$$crime_i = \beta_1 govparty_i + \beta_0 + e_i$$

The first thing to do is exclude states led by 'independent' governors. This is
done with the PROCESS IF or SELECT IF command, depending on the
implementation you are using, where NE means not equal. This exclusion
could have also been accomplished using other commands. Because
$govparty_i$ is equal to 0 for states lead by Democrats, the term $\beta_1 govparty_i$
is equal to 0 for all Democratic states. Therefore β_0 is the mean for the
Democratic states. β_1 is the difference between the Republican states and the
Democratic states. If it is positive then the Republican states had more

crime. If it is negative it means the Democratic states had more crime. It is the size of β_1 compared with the size of the residuals (e_i) that is being tested in a t test. To solve for these parameters directly we use the regression procedure. Depending on your computer implementation, the input should be something like this:

```
PROCESS IF (govparty NE 3).
REGRESSION /VARIABLES crime govparty /DEPENDENT crime.
```

6   The following output compares the amount of illegal software on five randomly sampled European personal computers and five randomly sampled South American personal computers. The variable software is the percentage of software on sampled computers that should not have been there. The variable contin is the continent (0 for Europe, 1 for South America). What conclusions can be made?

```
T TEST /GROUP contin (0,1) /VARIABLE software.
Group 1:  contin EQ   .00      Group 2:  contin EQ   1.00
t-test for:  software
```

	Number of Cases	Mean	Standard Deviation	Standard Error
Group 1	5	46.2000	16.769	7.499
Group 2	5	64.8000	22.565	10.092

		Pooled Variance Estimate			Separate Variance Estimate		
F Value	2-Tail Prob.	t Value	Degrees of Freedom	2-Tail Prob.	t Value	Degrees of Freedom	2-Tail Prob.
1.81	.579	-1.48	8	.177	-1.48	7.39	.180

7   You are trying to decide on a holiday. You want to choose somewhere that you expect will be comfortably warm. You look through the last year's newspapers and write down the temperatures (in degrees Fahrenheit) on 20 randomly sampled days for the resorts of Deserta and Tropica. These are denoted with the variable resort (0 for Deserta and 1 for Tropica). You run a t test on these and get the following output. Would this help you make your decision? Why?

```
T TEST /GROUPS resort (0,1) /VARIABLES temper.
Group 1:  resort EQ   .00      Group 2:  resort EQ   1.00
t-test for: temper
```

	Number of Cases	Mean	Standard Deviation	Standard Error
Group 1	20	78.2500	18.439	4.123
Group 2	20	80.2000	9.897	2.213

	Pooled Variance Estimate			Separate Variance Estimate		
F	2-Tail	t	Degrees of	2-Tail	t	Degrees of	2-Tail
Value	Prob.	Value	Freedom	Prob.	Value	Freedom	Prob.
3.47	.009	-.42	38	.679	-.42	29.11	.680

8   A random sample of 1000 people were divided into two equal groups. Those in one group were asked on how many days in the previous week they were 'satisfied' with life, and those in the other were asked on how many days they were 'very satisfied'. The means of the two groups were identical: 2.41 days per week. Suppose the researchers were interested in observing even a 'small' effect ($d = 0.2$). What was the power of their comparison if they were using an α of 0.05 (I recommend drawing a diagram!)? (With this many people the z table can be used.) Would it have been any different if the observed means were 2.15 and 3.21, respectively?

Further Reading

Cohen, J. (1992) A power primer. *Psychological Bulletin, 112*, 155–159.
This is a concise and excellent introduction to power analysis from a leader in the field. In this paper he gives the calculations for the simplest conditions for the tests (for the example, with the group *t* test it is assumed that the group sizes are equal and that the groups have the same standard deviations). His textbook (Cohen, 1988) goes into the more general cases.

5

Introducing Regression and Correlation

In the social sciences the relationship between two quantitative variables is often explored. In this chapter I explain how this is done, first graphically and then using the appropriate statistical technique(s). The technique is called regression analysis and the most common associated test of significance is the correlation.

One characteristic of this book that is different from many introductory textbooks is that the statistical tests thus far have all been presented, at least briefly, as equations. Having done this, introducing the logic behind regression analysis is greatly eased. Towards the end of the chapter these tests are compared.

Scatterplots

When exploring the relationship between two variables the most useful approach is graphing the data. Too often people use fancy statistical techniques without looking at their data. Scatterplots, sometimes called scattergrams, are easily made either with a pencil and graph paper or with a computer.

Suppose we were interested in the relationship between age and height for a sample of 20 people aged from zero to 30 years. The scatterplot might look something like Figure 5.1. Each individual is represented by a dot corresponding to her/his age, on the horizontal axis, and her/his height, on the vertical axis. The horizontal and vertical axes are often referred to as the x and y axes,

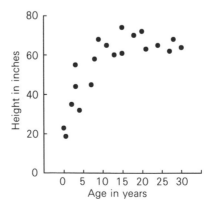

Figure 5.1   *A scatterplot of height versus age*

respectively. As can be seen, when people are young their height goes up rapidly, but when they are older it levels off. The statistical techniques I describe in this chapter allow us to say something about relationships like this.

One can easily talk about height increasing with age. It is trivially true that people in this age range tend to grow taller, not shorter. In most social science research the relationships are not as straightforward. Consider the scatterplot in Figure 5.2 from the states.sps data file (in Appendix A). It shows the relationship between the lowest temperature (in degrees Fahrenheit) recorded in the state and the high school dropout rate (percentage who drop out). There is a tendency for the colder places to have lower dropout rates, but the points appear fairly scattered throughout the plot.

We might think of various reasons for this relationship, for example that the students in the warmer states would rather be at the beach than at school or that in the colder states there is more emphasis on education. There are several possible reasons, but you would certainly not want to proclaim any direct causal relationship, either that increasing the dropout rate will raise the temperature

PLOT/PLOT dropout WITH lowtemp BY state.

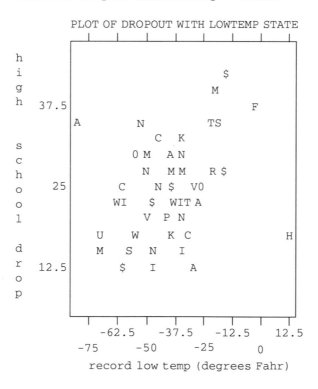

Figure 5.2 *A scatterplot of each state's high school dropout rate versus its record low temperature. The states are denoted by their first letter ($ for multiple occurrences)*

(which is nonsensical) or that if the temperature could be increased, the dropout rate would rise (which is quite speculative). The conclusion is simply that these are statistically related.

In SPSS, scatterplots are drawn with the PLOT procedure. To produce one, after writing PLOT/PLOT (which tells the computer which procedure to use), you write the variable you want on the *y* axis, then the word 'WITH' and then the variable for the *x* axis. Figure 5.2 is slightly more complex. I have added the phrase 'BY state', which tells the computer to denote each point with the first letter of the state (except where more than one state is at the same point, and this is shown with a $). The command is shown at the top of Figure 5.2. Other packages and implementations use similar commands.

Looking at this graph two points seem to stand out: the A on the upper left-hand side and the H on the lower right-hand side. These are *outliers*. They do not fit the general pattern of the rest of the data. A little exploration reveals that these are, not surprisingly, Alaska and Hawaii, the 49th and 50th states of the union and each separated from the other 48 states by thousands of miles. There are several ways to treat such outliers. Outliers can have a large impact on the statistics and can be the most important theoretically. Here, however, it might be argued that because of their spatial separation from the other states, any temperature-based comparisons should exclude the single state in the Arctic and the single state in the Tropics. In a later section I will discuss the impact of excluding these.

When making a scatterplot, either by hand or with a computer, it is important to make sure every part of the figure is as clear as possible. I discuss various aspects of graphing data throughout this book. Consider the following two basic rules and one moral for making graphs (see Wainer, 1984, for an excellent paper discussing these issues).

Rule 1: Graphs should be informative.
Rule 2: Graphs should be clear.
Moral: Making scientific graphs does not require artwork; prettiness doesn't count!

The moral should not be taken too negatively. Graphs *can* be artistic but that is not their purpose. Often graphs are both attractive and informative/clear. The point is, you should not ask if the graph looks nice, but whether it displays the information appropriately.

Regression

The word 'regression' is used to cover a whole family of techniques in which the researcher tries to find the best fitting model for a set of data. (The word has a related meaning in English, reverting or going back towards something. This meaning of the word is seldom used in statistics nowadays.) One of the simplest types of regression equation involves drawing a straight line through the data when they are presented as a scatterplot. This is called a simple linear regression and is the technique that will be discussed in this chapter. More complex regressions are discussed in later chapters.

There are equations that describe the statistically optimal line, but the first technique you should use is drawing a line yourself. This gives you the chance to get a feel for the data. Also, if the computer or the equation suggest a very different line, either you need to work on your feel for data or the suggested line is wrong (that is, you or the computer have made a mistake).

Consider the plot of the high school dropout rate versus record low temperature (Figure 5.2). Here, the straight line would probably go from somewhere near the bottom left-hand corner to somewhere near top right-hand corner. Recall from Box 1.4 that this can be represented by the following type of equation:

$$dropout_i = \beta_1 lowtemp_i + \beta_0 + e_i$$

where β_1 and β_0 are the parameters or constants we try to estimate. In this equation we are using *lowtemp* to predict *dropout*. As we are not assuming any causal direction in the relationship between these variables, it is arbitrary which is on the left-hand side of the equation and which is on the right. In other cases their placement is important. The variable on the left-hand side of the equals sign (=) is called the *regressed* variable. Those on the right-hand side I will call the *regressors*.[1] β_0 is the value on the y axis when *lowtemp* is zero. It is called the *intercept*. β_1 is the *slope* of the line. The slope is the value that describes the incline of the line (the slope is sometimes also called the *gradient*). The value of the y variable goes up β_1 units for each unit increase of the x variable. In this example a high positive slope would mean that for each increase of *lowtemp$_i$* we would expect *dropout$_i$* to go up quite a lot. A low positive slope means the increase in *dropout$_i$* would not be as large. Negative slopes occur when an increase in one variable is associated with a decrease in the other. More generally, we write

$$y_i = \beta_1 x_i + \beta_0 + e_i$$

when we regress the variable y on the variable x. We often say we are trying to predict the values of y using the variable x.

The technique used to estimate β_0 and β_1 is known as *least squares*. It involves finding the values of these parameters such that the sum of the squared residuals (Σe_i^2) is as small as possible. The estimated values for these parameters are unbiased estimates of the corresponding population values.

---

1 Sometimes these are called the dependent and independent variables, respectively. This is unfortunate because, as this case shows, the placement of variables is sometimes arbitrary and therefore the labels should not imply a specific causal relationship. The labels 'dependent' and 'independent' are usually only appropriate when conducting controlled experiments.

The resulting equations (which can be derived using calculus) are:

$$\beta_1 = \frac{\sum(x_i - \bar{x})(y_i - \bar{y})}{\sum(x_i - \bar{x})^2}$$

$$\beta_0 = \bar{y} - \beta_1\bar{x}$$

In words, the value of β_1 increases either when the values of $(x_i - \bar{x})$ *and* $(y_i - \bar{y})$ are both positive *or* when they are both negative. When one value is positive and the other value is negative, the value of β_1 decreases. Once the value for β_1 has been estimated, estimating the value for β_0 is fairly simple: multiply the estimate for β_1 by $\bar{x}$ and subtract this from $\bar{y}$. Consider the following data on ten people:

x	3	3	8	5	7	4	2	6	7	5
y	23	22	12	15	14	14	18	17	11	14

Suppose we were told to find the best-fitting straight line to describe the relationship between x and y. This would be the regression line. First, we would make a scatterplot like the one in Figure 5.3a. We might then draw the means of x and y (5 and 16 respectively) on the graph. From this, we could see that there are more points $(3 + 3 = 6)$ in the upper left and lower right quadrants (a quadrant being a quarter of the graph) than in the lower left and upper right quadrants $(1 + 1 = 2)$. The points in the former decrease the estimate of β_1, those in the latter increase the estimate. The points farthest away from the mean lines have the largest impact on the estimate. The difference between the number of values in these quadrants is a rough test of the association. When there are many more values in the upper left and lower right quadrants, as with these data, we would expect a negative value for β_1. To get a more precise indication, we solve for β_1 using the above equation. Table 5.1 shows the calculations involved. Next, to find β_0 we simply multiply our β_1 value (-1.53)

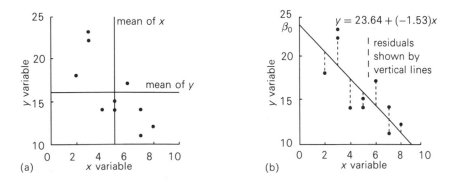

Figure 5.3   *A scatterplot of hypothetical x and y values, showing (a) the mean of each variable; (b) the regression line and residuals*

Table 5.1   *Calculating β_1 and β_0 for the data from Figure 5.3*

x_i	y_i	$(x_i - 5)$	$(y_i - 16)$	$(x_i - 5)(y_i - 16)$	$(x_i - 16)^2$
3	23	-2	7	-14	4
3	22	-2	6	-12	4
8	12	3	-4	-12	9
5	15	0	-1	0	0
7	14	2	-2	-4	4
4	14	-1	-2	2	1
2	18	-3	2	-6	9
6	17	1	1	1	1
7	11	2	-5	-10	4
5	14	0	-2	0	0
				$\Sigma = -55$	$\Sigma = 36$

$\beta_1 = -55/36 = -1.528$
$\beta_0 = 16 - (-1.528)5 = 16 + 7.64 = 23.64$

$y = 23.64 + (-1.53)x + e_i$

by $\bar{x}$ (5) and subtract this product from 16. The resulting value is 23.64, and the regression line is plotted in Figure 5.3b.

One of the main uses of regression is to predict values for a variable given information about other variables. Perhaps the most common textbook example is predicting academic success at university from 'entrance' variables (grades, standardised test scores, references, etc.). A regression model could be solved for previous years using the students' grades at university as a measure of academic success, and then this model could be used to help decide whether to accept or reject prospective students in future years.

In the example above we would be trying to predict values for y given certain values for x. Our predictions would be on the regression line. Thus, if we had a value of $x = 6$, we would predict a y of:

$$\hat{y} = 23.64 - 1.53 \times 6 = 14.46$$

This is our best guess for y. We use the ˆ (hat) symbol to denote that this is a predicted value. Because our estimate of β_1 is negative, as the values of x increase, our predictions of y decrease. Our predictions are not always going to be accurate, but they are our best guesses given our regressor variables and our assumptions (here, a linear relationship between x and y).

It is particularly important to be careful about making predictions of x scores outside the range of data collected. Suppose you were asked to predict the value of y for $x = 20$. The regression equation results in $y = 23.64 - 1.53 \times 20 = -6.96$. While mathematically there is no problem with predicted values less than zero, for some variables in the real world, such as height, a negative score is impossible. The problem is that the data used to derive this equation only had x values that went up to 8. Therefore when we make predictions outside the range of the original variable, we are extrapolating beyond what the equation was developed for. This *extrapolation* requires assuming that the straight-line relationship continues to points beyond those being considered. In general you should be wary making predictions beyond the range of your data. In many cases, the additional assumptions are not realistic and sometimes the predicted values do not make sense.

Partitioning Sums of Squares

Suppose we did not know the value of x for an individual and we still wanted to guess the value of y. What would be our best guess? We might simply guess the mean: 16. This would be a better estimate than randomly guessing. From a modelling perspective, this is our starting point. We would want to see how much our guesses (that is, our estimates) would improve knowing the value of x. If we just guess the mean, for the data above, a measure of the overall error is:

$$SST = \sum (y_i - \bar{y})^2$$

where *SST* is called the *total sum of squared deviations* (SST = Sum of Squares Total). If we divide this by $n - 1$ we would have the variance of y.

The role of the other variable (or, as described in later chapters, variables) is to minimise the sum of the squared residuals or *SSR*

$$SSR = \sum (y_i - \hat{y}_i)^2 = \sum e_i^2$$

The improvement due to the model is denoted *SSM* for the sum of squares accounted for by the model. It is based on the difference between the mean of y and the prediction for each case:

$$SSM = \sum (\bar{y} - \hat{y}_i)^2$$

SSM is simply the difference between *SST* and *SSR*. It describes the improvement due to the model. If it is large, then the x variable is useful in predicting y. If it is small then the model is not a large improvement over just using the mean. We use the percentage of improvement as a general measure of how the new variable helps. We denote this R^2:

$$R^2 = \frac{SSM}{SST} = \frac{\sum (\bar{y} - \hat{y}_i)^2}{\sum (y_i - \bar{y})^2}$$

In words, R^2 is the proportion of the total variance of y explained by the model. Figure 5.4 illustrates one way in which this can be presented. The circle on the left represents *SST*, the total sum of squares, of the y variable. The circle on the right represents the *SST* of the x variable (it is important to make the

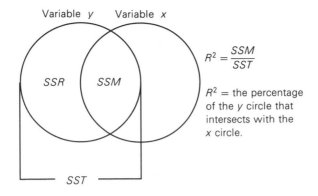

Figure 5.4 *Representing the proportion of variance accounted for by the model. The SSR and SSM refer only to the areas that they are enclosed within.*

circles the same size for each variable). Their intersection, *SSM*, is the amount of shared sums of squares. The residual sum of squares (*SSR*) is the amount left over within the *y* circle. Since we can divide all these sums of squares by $n - 1$ to create variance terms, we can also think of these circles as representing the variance of *x* and *y*. Their intersection is the proportion of *y* variance accounted for by the variable *x*. The ratio *SSM/SST*, the R^2 value, is the proportion of the total variance of *y* accounted for by *x*. As the intersection increases, so does the value of R^2. If *x* can account for *all* the variance of *y* then *SSM* is equal to *SST* and R^2 is equal to one. If there is no intersection, the R^2 value is equal to zero. R^2 cannot be negative. Even if the estimate for β_1 is negative, R^2 will still be positive.

Example: Pollution and House Prices

Let us consider a more concrete example that comes from a study by Harrison and Rubinfeld (1978; these data were made available through StatLib and at the time of writing are on http://lib.stat.cmu.edu/datasets/Boston) on 506 towns in the Boston area. One of the variables recorded was the median house price in each town (called medv). Suppose we wanted to see how this was related to the level of pollution due to the various oxides of nitrogen (NO_x). In this case we would probably be interested in trying to predict house prices from the levels of pollution (although it is plausible some people would be interested in predicting level of pollution from house prices). The mean of the median house prices (in units of $1000) was 22.53 (that is, $22,530). This would be our best guess if we knew nothing about any other variables. The total sum of squares is

$$SST = \sum(medv_i - 22.53)^2 = 42,716.29$$

This is the total variation. The variance of the median house price is 84.59. The variance can also be described as the mean of the *SST* which we denote M_{SST}. This model, without including any other variables, is,

$$medv_i = \beta_0 + e_i = 22.53 + e_i$$

To examine the relationship between pollution and house price we first construct a scatterplot. With this many cases a computer should be used. Using SPSS, the resulting scatterplot is shown in Figure 5.5 (with some additional text on the axes to make them clearer). Each number represents the number of cases at that point. When a letter is used that means there are more than nine cases at that point. (A for ten, B for 11, etc.). From this scatterplot, it is clear that the two variables are related. The towns with the most expensive houses are low on the pollution scale (upper left-hand corner) and those high on the population scale are in less expensive dwellings (lower right-hand corner). Therefore, if the pollution level was high we would predict house price to be below the mean, and

```
PLOT /TITLE 'House Prices and Pollution'
     /PLOT medv WITH nox.
              House Prices and Pollution
           |    |    |    |    |    |    |    |
 M  p           12    11   1 441 1
 e  r           1     2         1
 d  i   45 -    1 3   1    1
 i  c           11    1        1 1
 a  e             1 21
 n             3142312         2
              32261114         1
 h  i   30 -  42511124 1 1 3
    n          153 2241  11  1    1
 o            56H651E848 22521 1   3        1
 u  $         414E65 8C3D C341 2   5  3      2
 s  1         14461 373D 5637 1   32 2       3
 e  0            2    1A 5235 411A2          7
 0  0   15 -        3 3 21 154446            3
 0                    1 1    73313
                      1     162
           |    |    |    |    |    |    |
          .4        .56       .72       .88
             .48       .64       .8

                    concentration
                  (parts per million)
```

Figure 5.5 *A scatterplot of house prices versus pollution*

if the pollution level was low we would predict the price to be above the mean. We predict a negative value for β_1.

To find the line that best fits these data we use the following syntax (or some variant of it depending on your computer package). The command tells the computer that the variable `medv` (the median value of the houses) is the 'dependent' variable (what we are calling the regressed variable): the variable we are trying to predict. The `/METHOD ENTER` command tells the computer to input all other variables listed in the `/VARIABLES` command (`nox` is the level of the pollutant). I have shortened the output from SPSS. On the right are my comments.

REGRESSION /VARIABLES medv nox /DEPENDENT medv /METHOD ENTER.

```
Equation Number 1 Dependent Variable..
MEDV Median value of owner-occupi
Variable(s) Entered on Step Number

1..  nox  nitric oxides concentration

Multiple R          .42732
R Square            .18260
Adjusted R Square   .18098
Standard Error     8.32335
```

These are the R and the R^2 values described above. The adjusted value pertains to more complicated models described in Chapter 8.

```
Analysis of Variance
              DF   Sum of Squares   Mean Square
Regression    1      7800.12551     7800.12551

Residual     504    34916.16991       69.27811
```

This sum of squares is *SSM*.

This is *SSR*. *SSM* plus *SSR* is equal to *SST*. The mean squared errors are the sum of squares divided by the degrees of freedom (1 and 504 here). The 1 is for estimating one addition parameter (beyond the intercept) and the 504 is the number of cases minus the total number of parameters estimated.

```
F =   112.59148   Signif F =   .0000
```

The significance can be tested by dividing the two mean square errors.

——————————— Variables in the Equation ———————————

note that the B used here is what we have been calling β.
What SPSS calls beta is standardised to go from -1 to 1 in the same
way as the correlation, to be discussed in the next section.

Variable	B	SE B	Beta	T	Sig T	
NOX	-33.91606	3.19634	-.42732	-10.611	.0000	This is the estimate for β_1 and includes
(Constant)	41.34587	1.81119		22.828	.0000	a test to show it is different from zero. The same for β_0

From this, our regression equation is

$$medv_i = -33.9Nox_i + 41.3 + e_i$$

If we wanted to predict median house values we could put in the pollution level
and this would give our best estimate, based on this equation. But suppose there
was a town with 2 parts per million of NO_x. This is far higher than any of the
pollutant values used to derive the equation. If we assume that the equation still
holds at this level, our prediction would be that the median house price is *minus*
$26,500. Perhaps fair, but unlikely. You would also not want to input values of
nox less than zero, since these do not make sense. Extrapolation problems exist
in all areas of science.

Interpreting Regressions: the Overall Fit

The question most often asked about a regression is how good is the fit of the
model for predicting the regressed variable? The model in this case is of the form
$\beta_1 x_i + \beta_0$ and the variable being regressed is y. In this case (where there are only
two variables in total), the fit of the model tells us how related the variable x is to
the variable y: how they co-relate. One of the simplest ways of measuring this is
by seeing if, as one variable moves away from its mean, the other also moves
away from its mean. This is measuring how the two variables *covary* and
therefore is called the *covariance*. Recall the variance of a single variable is:

$$s^2 = \frac{\sum(x_i - \bar{x})^2}{n-1} = \frac{\sum(x_i - \bar{x})(x_i - \bar{x})}{n-1}$$

A similar equation is used to find the covariance of x and y, denoted $\text{Cov}(x,y)$:

$$\text{Cov}(x,y) = \frac{\sum(x_i - \bar{x})(y_i - \bar{y})}{n-1}$$

If the value is high then the tendency is that, when the value of one variable goes up, so does the value of the other. The two variables are then said to be positively associated. A negative value indicates that as the value of one variable increases, the value of the other tends to decrease. One problem with this measure is that its size depends on the scale of each variable. If we were measuring temperature in degrees Celsius, we would get a smaller covariance than if we were measuring temperature in degrees Fahrenheit. This problem is fixed by dividing the covariance by the standard deviations of each of the individual variables. This is called *Pearson's product moment correlation* or most often just *correlation*. The formula for it is:

$$r = \frac{\text{Cov}(x, y)}{(s_x)(s_y)} = \frac{\sum(x_i - \bar{x})(y_i - \bar{y})/(n - 1)}{\sqrt{\frac{\sum(x_i - \bar{x})^2}{(n - 1)}}\sqrt{\frac{\sum(y_i - \bar{y})^2}{(n - 1)}}}$$

$$r = \frac{\sum(x_i - \bar{x})(y_i - \bar{y})}{\sqrt{\sum(x_i - \bar{x})^2 \sum(y_i - \bar{y})^2}}$$

The correlation has many advantages over the covariance. First, it can range only from -1 to $+1$. A correlation of -1 means that there is a perfect (linear) negative relationship. A correlation of $+1$ means that there is a perfect (linear) positive relationship. A correlation of 0 means that there is no linear relationship. This does not necessarily mean that there is no relationship, only that a straight line does not describe it. The square of the correlation is interpreted most easily: r^2 is the amount of shared variance between the two variables. This is equivalent to the R^2 described earlier. Computer programs will usually print both r and r^2 (sometimes labelled R and R^2). You should use the r^2 as a conceptual guide to the size of the relationship.

Figure 5.6 illustrates some possible relationships. Figures 5.6a and 5.6b show a high positive and a high negative correlation, respectively. In each, while the points are not exactly on the same line, a straight line does appear to summarise the relationship adequately. In Figure 5.6c there is no apparent relationship between the variables, and the correlation would be approximately zero. In Figure 5.6d the two variables are clearly related, but the relationship is *curvilinear*. In this case the correlation is small because, although the variables are related, their relationship is not described by a straight line. Alternative forms of regression are suitable in this circumstance.

The values of r and β_1 are closely related. Positive values on these each indicate a positive relationship between the two variables. Negative values indicate the opposite. The r value is generally more useful in trying to describe the fit of the model: how well it works. When comparing just two variables, x and y, the r value is the same regardless of which variable you are using to predict which. The correlation between x and y is the same as between y and x: it is symmetric. The β_1 value is more useful when trying to predict y values for new cases or describing the impact of one variable on the other. It is asymmetric.

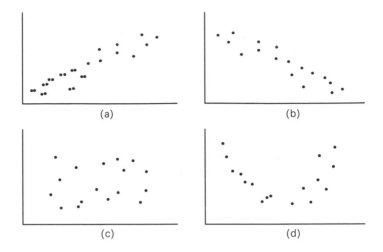

(a)　　　　　　　　　　　　　(b)

(c)　　　　　　　　　　　　　(d)

Figure 5.6 *Examples of different types of relationship depicted by scatterplots*

The value will change depending on which variable you are trying to predict. Mathematically the two are related as follows:

$$r = \frac{\sqrt{\sum(x_i - \bar{x})^2}}{\sqrt{\sum(y_i - \bar{y})^2}}\beta_1 = \frac{s_x}{s_y}\beta_1$$

Consider the data shown in Table 5.1. In this example $\sum(x_i - \bar{x})^2 = 36$, and $\sum(y_i - \bar{y})^2 = 144$. Depending on what information we have already collected, there are several ways to calculate r.

$$r = \frac{\sum(x_i - \bar{x})(y_i - \bar{y})}{\sqrt{\sum(x_i - \bar{x})^2(y_i - \bar{y})^2}} = \frac{-55}{\sqrt{36 \times 144}} = -0.76$$

or

$$r = \frac{\text{Cov}(x, y)}{s_x s_y} = \frac{\sum(x_i - \bar{x})(y_i - \bar{y})/(n - 1)}{\sqrt{\sum(x_i - \bar{x})^2/(n - 1)}\sqrt{\sum(y_i - \bar{y})^2/(n - 1)}}$$

$$= \frac{-55/9}{2 \times 4} = -0.76$$

or

$$r = \frac{s_x}{s_y}\beta_1 = \frac{2}{4}(-1.528) = -0.76$$

This is a fairly strong relationship: approximately 58% of the variance of y can be accounted for by x (-0.76 squared is 0.58). While this does leave 42% unaccounted for, most researchers would be pleased with such a figure (of course, what percentage is good depends on the situation).

Significance Testing

When we find a correlation, we are often interested whether it is significantly different from zero. In other words, we are interested to know if the size of the observed correlation is sufficiently large to make us doubt that the sample was drawn at random from a population in which there was no relationship between the variables. The population parameter for a correlation is usually denoted with the lower-case Greek letter ρ (pronounced 'rho'). A significant correlation means you can reject the hypothesis that there is no relationship between the variables in the population $(H_0 : \rho = 0)$. Researchers almost always use two-tailed tests when doing correlations. As I stressed before, in most circumstances a two-tailed test is better than a one-tailed test and doing a two-tailed test is seldom wrong. To know whether a correlation is significantly different from zero you must know the sample size. A correlation of $r = 0.1$ is significant with 500 people at $\alpha = 0.05$ (even though $r^2 = 0.01$ and therefore only 1% of the variance of y is accounted for by x), but is not with 300 people. Alternatively, a correlation of $r = 0.4$ (16% shared variance) is not significant at $\alpha = 0.05$ when there are only 20 people, but is when there are 30 people. Tables can be constructed for significance levels of r but it is probably simpler to use a transformation that allows its significance to be tested using the t table which you have already used. To test the hypothesis $\rho = 0$ we use the following equation:

$$t = r\sqrt{\frac{n-2}{1-r^2}}$$

and evaluate the result using t tables with $n - 2$ degrees of freedom.[2]
    From the example in Table 5.1,

$$t = -0.76\sqrt{\frac{9-2}{1-0.58}} = -3.10$$

We look up this value as we did for the t values in Chapters 3 and 4 . With 7 degrees of freedom, the absolute value of t exceeds the critical t value for $\alpha = 0.05$ which is 2.365. Therefore, we would conclude that the two variables are significantly correlated.

---

2   The number of degrees of freedom is the number of cases minus the total number of parameters estimated. In the procedures described here two parameters, β_0 and β_1, are estimated.

With the house price and pollution example we find

$$t = -0.427\sqrt{\frac{506 - 2}{1 - 0.18}} = -10.6$$

which is highly significant at all α levels shown in the t table. However, with an r^2 of only 0.18, it does not represent as large a percentage of shared variance as the last example. When you have big samples it is important to distinguish between statistical significance, which says a relationship has been detected, and substantial significance, meaning the effect is large enough to be of importance.

While the regression procedures in all major statistical packages produce correlation values, most packages also have procedures for just producing correlations. Suppose we were interested in the relationship among the following variables from the states data set in Appendix A: dropout rate, crime rate, low temperature and the natural log of the population (since the population is highly positively skewed, by states such as California, a transformation is usually used). To find the correlation and significance of these in SPSS you write:

```
CORRELATIONS /VARIABLES dropout crime lowtemp lnpop.

Correlations:  Dropout    Crime      Lowtemp  Lnpop

dropout        1.0000     .6247**    .3589*   .2239
crime          .6247**    1.0000     .4048*   .3215
lowtemp        .3589*     .4048*     1.0000   .2552
lnpop          .2239      .3215      .2552    1.0000
N of cases:    51      2-tailed Signif:   * - .01   ** - .001
```

This is called a *correlation matrix* and it is useful in some advanced statistical techniques, details of which are beyond the scope of this book (factor analysis, structural equation modelling and others). This matrix shows that although `Lowtemp` and `Dropout` are correlated, the correlation between `Crime` and `Dropout` is much higher. This relationship is discussed further in Chapter 8.

The significance can also be examined using the sums of squares discussed earlier. First we have to calculate the mean sum of squares. For the sums of squares accounted for by the model, this is *SSM* divided by the number of regressor variables. In the regressions described in this chapter there is only one. Therefore the mean, denoted M_{SSM}, is $SSM/1$. The mean for the sum of squared residuals, M_{SSR}, is *SSR* divided by its degrees of freedom. Its number of degrees of freedom is the total number of cases minus the number of parameters estimated. Here it is minus two for β_0 and β_1. The ratio of these two, M_{SSM}/M_{SSR}, is called the F ratio:

$$F(\mathrm{df}_{\mathrm{model}}, \mathrm{df}_{\mathrm{residual}}) = \frac{SSM/\mathrm{df}_{\mathrm{model}}}{SSR/\mathrm{df}_{\mathrm{residual}}} = \frac{M_{SSM}}{M_{SSR}}$$

Using the numbers already calculated from the house price and pollution example, we obtain

$$F(1,504) = \frac{7800/1}{34,916/504} = \frac{7800}{69.28} = 112.6$$

which is, up to rounding error, the F value printed in the output. The significance of an F value is determined using the F table which is described in more detail next chapter. Suffice it to say that large values of F mean the model is statistically significant and anything above about 5 is usually significant (112.6 is highly significant). Therefore we can reject the hypothesis that the model has no predictive value.

Having a significant correlation implies that the β_1 value, the slope, is significantly different from zero. We can construct a confidence interval for this parameter. This requires finding the standard error of this value. Conceptually, this is the same as finding the standard error of the mean. The equation for this is:

$$s_\beta = \sqrt{\frac{\sum(y_i - \hat{y}_i)^2/(n-2)}{\sum(x_i - \bar{x})^2}}$$

Consider the house price and pollution data. The top part of the equation is the mean of the sum of squared residuals (M_{SSR}). From the computer output we see that this is approximately 69.28. The value forming the denominator of the equation is the sum of the squared deviations for the x variable, here pollution. This is simply $n - 1$ multiplied by the variance. The variance, found using any of a number of different procedures, but not printed in the regression output, is 0.0134. Therefore, the standard error is:

$$s_\beta = \sqrt{\frac{69.28}{0.0134 \times 505}} = 3.20$$

which is the same as is printed in the output.

Constructing a 95% confidence interval for the parameter is done in the same way as for the mean. We look up the $\alpha = 0.05$ (two-tailed) value for t with 504 degrees of freedom. Since the table only goes up to 100 the value for ∞ (infinity) of 1.96 is adequate. We then add and subtract 1.96 multiplied by our observed s_β from the observed value of β_1 to produce the 95% confidence interval.

$$CI_{95\%} = -33.92 \pm 3.20 \times 1.96 = -33.92 \pm 6.27$$
$$= (-40.19, -27.65)$$

This allows us to say with some confidence that we believe that the value of the parameter, β_1, in the population is somewhere in this range.

We can also use the observed value and its standard error to test explicitly the hypothesis that $\beta_1 = 0$ in the population (or any other value; just subtract the observed value from the expected value and proceed). Divide the observed value by its standard error to give a t value that can be compared with the t table for $n - 2$ degrees of freedom:

$$t(n - 2) = \frac{\beta_1}{s_\beta} = \frac{-33.92}{3.20} = -10.6$$

With approximately 500 degrees of freedom this value far exceeds any of those in the t table. It is the same as the t value found by transforming r. For the cases described in this chapter, where you are using only one variable to predict one other, the three methods for testing significance (r, F and t) will produce the same result (up to rounding error). With more complicated designs they do differ.

Assumptions for Significance

As with the t tests described in Chapters 3 and 4, there are various assumptions that must be made before using a regression (or a correlation) and, in particular, before believing that the p values the computer churns out are accurate. Some of the assumptions are the same as those for the t test. For example, the sampling and/or random allocation must be done properly and it must make sense to talk about the variables as being continuous.

In plain English, the main assumption for regressions is that there is nothing strange-looking in the scatterplot or, more generally, in the residuals. One aspect that causes problems for p values is when the variance of y is markedly different for different values of the x variable. This is called *heteroscedascity*. When we were doing group t tests (Chapter 4) we also checked for this, but in that case we were simply looking for a difference between the two groups. There are complex ways of dealing with heteroscedacity in regressions, but these are beyond the scope of this book (for more detailed discussion see chapters in Lewis-Beck, 1993).[3] For us, the most important lesson is to recognise situations in which the homoscedacity assumption (that the variance remains approximately the same: the opposite of heteroscedacity) is untenable. Figure 5.7 shows an example with clearly heteroscedastic data.

Consider the pollution and house price example. Suppose we wanted to see if the variance in median house price was about the same in the high and low pollution areas. First, we have to divide the areas into high and low pollution regions. It is important to choose the dividing line carefully. Either it should be based on some theoretical reason or on a standard statistic. Here, I choose to

---

3 An important aspect of this assumption is that it affects the resulting p values, but the estimates for the β values will still be unbiased.

Box 5.1 Power for Correlation

When finding the significance of r we are testing $H_0 : \rho = 0$ (the null hypothesis) which means that there is no correlation between the two variables in the population. As with t tests, it is useful to examine the power of this test. This allows us to calculate the sample size necessary to give us a reasonable chance of detecting a certain size effect. It is also important, if we fail to reject the null hypothesis, to know how likely we would have been to reject different size effects.

As with t tests, Cohen (1992) has defined small, medium and large effects. These correspond to $\rho = 0.10$, $\rho = 0.30$ and $\rho = 0.50$. The sample sizes necessary to reject at the $\alpha = 0.05$ level the hypothesis $\rho = 0$ around 80% of the time for each of these effects are 783, 85 and 28, respectively. Thus, while large effects are easily detected with fairly small samples, small effects are more difficult to detect.

Suppose we were doing a study on children between the ages of 6 and 12 and were interested in the amount of television watched and the level of sugar intake between meals. Suppose that we wanted to detect even a small effect and decided that Cohen's prescription of $\rho = 0.10$ seemed appropriate. This would mean, in order to have an 80% chance of rejecting this size of effect, we would need to question 783 children.

For other relationships we might expect a much larger association. Suppose we wanted to compare the hours of watching television with hours spent on outdoor activities. Here we might expect a large negative correlation. If we were satisfied with Cohen's $\rho = 0.50$ then we would need only 28 children to give us a good chance of observing a significant effect. Cohen (1992) describes what to do for the simplest cases, and Cohen (1988) is recommended for more complicated examples. Of course, the effect sizes Cohen describes are just guidelines. In some cases you may be interested in different values of ρ. Since the r value can be transformed into a t value, power calculations for other effect sizes can be done using the logic presented for the t test power analyses in Chapter 4.

---

split the group roughly in half. The median is 0.538 so all the cases with levels less than this were put in group 1 ($n = 249$) and all the cases with this level or higher were placed in group 2 ($n = 257$). The standard deviations of these two groups are 7.53 and 9.19, respectively.

In Chapter 4 I described how we can formally test how likely this large a discrepancy is if the standard deviations in the population are the same. This is done by finding the ratio of larger variance to the smaller variance and comparing it with the F distribution. We will discuss the F distribution in greater detail next chapter. Here, the resulting value of 1.49 is significant at $p = 0.001$. This means that there is only a 1 in a 1000 chance of observing this

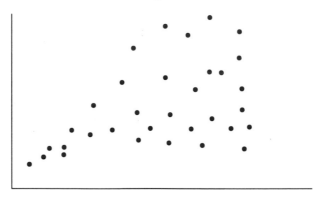

Figure 5.7   *An example of heteroscedastic data. The spread of the data along*
            the vertical axis differs depending on the value along the
            horizontal axis

large a difference if the price variances of the two populations (high and low pollution areas) are equal. Therefore we would reject the hypothesis that these groups have equal variances. However, the size of the difference is not large in absolute terms. The difference was detected because of the relatively large sample size.

$$F(257, 249) = \frac{9.19^2}{7.53^2} = \frac{84.45}{56.69} = 1.49$$

Another consideration, and the most important for this chapter, is that the pattern of the data should be described adequately by a straight line. Often this is not the case and in these circumstances linear regression and correlation are not appropriate. Figure 5.1 is a good example: as age goes up height also goes up but the increase is much more rapid when the people are young. This is called a curvilinear relationship. In the next few sections we discuss some rules for dealing with such cases.

Examining Residuals

As I have noted in several places throughout this book, it is important to look at residuals – cases that do not fit the general pattern – when doing statistical analysis. While there are some complex techniques of examining residuals, in most cases either you are looking for a couple of individual outliers (cases with large residuals) or you are looking for some kind of pattern in the residuals. I will examine both of these situations briefly.

   In the high school dropout rate and record low temperature example I noted that there were two outliers corresponding to Alaska and Hawaii. Here I will describe how these might be detected and what their impact is. Looking at the scatterplot (Figure 5.2), it is clear that these two states do not follow the same general pattern as the others. In any scatterplot there are bound to be some cases that have high residuals. The question is how large a residual should be for it to be of concern. Recall the discussion of z scores in Chapter 2 where we were calculating how extreme an individual's test score was compared with the population. In a similar way we can divide each residual by the standard error of the residuals to create studentised residuals ('student' refers to William Gossett, the person who developed the 'Student' t tests).

Fortunately SPSS and most other of the main packages will print the studentised residuals. Another useful measure is Cook's distance statistic. This measures the influence of each case on the overall model. In general, if Cook's distance is greater than 1 then it is considered large. You should also look to see if a few cases have much higher impact than any of the others. The following command produces these values (much of the output has been edited out).

```
REGRESSION /VARIABLES lowtemp dropout /DEPENDENT dropout /
METHOD ENTER
/RESIDUALS OUTLIERS (SRESID COOK) ID (state).
```

```
Multiple R          .35887
R Square            .12879
F =       7.24351        Signif F =      .0097
```

——————————— Variables in the Equation ———————————

Variable	B	SE B	Beta	T	Sig T
LOWTEMP	.16381	.06086	.35887	2.691	.0097
(Constant)	31.45851	2.64108		11.911	.0000

Outliers - Studentized Residual			Outliers - Cook's Distance			
Case #	STATE	*SRESID	Case #	STATE	*COOK D	Sig F
2	Alaska	2.43573	12	Hawaii	.56080	.5744
12	Hawaii	-2.19583	2	Alaska	.41474	.6628
4	Arkansas	-2.01599	19	Louisian	.10732	.8984
19	Louisian	1.91871	9	Wash_DC	.09913	.9058
9	Wash_DC	1.79196	10	Florida	.06411	.9380
33	New_York	1.60062	25	Mississi	.05861	.9431
15	Indiana	-1.57610	4	Arkansas	.05599	.9456
25	Mississi	1.54745	24	Minnesot	.04369	.9573
24	Minnesot	-1.38962	35	N_Dakota	.03906	.9617
16	Iowa	-1.34413	33	New_York	.03859	.9622

There are a few states that have fairly high residuals, but from this output alone there does not appear to be a large problem. With 51 cases we would expect some would have studentised residuals greater than 2 (you would expect by chance about one in 20 to be above 2). For Cook's distance, there also does not appear to be any large problem because none of the values is above 1.

However, two of the values are much larger than the others: Hawaii and Alaska. In these situations it is often worth seeing if the interpretation differs when these are excluded.

```
SEL IF (STATE NE 'Alaska ').
SEL IF (STATE NE 'Hawaii ').
REGRESSION /VARIABLES lowtemp dropout /DEPENDENT dropout /
METHOD ENTER.
```

```
Multiple R              .56169
R Square                .31549
F =      21.66260       Signif F =     .0000
```

	Variables in the Equation				
Variable	B	SE B	Beta	T	Sig T
LOWTEMP	.29305	.06296	.56169	4.654	.0000
(Constant)	36.56763	2.69072		13.590	.0000

The value of *r* is now much larger, 0.56 compared with 0.36. The β value is also larger, 0.29 compared with 0.16. The scatterplot in Figure 5.8 shows the data with both regression lines. It is important to make sure that your interpretation does not dramatically change when a few points are removed. If your results depend on a single case (or a couple of cases) then they are unreliable. If your conclusions do not change when a couple of extreme points are removed then your model is more robust. Here the regression lines are fairly similar.

All the regressions conducted in this chapter assume that there is a linear relationship between the two variables. It is therefore important to check this assumption. This can be done by making sure there is no pattern in the residuals. The age with height scatterplot (Figure 5.1) is a good example where the data do

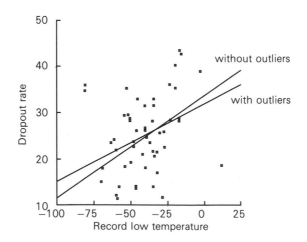

Figure 5.8   *Comparing the regression lines with and without Alaska and Hawaii*

not fit a straight line. Using the following commands, we can produce the scatterplot of the residuals (these are the actual residuals, the studentised residuals could also be used) with the predicted values. I have edited down the output considerably. As can be seen, there is a clear pattern in the scatterplot. This means that the relationship is not linear. You would need to run a nonlinear regression (which means fitting a curved line).

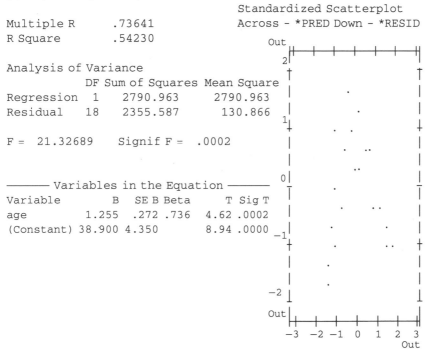

```
REGRESS /VAR height lage /DEPEND height /METHOD ENTER /
SCAT (*RESID, *PRED).
```

Multiple R   .73641
R Square   .54230

Analysis of Variance
              DF Sum of Squares Mean Square
Regression   1   2790.963   2790.963
Residual   18   2355.587   130.866

F = 21.32689   Signif F = .0002

———— Variables in the Equation ————
Variable   B   SE B Beta   T Sig T
age   1.255   .272 .736   4.62 .0002
(Constant) 38.900 4.350   8.94 .0000

Standardized Scatterplot
Across - *PRED Down - *RESID

Alternatives When Assumptions Are Not Satisfied

It's sad. In every chapter of this book that discusses the assumptions of a particular test, I have to include perhaps the most popular 'solution' when the data do not satisfy the assumptions. This 'solution' is to ignore the problem. The consequences of this depend on how severe the failures are. In general, when there are problems with the assumptions the reported p values are often lower than they should be. Therefore if there are problems with the regression assumptions you should lower your α level. With regard to nonlinear relationships, there is also a conceptual problem. If your model is linear, but the data are not, you should use a better model. This will increase the fit. In some cases this is easily done by transforming the variable as below.

A better solution than just ignoring the problem is to use tests that are specifically designed so that there are no distributional assumptions. The two main distribution-free correlations are Spearman's ρ (rho) and Kendall's τ (pronounced 'tau'). These each involve ranking the data for each variable and then comparing the orders. Spearman's ρ is the same as Pearson's correlation done on ranks, although there are a few extra modifications to take into account tied to ranks. Kendall's τ measures how similar the orderings of the two variables are. I refer interested readers to Siegel and Castellan (1988) for details on doing these tests by hand. A computer can calculate both of these. With the newer versions of SPSS these statistics are options in the main correlation procedure. In some versions there is a special non-parametric correlation procedure (called NONPAR CORR) that is used in the same way as the correlation procedure.

The final option is to transform one or both of the variables. This is the best option either when it is clear that there is a specific pattern in the data or when you have a good theoretical reason to suppose a particular nonlinear relationship. Both of these reasons apply for the relationship between height and age. We would not expect height to increase as rapidly for older people as for younger people. We can transform the height variable to account for this and then rerun the regression and look at the residuals. Here I have used the natural log transformation of age, although others could be used. The new scatterplot of the residuals does not exhibit any obvious pattern. Therefore we would probably

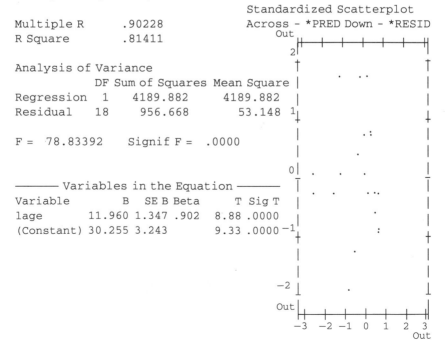

```
COMPUTE lage = LN (age)
REGRESS /VAR height lage /DEPEND height /METHOD ENTER /
SCAT (*RESID, *PRED).
```

Multiple R   .90228
R Square   .81411

Analysis of Variance

	DF	Sum of Squares	Mean Square
Regression	1	4189.882	4189.882
Residual	18	956.668	53.148

F = 78.83392   Signif F = .0000

——— Variables in the Equation ———

Variable	B	SE B	Beta	T	Sig T
lage	11.960	1.347	.902	8.88	.0000
(Constant)	30.255	3.243		9.33	.0000

Standardized Scatterplot
Across - *PRED Down - *RESID

be pleased with this transformation. It is also worth comparing the various indices of fit. The new R^2 is over 0.80, meaning over 80% of the variance in height can be accounted for by the transformed variable age. With the non-transformed variable only about half (54%) of the variance was accounted for.

Box 5.2   Representing Statistical Tests with Equations

All of the statistical tests that are introduced in this book can be written in an equation format. In this box both the paired and the group t tests, and the simple linear regression introduced in this chapter, are reviewed. The basic equation for a paired t test is:

$$x_{1i} - x_{2i} = d_i = \beta_0 + e_i$$

Here, x_{1i} and x_{2i} are the variables we are comparing. For each case, we subtract the value of one from the other to get a difference score (d_i) and use this to estimate the mean difference β_0. In this equation, each e_i is simply the difference between the observed score for that individual and the mean of the group.

For the group t test we are comparing the mean of one variable, call it y_i, between two different groups. Let us denote the different groups with the variable x_i. For one group let $x = 0$ and for the other let $x = 1$. In experimental research the control group is usually denoted by $x = 0$ and the experimental group by $x = 1$. The equation is then

$$y_i = \beta_1 x_i + \beta_0 + e_i$$

When $x = 0$ (for the control group), this equation is essentially the same as the previous one but just for the control group. β_0 is the mean of y for the control group. The parameter of interest is β_1. It is the difference between the means of the variable y for the two groups. If β_1 is positive then the experimental group has a higher mean, if it is negative then the control group has a higher mean. When we conduct a group t test we are testing the hypothesis that in the population there is no difference in the means between these two groups. In other words, $H_0 : \beta_1 = 0$.

In the regressions we discussed in this chapter a variable y was regressed on a variable x. This is equivalent to trying to predict the values of y with the variable x or to account for the variance of y with the variable x. The equation for this is

$$y_i = \beta_1 x_i + \beta_0 + e_i$$

which is exactly the same as the equation for the group t test. In this equation the β_1 value is the amount of increase in y for each increase in x. This is of course the same as for the previous equation.

Summary

In this chapter we discussed regressions and correlations. Regression analysis is the most common statistical technique used in the social sciences and in one form or another it can be used for almost any statistical technique in which you would be interested. Here I only presented the simplest form of regression. In the later chapters more complicated regression equations are introduced. Therefore it is necessary to make sure that you understand the basics here. In Box 5.2 it is explained how all the statistics thus far described can be written in a regression format.

The regressions discussed here are called simple linear regressions. One variable is regressed on the other and it is assumed that there is a linear relationship between the two. To examine whether this is true it is useful to produce a scatterplot and explore the residuals. In more complicated regressions some form of residual analysis is necessary.

I want to end this chapter with a discussion of a phrase that appears in almost every methodology book of the social sciences:

> Correlation does not imply causation.

This means that a large and statistically significant correlation (or β value or F value) does not mean that the regressor variable *causes* or even *explains* some change in the regressed variable. It is simply that when one variable varies, so does the other. They covary or correlate, hence the words covariance and correlation. In the real world two variables often correlate even when there is no clear causal link.

Assignment

1   Match the four scatterplots with the most appropriate descriptions.

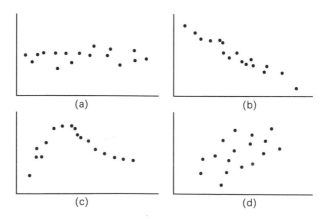

(a)

(b)

(c)

(d)

(i) The correlation would be approximately zero because, although there is a relationship, it is not linear.

(ii) There is a weak positive relationship.

(iii) There is a strong negative correlation.

(iv) There is no apparent relationship, the correlation is approximately zero.

2 (a) Draw, either by hand or with a computer package, a scatterplot from the following data. Make sure you label all the axes.

(b) By hand, superimpose a straight line that you feel describes the relationship. Circle any large residuals.

x	4	2	2	5	6	5	2	8	5	3
y	43	56	64	18	24	26	24	11	32	52

x mean $= 4.2$ sd $= 2.0$
y mean $= 35.0$ sd $= 17.7$

3 Using the data from Exercise 2, find the regression equation for the best-fitting line through the data. What percentage of the variance of y does the variable x account for? Would you reject the hypothesis that there is no relationship in the population between these variables? Show your work on this problem.

4 In a few brief sentences, describe why you would want to use regression analysis and give some example where it would be useful.

5 In a large-scale study, 5000 respondents were asked to rate their general life satisfaction. The researcher also recorded the temperature on the day that the interview took place. S/he found $r = 0.06$ which is statistically significant. What should s/he conclude?

6 A researcher was interested in the effects of the travelling distance to primary school on children's academic performance. S/he recruited a random sample of 200 children aged 8 to 9 in a local school and recorded the average time each child took to get to school and the child's academic performance (on a 0 (low) to 100 (high) scale). S/he found a highly statistically significant and substantial correlation of $r = 0.80$ ($r^2 = 0.64$) and concluded that increased travel time leads to higher grades. The researcher went on to advise parents and children to take less direct routes on their way to and from school in order to increase their children's performance. What is the *main* flaw in the researcher's argument?

7 Using the states.sps data file in Appendix A:

(a) Plot (using PLOT /PLOT popula WITH area BY state) the relationship between a state's population and its area. Circle any outliers and try to figure out which states these correspond to.

(b) Find the correlation of this relationship.

(c) Both of these variables are highly and positively skewed. Use the following commands to transform them into less skewed variables:

```
COMPUTE lnarea = LN (area).
COMPUTE lnpop = LN (popula).
```

Plot this relationship and find the correlation.

    (d) Using the distribution-free alternatives in the CORRELATION command (or the procedure NONPAR CORR) find the association between popul and area, and between lnpop and lnarea. Comment on these values.

8   The following data come Greaney and Kelleghan (1984), who were interested in educational transitions in Ireland. The data were made available by StatLib, a computer bulletin board that contains several data sets (this set can be found on http://lib.stat.cmu.edu/datasets/irish.edu). In the analysis below, the relationship between the prestige of the father's occupation and child's level of education attainment is explored. A higher score for fathers means a more prestigious occupation and a higher value of educ means a higher educational attainment for the child. Interpret the following excerpts from the output.

```
REGRESSION /VARIABLES educ fathers /DEPENDENT educ /METHOD
ENTER.
```

```
* * * * MULTIPLE  REGRESSION * * * *
```

(a)   Multiple R   .33448
       R Square   .11188
       Adjusted R Square   .11000

(b)   Analysis of Variance

	DF	Sum of Squares	Mean Square
Regression	1	574.80549	574.80549
Residual	472	4563.00885	9.66739

F =   59.45818 Signif F =   .0000

(c)   ———————————— Variables in the Equation ————————————

Variable	B	SE B	Beta	T	Sig T
fathers	.07189	9.32346E-03	.33448	7.711	.0000
(Constant)	3.37390	.39009		8.649	.0000

9   The four graphs shown below depict different possible statistical models. In each there are one or more letters (*f*, *g*, and/or *h*) that denote particular β values in the following equations. Match up the statistical tests with their graphical representation, and say which β value corresponds to which letter on the matching graph.

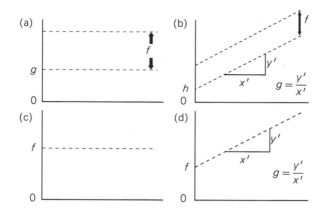

(i)   Paired t test

$$x_i = \beta_0 + e_i$$

(ii)   Group t test

$$y_i = \beta_1 x_i + \beta_0 + e_i$$

where x_i is zero for one group and one for the other.

(iii)   Linear regression

$$y_i = \beta_1 x_i + \beta_0 + e_i$$

(iv)   A combination of a group t test and a regression. This is called an analysis of covariance (or ANCOVA) and is discussed in Chapter 8.

$$y_i = \beta_2 x_{2i} + \beta_1 x_{1i} + \beta_0 + e_i$$

where x_{1i} is zero for one group and one for the other. You have not learned this technique yet, but try to figure out which letters correspond to which β values.

Comparing Many Means: the Analysis of Variance Approach

In Chapters 3 and 4 I discussed two different types of *t* test. In Chapter 3 this was the paired *t* test in which the scores for two variables were compared for each person. In Chapter 4 the group *t* test was described, where the people were split into two groups and the means of these groups were compared. These were fine for comparing two variables for a single group or the values of one variable between two groups. Often, however, you want to compare three (or more) variables or three (or more) groups. The procedures described in this chapter show how this is done. They are described as analysis of variance, or ANOVA, procedures. More advanced ANOVA models are described in Chapter 8.

The statistical methods described in this chapter involve a two-stage process. First you investigate whether there is a difference in the means, either among variables or among groups, and then you try to locate where these differences are. How the second stage is conducted depends on whether you have hypothesised any specific comparisons before conducting the study. While I describe the difference between these planned and unplanned comparisons in relation to the ANOVAs, be aware that the concepts are applicable to all types of statistics in which multiple comparisons can be made.

Before describing the techniques for comparing means it is worth repeating in general terms the difference between within-subject and between-subjects designs. In a within-subject design you are comparing the responses for several variables for everyone in a single group. Between-subjects designs compare the scores of a single variable among several groups. There are several different phrases used for referring to within- and between-subjects designs that are basically synonymous. I have listed some of these in Table 6.1.

Between-subjects Comparisons

Graphing Means

As is true with most statistical techniques, before performing any calculations, you should look at the data. Consider the following example from Abernethy *et al.* (1994). They were interested in differences among snooker (a type of pool) experts (six nationally ranked players), intermediates (seven club players) and novices (15 university students) in their strategies for playing the game. This is a between-subjects comparison because there are different people in each of the

Table 6.1   *The terms used for within- and between-subjects designs*

Within-subject designs	Between-subjects designs
Related	Unrelated
Dependent	Independent
Matched	Unmatched
Panel	Cross-sectional
Repeated measures	Between-group
Paired	

groups. A person cannot be both an expert and a novice. One of their comparisons was the maximum number of shots the player planned for in advance. The data shown in Table 6.2 are based on this study (I constructed them so they have the same means and similar standard deviations as those reported in Abernethy *et al.* 1994). The word 'grand' is used in Table 6.2 to refer to characteristics for the entire sample. Thus, the grand mean is the mean for all three groups together.

When graphing data we want to see if our statistical tests are likely to produce significant results. There are several ways this can be done. The EXAMINE procedure in SPSS can run many graphing techniques and most packages also offer similar techniques (it is worth reiterating that drawing graphs by hand is often the best procedure). One popular way involves graphing the means with their standard errors or confidence intervals. This is done by many computer programs, including the newer versions of SPSS, and is called an *error bar diagram*. If constructing one by hand, the 95% confidence intervals for each of the groups can be found using the techniques described in Chapter 3 (or having the computer do this for you). Draw a short line to denote each of the limits of the interval and connect these. Next mark where the mean is. This should be half-way between the two limits. Figure 6.1 shows the confidence intervals for the snooker data. The confidence intervals of the experts and intermediates overlap, so we would not confidently say that these groups differ. However, the novices do appear to think fewer shots ahead.

Table 6.2   *Data and some descriptive statistics for the maximum number of shots planned in advance by different level snooker players*

Experts	Intermediates	Novices
4, 8, 6, 11, 9, 8	11, 7, 3, 8, 14, 11, 10	4, 3, 7, 4, 6, 2, 3, 2, 7, 4, 3, 5, 4, 4, 4
$n = 6$	$n = 7$	$n = 15$
sum = 46	sum = 64	sum = 62
$\bar{x} = 7.67$	$\bar{x} = 9.14$	$\bar{x} = 4.13$
$s = 2.422$	$s = 3.532$	$s = 1.552$

Statistics for whole sample:
Grand $n = 28$ Grand mean = 6.14   Grand sum = 172
          Grand $s = 3.194$ Grand var = 10.20

Before doing any formal statistical tests you should have a good idea what the results will be. This safeguards you against any problem in the calculations and gives you a better understanding of the data. From Figure 6.1 there appears to be a relationship between expertise and thinking ahead. A rough test of this is seeing whether the confidence intervals of these groups overlap. This essentially compares the spread of the means of the different groups (what can be thought of as the variance between the groups) with the spread of the data within each group (or the variance within the groups).

Box 6.1   Why Can't I Just Do Lots of *t* Tests?

In Chapter 3 you learned how to do a *t* test for comparing the means of two groups. You probably do not want to learn another test if it is not necessary. I personally would not want to tell you about another test unless I thought it was worthwhile. Suppose you have three groups. You could just do a series of *t* tests to find out if there are differences between any pair of groups.

There are three reasons why a series of *t* tests will not suffice for multiple group comparisons. First, if there are three groups, as above, there are three possible pairs (experts and intermediates, experts and novices, intermediates and novices). This is not very many, but as the number of groups increases the number of possible pairs sky-rockets (what statisticians call a combinatoric explosion). If there were ten groups there would be 45 pairs; if there were 20 groups there would be 190 possible pairs and so on. So, the first reason why you should not do *t* tests on all the pairs is that it means less work for you. The second reason is that if you have several comparisons, it would be difficult to decide which α level to use. Clearly if you had 190 tests you would expect some comparisons to be significant by chance. Because of this you would have to lower your α level – say from 0.05 to 0.01 or even 0.001 – thus making it more difficult to detect differences (that is, increasing your chances of a Type II error). The ANOVA procedure gives you a single score and a single probability value. Finally, the ANOVA procedure can be extended to much more complicated designs, some of which are described in Chapter 8. It is more versatile than the basic *t* test.

The Oneway Between-subjects ANOVA

I have always felt the term analysis of variance, or ANOVA, is confusing. What you want to compare is the *means* of different groups, not their variances. In a nutshell, it is called analysis of variance because the procedure works by comparing the spread between the group means with the spread of values within each group. If the spread of the group means (often described as the between-groups sum of squares) is larger than is expected from the spread of

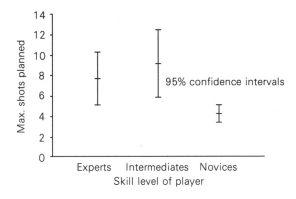

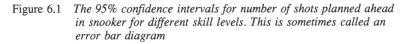

Figure 6.1   *The 95% confidence intervals for number of shots planned ahead in snooker for different skill levels. This is sometimes called an error bar diagram*

data within the groups (the within-group sum of squares) then this indicates the means differ. The technique was originally developed by the British statistician Ronald Fisher in the 1920s and 1930s. The ANOVA framework was originally designed to deal with experimental data in agriculture and has since grown popular within many experimental sciences.

Often the ANOVA framework is introduced separately from the regression approach and is described as a fundamentally different method for comparing the means of different groups. Historically, the ANOVA framework became popular because it could be done fairly easily without a computer (statistics has been around much longer than computers). The ANOVA framework has become very developed and the current computer programs are quite advanced. It remains popular for several reasons including that, at least when done by computer, you do not need to know much about how or why it works. This has enraged many statisticians. Running ANOVAs on a computer is often so user-friendly that it can be done without the user really understanding what is going on. Now, I feel strongly that user-friendliness is good. What these critics are arguing is that people can conduct several different ANOVAs and accumulate pages of output and not be able to recognise what is relevant or why. Further, when the computer runs an ANOVA, particularly for complex cases, it makes many assumptions. While these default assumptions can be overridden in most packages, many users do not realise what the assumptions are. For these reasons I urge readers to learn about ANOVAs both with the traditional approach and using an equation or regression format.

ANOVA as an Equation

At the end of Chapter 5 I showed how a group *t* test and a simple linear regression could be represented by the same equation. When there were two groups a single *dummy* variable was created that had the value zero for one group and one for the other. Consider the example in Figure 4.1 showing men's and women's attitudes towards nuclear disarmament. In that example we created a dummy variable for women: it had the value one for women and zero for men. We referred to men as the base or reference category. Here I show how to extend this to more groups.

Consider the snooker example where there are three groups. First we need to decide how many dummy variables should be used. In the two-group example we used one dummy variable. The parameter β_0 estimated the mean of the base category and the parameter β_1 was the difference between the two groups. In general we need one less dummy variable than categories. This is the degrees of freedom of the model discussed in Chapter 5 in relation to the F values of regression models. For this example, with three skill levels, we need two dummy variables. Next we have to decide on the coding and which group to use as the base category. In general, your base category is the one that you are comparing with the others. If you are doing an experiment, this is usually the control group. The choice of which category to use as the base depends on the particular theories in which you are interested. All things being equal, it is best to have the base category containing a fairly large number of cases. This makes the estimated β values more reliable. In our example the novice group has the most cases and will suffice. We create two dummy variables, call them EX_i and INT_i, to stand for the experts and the intermediates. Table 6.3 shows the codes for these two variables for the different groups. Each of the groups can be distinguished from the others by the values of these two variables. In the case of the novices it is by having the value zero for each of the variables.

The equation we model is:

$$Moves_i = \beta_2 EX_i + \beta_1 INT_i + \beta_0 + e_i$$

and its solution is

$$Moves_i = 3.54 EX_i + 5.01 INT_i + 4.13 + e_i$$

where β_0 is the mean for the novices. β_1 is the difference between the mean for the intermediates and the novices ($9.14 - 4.13 = 5.01$). β_2 is the differences between the mean for the experts and the novices ($7.67 - 4.13 = 3.54$). Figure 6.2 illustrates this model. Regression equations like this, with more than one regressor variable, are known as *multiple regressions*. They are described in more detail in Chapter 8.

Table 6.3 *Creating dummy variables for snooker skill*

Skill level	EX_i	INT_i
Expert	1	0
Intermediate	0	1
Novice	0	0

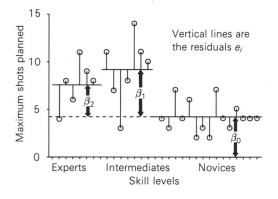

Figure 6.2   *Planning ahead: an equation/regression representation of the forward planning for differently skilled snooker players*

The values in Table 6.3 are perhaps the simplest way of coding the dummy variables. There are several others. It is important to realise, however, that while the different dummy variables will produce different β values, if properly designed each set should produce the same overall fit. We could have given the novices the value -1 for each of these variables instead of zero. This would also have tested whether the experts and intermediates were different from the novices, it is just that the β values would have been different. Often the dummy variables are designed to test specific differences between groups or particular relationships. For this example we might have wanted to use one β value to compare the combined group experts + intermediates with the novices and one β value to compare the experts with the intermediates. There are various rules for constructing these variables (what are sometimes called *contrasts*) when you want to test specific hypotheses (see Box 6.2). The main characteristic for testing the overall fit of the model is to ensure that each category is uniquely identified by the set of dummy variables. If not, the computer will give a zero for at least one of the values. This is a warning that there is a problem with your coding.[1]

Partitioning the Sums of Squares in an ANOVA

With an ANOVA our research question is 'Do the means of the groups differ?' In our snooker example, the null hypothesis was that the means for these three groups in the population are the same:

$$H_0 : \mu_{\text{EXPERTS}} = \mu_{\text{INTERMEDIATES}} = \mu_{\text{NOVICES}}$$

---

1   In some situations, a parameter estimate should be exactly zero, but you should check these cases carefully to make sure that this has not resulted from a coding mistake.

This equates with β_1 and β_2 *both* being zero, or at least not statistically significantly different from zero in the sample. If either of these is different from zero (in the population) we would want to reject the null hypothesis.

We are testing whether two parameters (that is, two of the three β values are of real interest; we are usually not interested in the value of the intercept β_0) are different from zero. Having two tests increases the likelihood of one of them being significant even if there are no differences in the population. It is important, therefore, to calculate a single probability value for the overall model before examining the individual comparisons. Recall from Chapter 5 that we can calculate the fit of a model against some baseline. In this case we would want to see how much our prediction of shots planned ahead improves when we include the two dummy variables as predictors. Recall from Chapter 5 that the definition of *SST*, the total sum of squares of the variable y_i, is:

$$SST = \sum(y_i - \bar{y})^2$$

Recall also its relation to the variance

$$s^2 = \frac{SS}{n-1} \quad therefore \quad SS = s^2(n-1)$$

Therefore if we want to calculate the total sum of squares all we need to know is the standard deviation (s), or the variance (s^2), of the entire sample and the sample size. From the data in Table 6.2 we can calculate the variance ($s^2 = 10.2$). The total sample size is 28 (6+7+15), therefore the total sum of squares is:

$$SST = (10.2)(27) = 275.4$$

The total sum of squares is the amount we try to account for. The more of this that the model accounts for the better. What we cannot account for are the residuals, the difference between the predicted and the observed score for each individual. The sum of squares of the residuals (*SSR*) is related to the amount of variation within each group (this is sometimes denoted by *SSW*, for within-group sum of squares). This is the variation not explained by the model. If we are using only skill level to predict shots, we would not be able to explain the variation within these levels. To calculate *SSR* we add up the individual sum of squares for each group:

$$SSR = 2.422^2 \times 5 + 3.532^2 \times 6 + 1.552^2 \times 14$$
$$SSR = 29.33 + 74.85 + 33.72 = 137.90$$

As in Chapter 5, the sum of squares explained by the model is the difference between these: $SSM = SST - SSR$ or $SSM = 275.40 - 137.90 = 137.50$. The larger the *SSM* the more the model explains.

As a test of your calculations, it is also worth calculating *SSM* directly. For these cases it is based on the differences among the groups. To calculate this, for each group, subtract each group mean from the grand mean. Square this difference and then multiply the result by the group size. Finally, add together the results of these for each of the groups and you get *SSM*. Conceptually, this is simply a measure of how different the group means are from the overall or grand mean. For the snooker data this would be

$$SSM = 6(6.14 - 7.67)^2 + 7(6.14 - 9.14)^2 + 15(6.14 - 4.13)^2 = 137.65$$

which is within rounding error of the previous estimate (more precise values are given later when this example is analysed by computer).

To test whether the model accounts for a statistically significant amount we have to find the *mean sum of squares* of the model and the residuals. These are the sums of squares divided by their degrees of freedom. For *SSM*, the number of degrees of freedom is the number of variables used in the model when presented as an equation. In general the number of variables is the number of categories minus one; here it would be two. The mean of the model sum of squares is $137.65/2 = 68.83$.

The degrees of freedom for the residuals are the total number of cases (28) minus the *total* number of parameters estimated (3), that is 25. An easier way to remember this is that the degrees of freedom of the residuals are equal to the sample size, minus the degrees of freedom of the model, minus one. The mean of the residual sum of squares is $137.90/25 = 5.52$. If n is the total sample size (for all the groups combined) and k is the number of groups, then

$$df_{model} = k - 1$$
$$df_{residual} = n - df_{model} - 1 = n - k$$

To see if there is significant difference among the groups we do an *F* test. This is the mean of the model sum of squares divided by the mean of the residual sum of squares.

$$F(df_{model}, df_{residual}) = \frac{SSM/df_{model}}{SSR/df_{residual}} = \frac{M_{SSM}}{M_{SSR}}$$

In our example $F(2, 25) = 68.83/5.52 = 12.47$. Recall from Chapter 5 that the value R^2 is *SSM/SST*, or the proportion of total variance accounted for by the model. In this case $R^2 = 137.65/275.40 = 0.50$, therefore 50% of the total variation in shots planned within this sample is accounted for by the skill level.

The final step is seeing whether this value is significant. To do this we need to use the *F* table in Appendix D. In general, the higher the *F* value the better the chance that it is statistically significant. If the null hypothesis were true (that is, all the means in the population were equal) we would expect the *F* value to be near 1. If the observed F value is less than 1 it means that there was less variation among the means than we would expect by chance.[2] When F is greater than 1 you have to use the table. In one way, the F test is one-tailed. It is testing whether the between-subjects sum of squares is greater than predicted from the within-subject, or residual, sum of squares. Therefore, the probabilities in the F table refer to just one side of the distribution. This is why we had to double the probabilities for two-tailed tests of differences in standard deviations in Chapter 4. However, it is worth bearing in mind that the F test is not one-tailed in the sense that there is a predicted relationship among the group means. It is asking just whether there are differences among the means.

The significance of F depends on the degrees of freedom of the model and of the residuals. First, choose the α level (only the values for $\alpha = 0.05$ and $\alpha = 0.01$ levels are printed, but most statistics programs print precise p values). Then go to the F table in Appendix D and find the column corresponding to the degrees of freedom of the model (here 2), and move down to the row for the degrees of freedom of the residuals (here 25). The top value is the critical F value necessary to reject H_0 at $\alpha = 0.05$. The bottom value is for $\alpha = 0.01$. In order for our observed F to be significant it must be higher than these values. The critical values for this example are 3.39 and 5.57, respectively. Our value exceeds both of these, therefore we can reject the null hypothesis at either of these levels.

It is worth noting that the calculations to find F do not require writing the model down as an equation, nor are they dependent on defining any specific contrasts. Learning about the equation format of an ANOVA is important for conceptual understanding and for exploring what specific differences exist. It is not strictly necessary for doing an ANOVA. In older textbooks, the equation or regression format was often not presented because the authors wanted to stress how to solve for F. In these days of fast computers, it is far more important that you get a conceptual grasp of statistics. Therefore, it is important to think about the ANOVA from both perspectives.

The output (slightly edited) and commands from SPSS are shown below for both approaches.[3] Due to rounding the numbers are slightly different from those found above, but the conclusions are identical. It is worth noting that the regression procedure gives individual t scores for each of the β values. Thus, it is in effect doing two t tests. The first one tests if the intermediates are different from the novices and the second whether the experts differ from the novices. Both are statistically significant, showing that these groups do differ.

---

2   When you obtain an F value for an ANOVA that is less than 1 do not look up its significance. Simply state that $F < 1$ and therefore the result is non-significant and you do not reject the null hypothesis. Doing this shows that you are aware conceptually of what F is, allowing you to impress your family and friends.

3   In SPSS there are several ANOVA procedures, ranging from the ONEWAY procedure, discussed here, which is suitable only for these situations but is relatively user-friendly, to the MANOVA procedure, which can do many things but is more complicated. You can get by fairly well with just these two so they are the only ones that are taught in this book (you could even get by just with MANOVA).

ANOVA

```
ONEWAY /VARIABLES shots BY skill (1,3).
- - - - - - - O N E W A Y - - - - - - - -
Variable    SHOTS  Maximum Shots Planned
By Variable SKILL  Snooker Skill Level

                Sum of  Mean    F     F
          D.F. Squares Squares Ratio Prob.
Between    2  137.50   68.75  12.46 .0002
 Groups
Within    25  137.92    5.52
 Groups
Total     27  275.43
```

Note that the results above are the same as those reported when using the regression approach. Also note the B values reported below. These are what we are calling the β values. The value for the constant is β_0, the value for ex is β_2 and the value for int is β_1. The t values for these β values show that each is significantly different from zero which in this case means that both the intermediates and the experts are statistically significantly different from the novices.

Regression

```
COMPUTE ex = 0.
IF (skill EQ 1) ex = 1.
COMPUTE int = 0.
IF (skill EQ 2) int = 1.
REGRESSION /VARIABLES shots ex int
/DEPENDENT shots /METHOD ENTER.


Multiple R          .70657
R Square            .49924
Adjusted R Square   .45918
Standard Error      2.34882


Analysis of Variance
                   DF   Sum of     Mean
                         Squares
Regression    2  137.50476  68.75238
Residual     25  137.92381   5.51695

F =    12.46202  Signif F =  .0002

——— Variables in the Equation ———
Variable   B    SE B  Beta    T   Sig T
INT       5.01  1.08  .6916  4.66 .0001
EX        3.53  1.13  .4623  3.11 .0046
(Constant)4.13   .61         6.82 .0000
```

Another Example: Study Habits

Suppose we were interested in how study habits affect performance on knowledge retention. Fifteen students volunteered to take part in the study. Five were randomly allocated to a control condition and were simply told to read a chapter from a book. Students in a second condition were told to read the chapter and then to write an outline of it. The third group had first to skim through the chapter, thinking of the key questions, and then to read it. The exam had 50 multiple choice questions based on the chapter. The number of correct answers is given in the columns headed x_i shown in Table 6.4, and below these are the calculations for the sum of squares within each group, used to calculate *SSR*, and the total sum of squares, for *SST*.

The larger the value of *SSM* the more the model explains. If we were going to use a regression approach we might use the equation:

$$y_i = \beta_2 outline_i + \beta_1 skim_i + \beta_0 + e_i$$

where *outline*$_i$ has the value one for everyone in the second group and zero for everyone else and *skim*$_i$ has the value one for everyone in the third group and zero for everyone else (here, $\beta_2 = 6$ (the difference in the means of *outline* and *control*), $\beta_1 = 12$ (the difference in the means of *skim* and *control*) and $\beta_0 = 26$ (the mean of *control*)). The response variable, y_i, is the number of correct responses. To test whether this model is statistically significant we have to find the mean sum of squares of the model and of the residuals. The means of these are found by dividing by their degrees of freedom, 2 and 12, respectively. Therefore the mean of the model sum of squares is $M_{SSM} = 360/2 = 180.0$ and the mean of the residual sum of squares is $M_{SSR} = 612/12 = 51.0$. Therefore, in this example, $F(2, 12) = 180.0/51.0 = 3.53$.

The final step is seeing whether this value is significant using the F table. We find the column corresponding to the degrees of freedom for the model (2), and move down the row of the degrees of freedom for the residuals (12). For $\alpha = 0.05$, the value shown is 3.89. This is the critical value. If the observed F is *higher* than this then it is significant at $\alpha = 0.05$. Here, 3.53 is less than 3.89 so if we were using $\alpha = 0.05$ we would fail to reject the null hypothesis that there is no difference between groups. We would say the result is non-significant. It is important to stress that we do not accept the null hypothesis, we only fail to reject it.

Planned and Unplanned Comparisons

The ANOVA procedures involve two stages. First, you need to find out if there are any differences in the means of the groups. This is done by calculating the F value and testing its significance. Next, you need to find out where the

Table 6.4 *Comparing different study schemes with an ANOVA*

Control ($\bar{x} = 26$)			Outline ($\bar{x} = 32$)			Skim first ($\bar{x} = 38$)		
x_i	$(26 - x_i)$	$(26 - x_i)^2$	x_i	$(32 - x_i)$	$(32 - x_i)^2$	x_i	$(38 - x_i)$	$(38 - x_i)^2$
24	2	4	32	0	0	42	−4	16
31	−5	25	37	−5	25	36	2	4
15	11	121	42	−10	100	47	−9	81
29	−3	9	28	4	16	34	4	16
31	−5	25	21	11	121	31	7	49
	SS	184			262			166

Grand Mean = 32

$(32 - 24)^2 =$	64	$(32 - 32)^2 =$	0	$(32 - 42)^2 =$	100
$(32 - 31)^2 =$	1	$(32 - 37)^2 =$	25	$(32 - 36)^2 =$	16
$(32 - 15)^2 =$	289	$(32 - 42)^2 =$	100	$(32 - 47)^2 =$	225
$(32 - 29)^2 =$	9	$(32 - 28)^2 =$	16	$(32 - 34)^2 =$	4
$(32 - 31)^2 =$	1	$(32 - 21)^2 =$	121	$(32 - 31)^2 =$	1
	364		262		346

$SST = 364 + 262 + 346 = 972$
$SSR = 184 + 262 + 166 = 612$
$SSM = SST - SSR \quad = 360$

differences are. In the snooker example, all the significance of the F value tells us is that if all the means in the population are the same, then getting differences as large as the ones observed is unlikely. This, on its own, is not very revealing because we do not know which means differ from each other. The second stage involves locating the differences. There are two ways of doing this. The first is called *planned* or *a priori* comparisons. These are appropriate if, before you collect any data, you have specific comparisons you want to make. The second is called *unplanned* or *post hoc* comparisons. These are appropriate when you have looked at the data and you want to explore where the differences are. The distinction between these two types of comparisons is important.

When you design a study with multiple groups, you usually have some notion about how these groups will differ. In the example above we would probably have expected the novices to be different from the two experienced groups. This would be one planned comparison. Another comparison would be that the two experienced groups differ from each other. Planned comparisons are equivalent to testing different β values in the same model. Therefore, many of the same rules apply. In particular, if you have k groups there should be $k - 1$ dummy variables or what are called *contrasts* in the ANOVA literature. Contrasts are denoted by a series of *weights*. The weights specify which groups should be compared with which. Groups with positive weights are contrasted with groups with negative weights (these weights could be used as the values for the dummy variables in the regression format). Two contrasts are listed below.

	Novices	Intermediates	Experts
Novices v experienced groups	−2	1	1
Intermediates v experts	0	−1	1

The first contrast compares the novices with the more experienced players. This is because the novices have a negative weight (-2) and the other two have positive weights. In the second, the intermediates (-1) are compared with experts $(+1)$.

An important characteristic of these contrasts is that the sum of the weights for any individual contrast is equal to zero. If we sum within each contrast we get zero $(-2 + 1 + 1 = 0$ and $0 + -1 + 1 = 0)$. If this is done (using the oneway procedure), then the computer does a t test for each of these contrasts.

As discussed for the equation-based models, each group should be uniquely identified by the contrasts. The ANOVA models further specify that each contrast should be *orthogonal*.[4] This basically means that each of the individual tests of significance are independent of each other. This is important for interpreting the resulting p values. There are some basic rules for determining

4 For students who have studied vectors, this means the vectors defined by the contrasts are all at right angles to each other. If you haven't studied vectors, don't worry.

if a set of contrasts is orthogonal. Suppose you had the following sets of contrasts for the snooker example:

	Set A: orthogonal			Set B: non-orthogonal		
Contrast 1	-2	1	1	-2	1	1
Contrast 2	0	-1	1	-1	0	1

In set A, if the first contrast is significant (the novices being different from the other two groups combined) it would not give us any information about whether the second contrast is significant. For set B, on the other hand, if the first contrast is significant, it would increase our belief that the second is also significant. Comparing the novices and the combined group tells us something relevant about whether the novices may differ from the experts. The first set of contrasts is orthogonal, the second set is non-orthogonal. To test for orthogonality multiply the weights for each group together and then sum these products. If the result is zero then the set is orthogonal.

	Set A: orthogonal			Set B: non-orthogonal		
Contrast 1	-2	1	1	-2	1	1
Contrast 2	0	-1	1	-1	0	1
Products	0 $+$	-1 $+$	1 $= 0$	2 $+$	0 $+$	1 $= 3$

In some cases it may still be worthwhile using non-orthogonal contrasts if these contrasts are the ones of most interest. Using non-orthogonal contrasts means that the p values of the different contrasts will be correlated. Because of this more caution is necessary when interpreting the p values and conservative methods for adjusting the α level should be used (see below).

To summarise, there are three basic rules for constructing contrasts for the ANOVA. The second two are not necessary for constructing useful β values in the regression format, but they are important for the ANOVA approach and the computer will expect you to follow them.

- If you have k groups you should have $k - 1$ contrasts that uniquely specify each group
- The sum of the weights for any contrast should be zero
- The set of contrasts should be orthogonal.

In SPSS the planned contrasts can be specified within the oneway procedure using the /CONTRAST command followed by the values for the contrasts, or the weights. SPSS checks that the weights within each contrast sum to zero but does not check to make sure they are orthogonal. The computer assumes that they are orthogonal. It also assumes that only one test is conducted. Therefore the p values are not appropriate if there are several contrasts. If you have many contrasts, you should adjust your α level. Some statisticians suggest dramatically lowering the α level as the number of contrasts increases. Sometimes this is necessary, but more importantly you should be cautious interpreting any significant result when multiple tests are done.

For the snooker data, the two most probable planned contrasts are the novices versus the experienced players and the intermediates versus the experts. After the normal analysis of variance output, SPSS essentially does a t test on these comparisons and shows that the first contrast is statistically significant, while the second is not. Therefore we can conclude the intermediates and the experts differ from the novices, but we cannot conclude that the intermediates and the experts differ. Here are the command and the t test results.

```
ONEWAY shots BY skill (1,3) /CONTRAST -2 1 1 /CONTRAST 0 -1 1.
                          Pooled Variance Estimate
                 Value   S. Error  T Value  D.F.   T Prob.
Contrast 1  8.5429   1.7829    4.791   25.0   .000
Contrast 2 -1.4762   1.3068    1.130   25.0   .269
```

It is worth noting that the computer prints both the pooled and the separate variance estimates. While the separate variance estimate is the same as that printed by the t test procedure, the pooled estimate also uses the variance of any groups not being compared in the contrast. This is why it shows 25 degrees of freedom even for the second contrast when only 13 people are being compared.

Often researchers are interested in group differences but they are not really sure what comparisons are of the most interest. In these cases *unplanned* comparisons are conducted. Suppose, for example, you wanted to explore whether there were differences in interest in science in the different geographic regions of Britain and suppose you had no specific planned comparisons. In this case if you get a significant F value, you want the computer to search around to find the differences. You want the computer to do a little fishing expedition (sometimes called *data mining* or *exploratory data analysis*). Consider the following analysis (the data come from research reported in Gaskell *et al.*, 1993) showing scientific interest (on a 1 to 5 scale) by nine geographic regions of Britain. The means and standard deviations are listed below as well as the basic output from a oneway analysis of variance. The significance of the F test $(F(8, 2084) = 7.19, p < 0.001)$ tells us that the regions differ significantly among themselves, but it does not tell us which regions differ from which.

```
ONEWAY inter BY stand (1,9) /STATISTICS DESCRIPTIVES.

   Variable   INTER   INTEREST IN SCIENCE
By Variable   STAND   STANDARD REGION

ANALYSIS OF VARIANCE
                        SUM OF     MEAN      F        F
SOURCE          D.F.    SQUARES    SQUARES   RATIO    PROB.
BETWEEN GROUPS     8    99.8094   12.4762   7.1874   .0000
WITHIN GROUPS   2084  3617.5007    1.7358
TOTAL           2092  3717.3101
```

| | | | STANDARD | |
GROUP	Grp	COUNT	MEAN	DEVIATION
LONDON/S'EAST	1	663	2.9744	1.3160
SOUTH & WEST	2	158	2.9747	1.2258
EAST ANGLIA	3	79	2.8987	1.2669
MIDLANDS	4	353	2.7479	1.3469
WALES	5	103	2.4951	1.3422
NORTH WEST	6	220	2.6318	1.3467
YORKSHIRE	7	192	2.6458	1.2942
NORTH	8	115	2.3739	1.3143
SCOTLAND	9	210	2.3810	1.3369
TOTAL		2093	2.7511	1.3330

In order to conduct unplanned comparisons the /RANGES command must be used and one (or more) of the many tests for unplanned comparisons can be done. Most of these calculate the difference between each pair and then adjust the necessary α level by how many comparisons it makes (or they calculate the critical difference with the adjusted α and see which differences are larger). With nine groups there are 45 pairs that can be compared. The computer will lower the α level for each pair (what is called the *per comparison α*) so that the α level for the whole analysis (the *familywise α*) remains at $\alpha = 0.05$ (or whichever level you have set). The main difference among most of these tests is how they adjust the α level. Two of the most common tests for unplanned comparisons are the Scheffé test and Tukey's HSD (honest significant difference) test. The results from these two tests are shown below. Both produce tables with asterisks denoting whether two groups are statistically different. Here the familywise α is 0.05. For the Tukey test, there are seven statistically significant pairwise differences. For the Scheffé test there are only three significant comparisons. The Scheffé will usually produce fewer significant differences than the others (see Zwick, 1993, for a detailed discussion of the issues). It is generally thought of as being too conservative (that is, it is likely to miss many significant pairwise differences), but it is still useful for cautious researchers.

It is important to understand the difference between *familywise α levels* and *per comparison α levels*. The familywise level is that set for an entire model. It assumes that there is only one test being done. With a priori comparisons, there are usually only three or four comparisons. Because of this, in order to keep your familywise α level at 0.05 you should use a lower level when assessing the significance of each individual comparison. When you do *post hoc* tests there are often 20 or 30 (or more) comparisons. Therefore to keep the familywise α equal to 0.05, the per comparison α level for each individual comparison should be made quite a bit smaller. These *post hoc* tests do this in various ways. The convention for a priori tests is either to use a per comparison α level of 0.05 but treat any significant values cautiously or to use more stringent α level. The first option controls for Type II errors but increases the likelihood of Type I errors. For the second option researchers usually calculate the per comparison α by dividing the familywise α by the number of contrasts. This calculation is based on Bonferroni's inequality. It controls for Type I errors but greatly increases the chance of Type II errors. It is the more popular option (since researchers tend to worry about Type I errors more than Type II errors). However, when there are many comparisons it is less useful because many relationships will not be detected.

(*) DENOTES PAIRS OF GROUPS SIGNIFICANTLY DIFFERENT AT THE 0.050 LEVEL

MULTIPLE RANGE TEST	MULTIPLE RANGE TEST
TUKEY-HSD PROCEDURE	SCHEFFE PROCEDURE

Mean	Group	G G G G G G G G G r r r r r r r r r p p p p p p p p p 8 9 5 6 7 4 3 1 2	Group	G G G G G G G G G r r r r r r r r r p p p p p p p p p 8 9 5 6 7 4 3 1 2
2.3739	Grp 8		Grp 8	
2.3810	Grp 9		Grp 9	
2.4951	Grp 5		Grp 5	
2.6318	Grp 6		Grp 6	
2.6458	Grp 7		Grp 7	
2.7479	Grp 4	*	Grp 4	
2.8987	Grp 3		Grp 3	
2.9744	Grp 1	* * * *	Grp 1	* *
2.9747	Grp 2	* *	Grp 2	*

Assumptions and Alternatives for a Between-subjects ANOVA

The assumptions for a between-subjects ANOVA are similar to those of the between-subjects (that is, group or independent) *t* test:

- The variable whose mean you are exploring should be interval level
- The variances or standard deviations should be about the same for each group
- The variable should be Normally distributed for each group
- The scores should be independent of each other.

If the first of these, that the variable whose means you are comparing is interval, is not valid, then strictly speaking you should not be calculating means or trying to compare them. Statisticians describe this as the tests not being *meaningful*. In practice it can be argued that very few variables in the social sciences are interval. Some statistical approaches square up to this directly and have developed intricate methods to take it into account (see, for example, Cliff, 1993), while others have quite purposefully developed methods circumventing such questions (see van de Geer, 1993a; 1993b). Most researchers are more relaxed about this requirement and continue to use the standard approaches.

In the *t* test, recall that there were various tests to investigate whether the variances (or standard deviations) were the same: what is called the assumption of homogeneity. Similar tests exist for comparing multiple groups. These include the Bartlett–Box F, Cochran's C and Levine's test which are available on different implementations of SPSS and also in other packages. They can be tested using the /STATISTICS command and checking for homogeneity. If the variances are different, one option is to try to transform the variable so that the variances are more similar. A common practice is to use the ln or natural logarithm transformation discussed in previous chapters. A simpler option is to use a statistical test that does not have any distributional assumptions. The main test for this situation is the Kruskal–Wallis test. In SPSS this is run from the NONPAR TEST procedure selecting, depending on the implementation, either the K-W option (for Kruskal–Wallis) or the k independent groups option. The Kruskal–Wallis test produces a χ^2 (chi squared) value and its significance (use the value that has been corrected for ties). A χ^2 table is given in Appendix E and is discussed in detail in the next chapter. A significant score means that there is a difference in central tendency among the groups. There are several other so-called *robust* techniques described in Wilcox (1995).

Box 6.2   Combining ANOVA and Regression

In an important paper in 1968, Jacob Cohen remarked that if statisticians were told that ANOVA and regression were essentially the same thing they might respond with something like 'of course – general linear model' (Cohen, 1968: 426). However, Cohen said that many social scientists at that time would have looked on 'with incredulity'. Cohen (1968: Table 1) produced sets of contrasts for the four-group situation in which three variables are used in the regression. Although he was not the first to note this equivalence, his paper has become important for introducing many researchers who used ANOVAs to the flexibility of regression.

By now, most (not all) social scientists are aware of their equivalence. ANOVA and regression have grown out of very different traditions and therefore there are still some practical differences between the approaches, but they can be used to perform the same tests. The ANOVA framework has developed hand-in-hand with the experimental method starting with Fisher's work in the Rothamsted Experimental Station of Agriculture (in England) and continuing today with the complex designs in many psychology laboratories. Many statisticians would argue it is only appropriate when using controlled experiments, but because of its historical roots it is a frequently used technique throughout the social sciences. The regression and correlation techniques have developed mostly from non-experimental research. They are more general statistical techniques and now can be run relatively easily (and quickly) with modern computers. Therefore many researchers now prefer them to be used when both approaches are possible. As both are used in the literature that you are likely to encounter, it is important that you understand both.

Similar arguments can be made for problems with the Normality assumption. In general, if the variable is skewed, not only are the distribution-free statistics more correct to use, they are more powerful. Consider the example of elapsed time between a crime and a line-up first discussed in Chapter 4 (I used a subsample in that chapter; here I use all the cases where elapsed time was available – these data are reported in Wright and McDaid, 1996). Suppose we wanted to see if the elapsed time in weeks differed according to the outcome of the line-up (no identification, picking the suspect or picking someone other than the suspect). If we use the oneway ANOVA we get $F(2, 1558 = 1.79, p = 0.17)$, which is non-significant. The data are heavily skewed. If we use the Kruskal–Wallis test we get $\chi^2(2) = 9.53$, $p < 0.01$, which is significant. This illustrates how the distribution-free alternatives often produce significant test statistics when the distributional assumptions are not satisfied.

The final assumption is that all the scores are independent of each other. This means that the score of one person should not affect the score of another. While this assumption exists for most statistical tests, it is often questionable. For example, if you are doing an experiment, like the control/outline/skim one described above, you might use different lecture groups for these conditions: allocating all the students from each class to a condition. However, it is likely that these groups differ naturally (a vastly different type of human opts for an 8 a.m. lecture than opts for a 4 p.m. lecture). Even when these differences are small, the real α level can rise well above the α level you report. In other words, if you set your α level at 0.05, in actuality it may be very much higher. Even with small differences between groups, the true α level can rise to 0.25 or higher even when the reported or nominal α level is 0.05 (Scariano and Davenport, 1987). In these cases, if the null hypothesis is true, you would errantly reject it much more than 5% of the time. The best solution to this problem is to try to ensure that the measurements are independent. If this is not possible then it is advisable to lower your α to 0.01 or even 0.001 or to use the superordinate groups (like the students' lecture classes) as the cases. There are some advanced techniques (see Kreft and de Leeuw, forthcoming) that can be used, but these are beyond the scope of this book.

It is worth mentioning that it is best to have roughly equal numbers of cases in each group. Otherwise, some of the comparisons (or if done using the regression approach, some of the parameters) will be less reliable than others. Also, it can affect the overall p value particularly if some of the other assumptions are not satisfied. However, clearly in many cases when comparing naturally occurring groups it is impossible to have equal numbers in different groups.

Repeated Measures or the Within-subject ANOVA

In many cases researchers want to compare the means of different variables for the same group. This often occurs in time series (that is, longitudinal) studies where the researcher is investigating if people change over time or when the researcher measures a series of variables and wants to see if these differ. The techniques for these repeated measures designs are more complex than the between-subjects designs. In this section I describe some examples and try to impart the conceptual understanding needed for these techniques. In the next section I briefly describe some of the underlying mathematics. Then I go through, again in brief, how to compare individual variables using a computer. Finally, I discuss the assumptions made when doing a repeated measures ANOVA and some approaches when these assumptions are not satisfied.

Within-subject designs are often useful because much of the individual variation can be factored out. The first example will demonstrate how this is more powerful. Because of this power, fewer participants are necessary. There are some problems with within-subject designs that were discussed in Chapter 4, but they often are the best method. Suppose a researcher was interested in whether company efficiency varied at different points of the year. S/he would first construct or find an appropriate scale for measuring efficiency and then measure this construct (let us say it ranges from 0 to 100, 100 being spectacularly efficient) for several companies at different points in the year. Consider the data in Table 6.5 on efficiency at six companies for the four seasons.

The main conceptual idea behind within-subject designs is to improve the power by taking into account the differences between people or cases. In this example, much of the variation in the efficiency scores is due to differences among the companies. Some companies are more efficient than others. In a between-subjects design we cannot do anything about this; it simply is part of the error term. When using a within-subject design we can remove this from our error term. In essence, we try to model the variation *within* the companies rather than *between* them. This makes within-subject designs usually more powerful than between-subjects designs because between-subjects variation is accounted for. The increase in power is related to the correlation among the variables: the greater the correlations, the greater the advantage for a within-subject design.

Table 6.5 *Company efficiency and season*

Company	Autumn	Winter	Spring	Summer	Mean	Variance
1	40	34	45	38	39.25	20.92
2	34	31	52	47	41.00	102.00
3	30	45	41	42	39.50	43.00
4	51	58	66	52	56.75	47.58
5	57	45	67	59	57.00	82.67
6	35	56	58	61	52.50	140.33
Mean for season	41.17	44.83	54.83	49.83		
Variance for season	112.57	121.37	115.77	84.57		

Grand mean (A mean for all seasons) = 47.67   Grand variance = 122.14

Graphing Within-subject Means

As with most statistical problems, you should begin by graphing the data in order to get a feel for them. With the between-subjects ANOVA you graphed the means with their confidence intervals. You could do the same here for the season data (see Figure 6.3), but this does not take into account the increased power of a within-subject design. From Figure 6.3 it does not appear as if there is much difference among these means because the confidence intervals all overlap considerably. In fact, if these data were treated as if each number came from a different company (that is, as a between-subjects design), then the result is non-significant $(F(3, 20) = 1.96, p = 0.15)$.

It is important to capture the within-subject element in graphing these data (see Loftus and Masson, 1994, for a more thorough discussion). When there are not many cases, one within-subject method is to draw a separate line for each case. This is shown in Figure 6.4 and it does seem to show more of a pattern: an increase in the spring.

Figure 6.4 still includes information about differences between the companies. Because we are interested just in differences within each company we want to take out the differences between companies. To do this, subtract each company's mean from the grand mean (47.67) to make the adjustment value. For the first company this would be $47.67 - 39.25 = 8.42$. Each efficiency score for company one has this value added to it. For autumn, this gives $40 + 8.42 = 48.42$. For these adjusted scores, all the companies have the same mean. Figure 6.5 shows the graph of these adjusted scores.

In Figure 6.5, the relationship is much clearer, showing a steady increase from autumn to spring, tapering off in the summer. It is worth noting that this could be due to either a seasonal effect or a general trend in improved efficiency. To know which of these reasons is responsible for the observed pattern, data would have to be collected over several years. These sorts of problem are discussed with respect to *time series analysis* and are often used in economics,

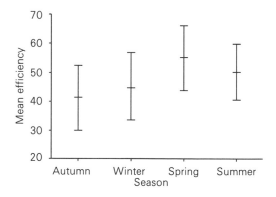

Figure 6.3   *The means and 95% confidence intervals for the data in Table 6.5 by the between-subjects approach*

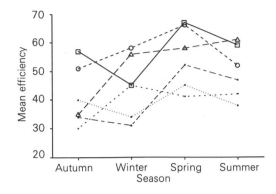

Figure 6.4   *The efficiency scores for the six companies*

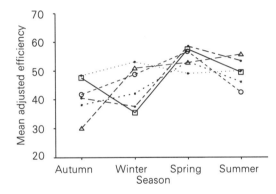

Figure 6.5   *Graphing the efficiency scores adjusted for each company's overall mean*

meteorology and other disciplines where seasonal (or more generally cyclical) effects are likely to be present.

The final step is to graph the confidence intervals of these adjusted scores. This is done in Figure 6.6. These graphs illustrate the basic logic of within-subject designs. As we moved from Figure 6.3 to Figure 6.6 we accounted for the overall performance of each company. We expect variation in overall efficiency among companies, and essentially we have factored this out. The greater the differences among companies, the greater the advantage (statistically) of using a within-subject design and the more the width of the confidence interval will shrink when applying these procedures. It is worth noting that the means shown in Figures 6.6 and 6.3 are the same.

This can be done with any size of sample. The procedures described here can easily be implemented in SPSS by computing new variables adjusted for the

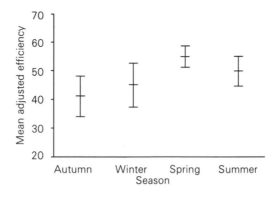

Figure 6.6   *The confidence intervals for efficiency, taking into account variation of overall efficiency among companies*

subject's mean. This basic procedure can be extended to more complex designs (see Loftus and Masson, 1994, which was the principal source for this section).

Calculations for Within-subject ANOVA

The first step in the calculations is adding together the sums of squares within each of the companies. I will refer to this as *SSW*, for sums of squares within the companies. Because there are four measurements for each company, to calculate *SSW*, each variance is multiplied by 3. Therefore *SSW* is [5]

$$SSW = 20.92 \times 3 + 102.00 \times 3 + \ldots + 140.33 \times 3 = 1309.50$$

This is the value we try to explain. Our hypothesis is not concerned with whether the companies differ among themselves, only if the efficiency varies by season. We try to model all of the variation within each company. If we tried to explain *all* the variation (within groups and between groups), this would be the grand variance multiplied by the number of data points (24) minus one: $122.14 \times 23 = 2809.22$. This is much larger than the value we try to explain. About half of the variation in efficiency scores can be attributed to differences among the companies. The between-companies sums of squares is about 1500. Using the smaller value makes this test more powerful.

The null model is that the means for the seasons are all the same: the null hypothesis. The sum of squares for the model is based on the difference between the mean for each season and the grand mean. We multiply the squared difference by the number of cases, here 6. The result is:

---

5   The '. . .' between two terms in an equation means that the values between those terms are also included in the expression.

$$SSM = 6(41.17 - 47.67)^2 + 6(44.83 - 47.67)^2 + 6(54.83 - 47.67)^2$$
$$+ 6(49.83 - 47.67)^2 = 637.48$$

The sum of squared residuals is the difference between SSW and SSM, or $SSR = 672.02$.

To find the F value we need to know the degrees of freedom. In total there are 24 different data points (four for each of the six companies). How each of the degrees of freedom is used becomes clearer when representing this as an equation (see Box 6.3) but I will describe in words how they are used. When we focused just on the variation across the seasons for each company, we were effectively ignoring the mean efficiency rating of each company. This is six degrees of freedom used; one for the mean of each company. This leaves 18 degrees of freedom and it is the sum of squares of this (SSW) that we focus on. The model used three. This is because we could use three dummy variables to represent the four variables (see Box 6.3). The remaining 15 degrees of freedom are for the residuals.

The degrees of freedom are used to calculate mean sums of squares. As with the between-subjects ANOVA, these are simply the sums of squares divided by their degrees of freedom. The F value is then M_{SSM}/M_{SSR}. Table 6.6 shows how these are usually represented. I have added formulae for calculating the degrees of freedom. Let n be the number of subjects and k the number of variables (therefore there are kn data points in total).

The F table (Appendix D) is used in the same way as for the between-subjects ANOVA. Go along the top row until you come to the degrees of freedom for the model (here 3). Then go down the row corresponding to the residual degrees of freedom (here 15). If the precise number of degrees of freedom required is not shown, use the next larger one for the model df (if the model df is not shown) or the next smaller df for the residual df (if its value is not shown). The critical value for 3 and 15 degrees of freedom for $\alpha = 0.05$ is 3.29 and 5.42 for $\alpha = 0.01$. Since our observed value is *greater* than the first of these we can reject the null hypothesis (that there is no difference between the means of the seasons) at an $\alpha = 0.05$ level. It is not as large as the critical value for the $\alpha = 0.01$ test and therefore we would fail to reject the null hypothesis if we were using this more stringent level. When these tests are done by computer (as below), a precise p value is printed and should be reported.

Table 6.6   *A summary table for the efficiency across seasons example (k=number of variables, n=number of cases)*

Sums of squares for	df	SS	MSS	F	Sig.
Model	$k - 1 = 3$	637.48	212.49	4.74	<0.05
Residuals	$(k-1)(n-1) = 15$	672.02	44.80		

Box 6.3 Repeated Measures Designs as Equations

Now, I promised that all the statistical tests that are presented in this book can be represented as equations. The repeated measures or within-subject ANOVA can – but it is more complicated. For this reason I will describe it only briefly. Recall the equation for the paired t test:

$$d_i = \beta_0 + e_i$$

where d_i is the difference between the two variables and β_0 is the mean of this difference. For the efficiency example there are four variables: call them Win_i, Spr_i, Sum_i and Aut_i. In general when we have k variables we need $k - 1$ equations to describe the model. Conceptually, we can think of the model as three separate equations (depending on the assumptions, the residual terms can be more complex):

$$D_{1i} = Win_i - Spr_i = \beta_1 + e_{1i}$$
$$D_{2i} = Win_i - Sum_i = \beta_2 + e_{2i}$$
$$D_{3i} = Win_i - Aut_i = \beta_3 + e_{3i}$$

where the three β values are the mean of $Win_i - Spr_i$, $Win_i - Sum_i$ and $Win_i - Fall_i$, respectively. These three differences are the variables on which we focus. In general, if we had k different variables we would need $k - 1$ equations for modelling purposes. The significance of the overall statistic tells us whether, as a group, the β values are significantly different from zero. These are the three degrees of freedom associated with the model, the differences among the seasons.

To calculate these parameters in SPSS the MANOVA procedure is used (or the repeated measures procedure in some implementations). This model, which is often referred to as a system of equations, is a type of *multivariate regression* (multivariate, not multiple) because there is more than one regressed variable (here D_{1i}, D_{2i} and D_{3i}).

SPSS does not print the estimates of the parameters by default, but it will if you input /PRINT TRANSFORM ESTIMATES. SPSS has default variables it uses. As with the between-subjects ANOVA, calculating F does not depend on the specific dummy variables you use, though knowing how to do this is important for partitioning the overall effect into its components. You may choose your own set of variables using the /CONTRAST command to allow for specific planned comparisons.

Computer Output and Syntax

The MANOVA command is used for within-subject analysis. This is a fairly versatile procedure. It can do a wide variety of analyses and is particularly useful if you are doing complex experimental designs. Below is the simplest 'no frills' code for running the above repeated measures analysis of variance and the output (slightly edited). To the right of the output I describe what the different parts mean.

MANOVA autumn winter spring summer /WSFACTOR season (4)
   /WSDESIGN.

```
Tests of Between-Subjects Effects.
  Tests of Significance for T1
                  SS      DF    MS        F     Sig of F
WITHIN CELLS    1499.83   5    299.97
CONSTANT       54530.67   1  54530.67  181.79   .000
```
This tests if the grand mean differs from zero.

```
Tests involving 'SEASON' Within-Subject Effect.
Mauchly sphericity test, W =       .288
Chi-square approx. =               4.631 with 5 DF
 Significance =                    .463
 Greenhouse-Geisser Epsilon =      .628
 Huynh-Feldt Epsilon =             .996
 Lower-bound Epsilon =             .333
```
These test for various assumptions discussed below. They dictate whether the multivariate or univariate estimates should be used.

```
EFFECT .. SEASON
Multivariate Tests of Significance (S = 1, M = 1/2,
  N = 1/2)

Test Name    Value    Approx.  Hypoth.  Error  Sig of F
                      F        DF       DF
Pillais      .90371   9.38520  3.00     3.00   .049
Hotellings   9.38520  9.38520  3.00     3.00   .049
Wilks        .09629   9.38520  3.00     3.00   .049
Roys         .90371
```

```
Tests involving 'SEASON' Within-Subject Effect.
                SS      DF    MS      F    Sig of F
WITHIN CELLS   671.50   15   44.77
SEASON         638.00   3   212.67  4.75   .016
```
These are numbers that are usually reported.

The MANOVA procedure does not have a built-in option for unplanned comparisons as existed with the ONEWAY procedure. However, we can calculate the per comparison α level for a given familywise α and conduct the appropriate tests. As discussed earlier, one method is simply to divide the familywise α by the number of possible comparisons. In this example, with four seasons, there would be six pairwise comparisons. Therefore the adjusted per comparison should be 0.008 if using Bonferroni's inequality (that is, per comparison α = familywise α/no. of pairs). As mentioned, there is some flexibility in this method, and this will suffice here. The next step is checking the p values of all the comparisons using a standard t test. In the old days you would begin with the pair with the largest difference and check if this was significant with the per comparison level. If it was significant then you would try the next biggest, and so on. These days, it is easy enough to do all the comparison by computer (if you think this takes a lot of time, think about those social scientists in the old days doing it by hand!). You can also use the /CONTRAST command in the MANOVA procedure to test comparisons.

The *t* values and their associated *p* values, as printed by the *t* test procedure, are shown in Table 6.7. The only one of these that is significant at the adjusted per comparison α level is the difference between autumn and spring.

Assumptions for the Repeated Measures ANOVA

The assumptions for the repeated measures ANOVA are that the observations are all independent (an assumption for almost all statistical tests); that the variables are interval; that variables are all roughly Normally distributed; that the variables are *multivariate Normal*; and that there is *sphericity*. Sphericity is a rather difficult concept. It requires that if you calculate the differences between each pair of variables, the variances of these differences are about the same.

While multivariate Normality and sphericity sound complex, in practice most researchers just examine the individual variables to make sure each is Normally distributed and examine the printed tests of sphericity. In SPSS the Mauchly sphericity test is printed. If it is significant, then it means the sphericity assumption is *invalid*. When this happens it is best to look carefully at the variables because something of considerable interest might be happening. In particular, one of the variables may have a substantially larger variance than the others or the correlations among the variables may be peculiar. When the sphericity assumption does not hold, the *p* values printed are incorrect and should be adjusted upwards. There is some debate on what should be done. SPSS prints out the Greenhouse–Geisser ϵ and the Huynh–Feldt ϵ (epsilon). The more conservative approach involves multiplying the degrees of freedom for both the model and the residuals by the Greenhouse–Geisser ϵ and then evaluating the significance. The Huynh–Feldt ϵ is less conservative. These values are printed if requested using the /PRINT SIGNIF (GG HF) command. An alternative method to use when the sphericity assumption does not hold is to use the multivariate test statistics that are printed. There are several issues that arise with these that are beyond the scope of this book (see Stevens, 1992).

Table 6.7 *The t values and p values levels (in parentheses) for all pairwise comparisons in company efficiency example (all have 5 df)*

	Winter	Spring	Summer
Autumn	0.70 (0.515)	5.25 (0.003)	2.03 (0.098)
Winter		2.38 (0.063)	1.39 (0.223)
Spring			1.97 (0.106)

There is also a distribution-free test, Friedman's ANOVA, that can be used in situations where the assumptions are not valid. This procedure involves ranking, for each case, the values of the variables, and then comparing the sums of the ranks. To use this within SPSS use the NPAR TESTS procedure and run Friedman's test.

Summary

When comparing means either among several variables or among several groups, the ANOVA approach is often used. It involves two stages. First the researcher must determine if there is a difference among the means. This is done using the F test. The F test simply checks whether the null hypothesis, that all the means are the same, can be either rejected or not.

The second step involves finding out where any differences are. The simplest way to do this is by conducting t tests on the various pairs. The one problem with this is that the p values that are printed are appropriate if each comparison was the only test. If the α level was not changed it would greatly increase the chances of finding something that appeared statistically significant but was not (that is, it increases the chance of making a Type I error). To compensate for this, it was recommended that the α level be lowered. How much it is lowered is a matter of some debate. To control completely for Type I error, some researchers suggest using Bonferroni's inequality which involves dividing the familywise α by the number of comparisons. If there are ten groups and you tested all 45 comparisons, and if you were using a familywise α of 0.05, the per comparison α (the new critical value for the individual t tests) would be approximately 0.001. This is a conservative approach and will increase the chance of making a Type II error. A more liberal approach is simply decreasing the α from 0.05 to 0.01, or from 0.01 to 0.005, but to be cautious when interpreting the p values. As I have stressed in several places in this book, care must be taken in interpreting the p values. You should be more concerned with your model than with the precise p value the computer churns out.

Assignment

1   Much health research demonstrates differences among the social classes. Consider the following data in which people were asked, on a 1–10 scale, how often they felt ill (1 being hardly ever, 10 being almost always). The table below shows the sample sizes, the means and the variances for four social classes (AB being the 'highest', DE the 'lowest'). Conduct the appropriate analyses for testing whether the different social classes have different levels of feeling ill.

	n	$\bar{x}$	s^2
AB	26	4.12	9.55
C1	52	5.02	6.29
C2	44	5.18	6.66
DE	53	6.04	5.73
Total	175	5.23	6.97

2　The data from Exercise 1 can be represented by the equation

$$Health_i = \beta_3 AB_i + \beta_2 C1_i + \beta_1 C2_i + \beta_0 + e_i$$

where AB_i is equal to 1 for people in class AB and 0 for everyone else. Similarly, $C1_i$ and $C2_i$ are dummy variables for C1 and C2, respectively. What is the base, or reference, category? What are the values for the four β values?

3　The following is the partial output from a between-subjects ANOVA.

```
Variable SCORE
By Variable GROUP
Analysis of Variance
```

		Sum of	Mean	F	F
Source	D.F.	Squares	Squares	Ratio	Prob.
Between Groups	X	423.3333	X	X	X
Within Groups	X	612.0000	X		
Total	X	1035.3333			

Group	Count	Mean	Standard Deviation	Standard Error
Grp 1	5	25.0000	6.7823	3.0332
Grp 2	5	32.0000	8.0932	3.6194
Grp 3	5	38.0000	6.4420	2.8810
Total	15	31.6667	8.5996	2.2204

(a)　Fill in the appropriate numbers for the Xs.
(b)　What would you conclude?

4　In the states.sps data set from Appendix A, there is a variable called region which divides the states into east coast, central and mountain/west coast states. Using an ANOVA, compare the dropout rates among these three regions.

5　Using the states.sps data set, compare the record low temperature (lowtemp) by the region. You should begin by making sure the assumptions of an ANOVA are satisfied before actually running an ANOVA (in particular, remember the variances are supposed to be approximately the same). Choose either an ANOVA or a Kruskal–Wallis test for comparing these regions.

6   There is much interest in people's ability to perform complex tasks at different points in the day. Every student knows that some people are better workers at night and others in the day. Ten students volunteered to take part in a study exploring time of day effects. At 6 a.m., 11 a.m., 3 p.m., 9 p.m. and 1 a.m., the volunteers answered a group of 15 algebra problems at each one of these five times. All the problems were ones that all the students were able to answer. The variable of interest was how many minutes it took. The data, and some preliminary calculations (the means and variances for individuals, the times and the grand mean and variance in the lower right-hand corner), are shown below.

(a)   Draw an appropriate graph with 95% confidence intervals shown.

(b)   Can you reject the hypothesis that time of day does not affect performance?

(c)   Can you think of any problems using a repeated measures design here as opposed to a between-subject design?

			Time of test				
	6 a.m.	11 a.m.	3 p.m.	9 p.m.	1 a.m.	$\bar{x}$	s^2
	2	3	3	4	4	3.20	0.70
	4	4	5	4	5	4.40	0.30
	6	7	6	5	8	6.40	1.30
	7	6	5	3	5	5.20	2.20
	2	2	3	2	5	2.80	1.70
	8	6	7	9	10	8.00	2.50
	7	4	6	4	9	6.00	4.50
	3	4	2	3	2	2.80	0.70
	9	6	7	4	5	6.20	3.70
	4	6	7	4	3	4.80	2.70
$\bar{x}$	5.20	4.80	5.10	4.20	5.60	4.98	
s^2	6.40	2.62	3.43	3.51	6.71		4.39

7   A representative sample of 100 voters was asked to rate four issues (taxation levels, environmental issues, foreign policy, political sleaze levels) for how likely it was that policies about these would affect their voting choice. The scale ranged from 1 to 9, with 1 being 'no impact' and 9 'much impact'. The analysis of variance table is partially listed below. Fill in the correct numbers where the Xs appear.

```
Source of Variation SS      DF    MS    F    Sig of F
WITHIN+RESIDUAL    3133.48  XXX   XXX
POLICY              228.77  XXX   XXX   XXX     XXX
```

```
Variable  Mean  Variance  N
SLEAZE    3.05    8.94    100
ENVIR     3.51   11.89    100
FOR       4.43   12.87    100
TAX       4.98   10.97    100
```

The researcher had no a priori comparisons. Therefore, s/he ran *t* tests on all possible pairs. The *t* values and associated *p* values that the computer reported are shown below. Describe how you would interpret these *p* values and say why. The negative values for the *t* values indicate that the column variable is smaller than the row variable.

	Sleaze	Environment	Foreign
Environment	$t(99) = -1.00$ $p = 0.319$		
Foreign	$t(99) = -3.23$ $p = 0.002$	$t(99) = -1.93$ $p = 0.057$	
Tax	$t(99) = -4.42$ $p = 0.000$	$t(99) = -3.13$ $p = 0.002$	$t(99) = -1.14$ $p = 0.258$

Further Reading

Lovie, A. D. (1981) On the early history of ANOVA in the analysis of repeated measure designs in psychology. *British Journal of Mathematical and Statistical Psychology*, *34*, 1–15.

Rutherford, A. (forthcoming) *Introducing ANOVA and ANCOVA* (provisional title). London: Sage.

Stevens, J. (1992) *Applied multivariate statistics for the social sciences*. London: Lawrence Erlbaum Associates.

7

Comparing Proportions

In this chapter I describe the statistical tests that are used when the data are proportions or counts. The level of these data is categorical or nominal. The basic operation of the statistical tests for this type of data is similar to the others discussed in this book: construct a model, see how closely the observations fit the model, and if the differences (that is, the residuals) are large enough then reject the model. I will show how this can be done when there is a single variable and when there are two variables. In Chapter 8, I show how this can be extended to situations with more than two variables.

Single Variables

Confidence Intervals

In a number of countries, including the United Kingdom, the government in power can control to some extent when to hold an election. Governments obviously try to choose a time in which their public opinion is higher than their opponents'. Because of this they follow the opinion polls very closely. When market researchers report that, for example, 54% of a sample of people say that they would vote for the Labour Party if there were a general election tomorrow, they usually say something like 54±3%, which means that the confidence interval goes from 51% to 57%. This is the confidence interval around the observed proportion. In this section I discuss how this is calculated.

When calculating a 95% confidence interval for a mean (Chapter 3), you multiplied the standard error of the mean by the critical value of t for $\alpha = 0.05$. The same logic applies here except that the formula for the standard error of a proportion is different. Let $prop$ be the proportion of the sample in one category (like voting for the Labour Party) and n be the total sample size. The standard error is

$$se = \sqrt{\frac{prop(1 - prop)}{n}}$$

As with all estimates, as the sample size increases, both the standard error and the width of the confidence interval decrease, meaning the estimates become more precise. The formula for the confidence interval is

$$CI_{1-\alpha} = prop \pm z_\alpha se = prop \pm z_\alpha \sqrt{\frac{prop(1 - prop)}{n}}$$

If we want to calculate the 95% confidence interval we first have to find the appropriate z value from the table of the Normal distribution in Appendix B. For a 95% confidence interval, we look up the two-sided value for $\alpha = 0.05$ and find 1.96. This value (z for $\alpha = 0.05$) occurs often enough that it is worth remembering. Suppose 100 people were asked who they would vote for and 54% said they would vote for the ruling party. The confidence interval would be

$$CI_{0.95} = 0.54 \pm 1.96 \sqrt{\frac{0.54 \times 0.46}{100}} = 0.54 \pm 0.10$$

which means the confidence interval ranges from 0.44 to 0.64. This is a rather large range because, in terms of political opinion polls, 100 people is a small sample. The government would not feel confident securing a majority if there was a general election. If 1000 people had been asked, and the observed percentage was still 54%, the confidence interval would be 54±3%. The government would then feel more confident of winning the election. Table 7.1 shows some examples of the widths of 95% confidence intervals for different sample sizes and proportions.

Hypothesis Testing

There is much discussion, both at parties and in academia, about extra-sensory perception (ESP). Suppose a group of researchers wanted to test whether an individual could control the outcome of a coin toss and they had that person flip a coin 100 times. The final outcome was 58 heads and 42 tails. The researchers wondered whether this was significantly different from chance. In other words, they wondered how likely an outcome as extreme as this would be if there was

Table 7.1 *The width of the 95% confidence interval around a proportion for different sample sizes and proportions. Note: an observed proportion of 0.90 will produce the same width as a proportion of 0.10*

Sample size	Proportion observed		
	0.10	0.25	0.50
25	±0.12	±0.17	±0.20
50	±0.08	±0.12	±0.14
100	±0.06	±0.08	±0.10
250	±0.04	±0.05	±0.06
500	±0.03	±0.04	±0.04
1000	±0.02	±0.03	±0.03
10,000	±0.006	±0.008	±0.01

no ESP. The model the researchers would compare with the observations is the null model. In this case the null model is that the coin is equally likely to land heads up as to land tails up: half heads and half tails. To come up with the expected values we multiply this expected proportion (0.5) by the sample size, 100, and find the expected values to be 50 heads and 50 tails. Like all the statistical techniques discussed, we compare the observations with the predicted values from the model and calculate the difference, the residuals.

It is useful to present the data as in Table 7.2; tables like this can be made with most statistical packages and spreadsheets. Each possible outcome, here heads and tails, has a *cell*. There are two cells in this example. Within each cell various percentages and other useful information can be printed. Here, I have included the observed frequency, the value expected from the model, and the difference between these. I have also included the row totals or what are sometimes called the row marginals.

For the model to be good, the residuals should be as small as possible. If the residuals are large then the model does not fit the data well. There are two statistics that are usually used in this situation to see if the residuals are sufficiently large to reject the null hypothesis. The first is more common in this situation and I will go through it in some detail here. It was originally devised by Karl Pearson, the father of Egon Pearson who was mentioned in Chapter 2. It is:

$$\chi^2 = \sum \frac{Residual^2}{Model} = \sum \frac{(Observed - Model)^2}{Model}$$

This is called the Pearson χ^2 (chi-square) statistic or because of its popularity sometimes just the χ^2 statistic. It is a measure of deviance; the higher it is the less well the model fits the data. For each cell in Table 7.2 you subtract the value predicted by the model from the observed to get the residual and you square this residual. Then you divide this value by the value expected from the model and add these together for all of the cells. In this case it is

$$\chi^2 = \frac{(58 - 50)^2}{50} + \frac{(42 - 50)^2}{50} = 1.28 + 1.28 = 2.56$$

The question is whether the deviance from the model, as measured by the χ^2 value, is large enough to reject the model. To answer this we need to use the χ^2 table in Appendix E. This requires knowing the degrees of freedom. In Table

Table 7.2 *The observed and expected frequencies for the ESP study*

	Heads	Tails	Row totals
Observed	58	42	100
Expected from Model	50	50	100
Residual (Observed − Model)	+8	−8	0

7.2, there are several pieces of information, but all of them can be constructed from just two: the total sample size (100) and the number of heads (58). The number of tails can be calculated by subtracting the number of heads from the total number of tosses. This means that in total there are only two degrees of freedom. For the null model we use one of these, the sample size, to calculate the predicted values. Our model is that the total sample of size 100 is split evenly between the two groups. The number of degrees of freedom of the residuals is the total number of pieces of information minus the degrees of freedom of the model. The residuals in this example have only one degree of freedom $(2 - 1 = 1)$. We look up the critical χ^2 value for one degree of freedom and find that it is 3.84 for $\alpha = 0.05$. Because our observed value is less than this, we would fail to reject the null hypothesis. Like the F table, the χ^2 prints the probabilities of one end of the distribution. Like the F test, this is simply testing whether the deviations from the model are large enough to reject the null hypothesis, but no directional predictions are made.

The second equation is called the likelihood ratio statistic, here denoted $L\chi^2$ although in some places it is denoted by G^2. The formula for it is:

$$L\chi^2 = 2 \sum Observed \ln\left(\frac{Observed}{Model}\right)$$

where ln is the natural logarithm (the transformation that has been used in several places in this book). There is a button marked ln on most scientific calculators and an ln function in the syntax of most statistics packages (sometimes called log or $\log_e$). Plugging in the numbers for this example yields

$$L\chi^2 = 2(58 \ln(58/50) + 42 \ln(42/50)) = 2.57$$

Its significance is looked up in the same way as Pearson's χ^2 and in this case, as in most cases, the conclusions are the same (it is also non-significant). Particularly when the sample size is large, the two formulae give nearly equivalent results. Pearson's χ^2 is usually preferred for simple examples, like most of those discussed in this chapter, while the likelihood ratio $L\chi^2$ is usually preferred for more complicated designs, as will be discussed next chapter. The reason for this is that $L\chi^2$ allows the overall effect to be partitioned into its components in a similar way to how we partitioned the sums of squares in Chapter 6. Since both are printed by most computer packages, I will list both here.

Consider a slightly more complex example that is based on Kubovy and Psotka (1976). Forty people were stopped in the street and asked to name a number between 0 and 9. The results are shown in Table 7.3. One model that might be worth entertaining is that each number is chosen equally often. Since there are ten numbers you would expect that about one-tenth of the people would say each number. Because there are 40 people in this example, you would expect about four people to say each number.

Table 7.3   *Choosing a number between zero and nine (based on Kubovy and Psotka, 1976)*

	0	1	2	3	4	5	6	7	8	9	Total
	\multicolumn{11}{c}{Number chosen and model prediction}										
Observed	2	2	3	4	4	4	5	10	4	2	40
Model	4	4	4	4	4	4	4	4	4	4	40
Residual	−2	−2	−1	0	0	0	1	6	0	−2	0

For these data, Pearson's χ^2 statistic is 12.50, while $L\chi^2 = 10.51$. We now have to calculate the degrees of freedom. Although there are 40 people, the data in Table 7.3 are completely described by ten numbers. Therefore, we start with ten degrees of freedom. Our model uses one degree of freedom: the total sample size (40). This leaves nine degrees of freedom left for the residuals. Remember, the χ^2 value refers to what is left over after the model; it has the degrees of freedom of the residuals. If we go to Appendix E, we see that the critical value for $\alpha = 0.05$ and nine degrees of freedom is 16.92. Both the observed values are smaller than this critical value and thus are non-significant. This means that the data do not allow us to reject the hypothesis that each of the numbers is equally likely to be chosen.

One aspect of Appendix E that is important to notice is that as the number of degrees of freedom increases the χ^2 value necessary to reject a hypothesis also increases (see Figure 7.1). Each degree of freedom, which is a degree of freedom of the residuals, represents some information that could be used to improve the model. In this example, there are nine pieces of information in the residuals, each being treated separately. In many cases you are only interested in particular degrees of freedom.

Kubovy and Psotka (1976) were aware that 7 seems a special number. Therefore, they might have just wanted to see if the proportion picking 7 differed from chance. They would have collapsed Table 7.3 so that there were

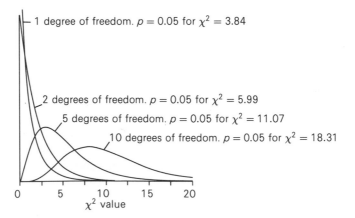

Figure 7.1   *The χ^2 distribution for different degrees of freedom*

only two cells: those choosing seven (10) and those choosing something else (30). Their model would be a 10% to 90% split and they would use the total sample size (100) in calculating the expected values. This leaves only one degree of freedom for the residuals and therefore requires a smaller χ^2 value to reach significance (see Figure 7.1). The expected value for choosing seven is 4, and the expected value for the others is 36. Here are the equations:

$$\chi^2 = \left(\frac{(10-4)^2}{4} + \frac{(30-36)^2}{36} \right) = 10.00$$

$$L\chi^2 = 2\left(10\ln\left(\frac{10}{4}\right) + 30\ln\left(\frac{30}{36}\right) \right) = 7.39$$

Now there is only one degree of freedom in the residual. When we look up the critical χ^2 values for both $\alpha = 0.05$ and $\alpha = 0.01$ we find 3.84 and 6.63, respectively. Therefore, the result is significant at either of these levels. We can reject the null hypothesis and conclude that the number 7 is chosen more than expected by chance. We would write this, using the value for the first equation, which is more common in this situation, as

$$\chi^2(1) = 7.39, \; p < 0.01$$

where the (1) tells readers that there is one degree of freedom in the residuals. It is important to note with this example that if, for example, many people responded with the number 3, this test would not have picked up this deviation because all the non-7 responses are clustered together. It is also important to stress that this approach is only valid if before collecting the data you had good reason to believe that 7 would be different.

Using a Computer

There are several different procedures in SPSS for running these tests. I am going to describe one of the more general ones. Sometimes it is suggested that you should use a specific procedure designed just for the cases when there is only one variable, one designed for two variables and then another when there are more than two variables. To avoid forcing you to learn multiple procedures I will show you how to work the examples above with what is called the LOGLINEAR procedure. This will also be able to run more complex problems. It has a frightening-sounding name, but it is not hard to use. Its name has to do with how these problems are represented as equations, which I explain towards the end of this chapter.

SPSS allows the data to be stored in two different ways. The first is to have a line (or more) of data for each case. This has been the method used for all the procedures discussed thus far. However, there is another method that is often much easier for these types of problems. It involves the WEIGHT command.

Consider Table 7.2. There are only two degrees of freedom, only two pieces of information necessary to describe everything in the table. It would be inefficient to have to put in a data point for each of the 100 tosses. Instead, we can simply tell the computer how many observations there are in each cell. The following syntax does this (recall from Chapter 1 that FREE tells the computer that each data point is separated by a space or a comma).

```
DATA LIST FREE /coin w.
BEGIN DATA
1   58
2   42
END DATA.
WEIGHT BY w.
```

To run this test we first have to compute a constant, a variable with the same value for all cases. This can be done with the COMPUTE command. You could let it equal anything but the convention is to let it equal one. Then you input the command printed below for LOGLINEAR. The '/DESIGN const' tells the computer that you want it to test the model which has the expected values being equally likely. The commands and the edited output are below. With the LOGLINEAR procedure the /DESIGN command should always be last.

```
COMPUTE const = 1.
LOGLINEAR coin (1,2) WITH const /DESIGN const.
```

```
* * * * * * * * * * LOG  LINEAR  ANALYSIS * * * * * * * * * *
```

Note: for saturated models .500 has been added to all observed cells. This value may be changed by using the CRITERIA = DELTA subcommand.

Observed, Expected Frequencies and Residuals

Factor	Code	OBS count	EXP count	Residual	Adj Resid
COIN	1	58.50	50.50	8.000	1.592
COIN	2	42.50	50.50	-8.000	-1.592

Goodness-of-Fit test statistics

```
Likelihood Ratio Chi Square =   2.54536    DF = 1   P =   .111
            Pearson Chi Square =   2.53465    DF = 1   P =   .111
```

You will notice that the observed counts and the expected counts, which are the values predicted by the model, are slightly higher than we had calculated. In some cases (I will explain which when discussing comparisons of two variables) the LOGLINEAR procedure adds a small amount, called a flattening constant, to each cell. This constant is denoted by the Greek letter δ (lower-case delta). For most problems, when SPSS does this, it raises the p value a little and should be used. The difference, however, is usually quite small, particularly if the cell sizes are large. As the note in the output says, if you want to obtain exactly the same output as calculated earlier you can add /CRITERIA DELTA (0) before /DESIGN const so the command reads:

LOGLIN coin (1,2) WITH const /CRITERIA DELTA (0) /DESIGN const.

   The code for the numbers example, when comparing all ten possible numbers, is similar to the above. A slightly more complex procedure is necessary for comparing the model of 10% of the people choosing 7 and 90% choosing something else. It involves creating a new variable to denote whether a person chooses 7 or not, and a variable that has a value that is nine times as big for the people who do not choose 7 than for those who do. One fairly simple way of doing this is by making a variable that is equal to one for everybody and then changing it to nine for all the people who choose a number other than 7 (there are actually several ways to do this in SPSS). The LOGLINEAR procedure is then told to weight the cells by this variable (here called choice). In this case we let $\delta = 0$ so that we get the same results as before.

```
COMPUTE const = 1.
COMPUTE sev = 0.
IF (number = 7) sev = 1.
COMPUTE choice = 1.
IF (sev = 0) choice = 9.
```

This creates a new variable that is 1 if 7 was chosen and 0 otherwise. This sets up the appropriate cell weight; a 1 to 9 split.

```
LOGLINEAR sev (0,1) WITH const /CWEIGHT choice
   /CRITERIA DELTA (0)   /DESIGN const.
```

```
* * * * * * * * * * LOG LINEAR ANALYSIS * * * * * * * * * *
```

```
Observed, Expected Frequencies and Residuals
   Factor    Code   OBS count   EXP count   Residual   Adj Resid
SEV            0      30.00       36.00      -6.000      -3.162
SEV            1      10.00        4.00       6.000       3.162
```

```
Goodness-of-Fit test statistics
   Likelihood Ratio Chi Square =   7.38652   DF = 1   P =   .007
               Pearson Chi Square = 10.00000   DF = 1   P =   .002
```

Two-variable Problems

Suppose you had two variables and you wanted to know if they were related. If they were interval variables, like height and weight, you could do a scatterplot, a correlation and/or a regression. But suppose they were categorical, like social class and marital status. Consider Table 7.4 showing hypothetical data for 1000 people comparing social class and marital status.

There are, in total, 16 cells with numbers in them, not counting the row and column totals. This is the *total* degrees of freedom. If we wanted to test the model that all cells had equal chance of someone being in them, we could do the same as before with /DESIGN const. We would use one piece of information in constructing our expected values, the sample size. There are 16 cells and 1000 people, therefore our predicted value for each cell would be $1000/16 = 62.50$. The computer command (assuming both class and marital are coded from 1 to 4) is

```
COMPUTE const = 1.
LOGLINEAR class (1,4) marital (1,4) WITH const /DESIGN const.
```

This produces a $L\chi^2$ of 910.17. Because we have used one piece of information in the model, there are 15 degrees of freedom left for the residual. This value is statistically significant for $\alpha = 0.01$ with 15 df. This means we could reject the hypothesis of equal cell values.

The way in which people are assigned to different social classes is somewhat arbitrary. Therefore the percentage of people assigned to each class is not very interesting. While there may be some interest in the numbers of people in different marital situations, this also is not the focus of interest. We want to take into account the number of people in each social class and in each marital category and see how well we can predict all the cell values. What is left over is the association between class and marital status. The model being tested is that the breakdown of marital status is the same for all the different social classes (or alternatively the breakdown of social classes is the same for people in each marital status group).

The first step in the calculations is finding the expected values for the model. The model uses the number of people in each class and each marital status

Table 7.4 *Comparing social class and marital status. In parentheses are the expected values for the model of no association between class and marital status*

	Social class				
	I	II	III	IV	Row totals
Married or cohabiting	215 (192.4)	156 (154.3)	128 (131.6)	169 (189.7)	668
Single	45 (54.7)	37 (43.9)	49 (37.4)	59 (54.0)	190
Widowed	12 (24.2)	25 (19.4)	10 (16.6)	37 (23.9)	84
Divorced or separated	16 (16.7)	13 (13.4)	10 (11.4)	19 (16.5)	58
Column totals	288	231	197	284	1000

group. How many people, for example, would we expect to be in the married/ cohabiting group from social class I if the breakdown of marital status was the same in this group as in the whole sample? In the sample, 668 of 1000 (66.8%) of the people are either married or cohabiting. Therefore, we would expect the same percentage in class I. There are 288 people in class I. We would expect 66.8% of these people to be married or cohabiting if there was no association between class and marital status; 66.8% of 288 is 192.4. Do not worry that this is not a whole number. This is the expected value of the model, often denoted E. A formula for calculating this is

$$Model_{ij} = E_{ij} = \frac{RT_i CT_j}{n}$$

I have added some notation here that is worth explaining. $Model_{ij}$ and E_{ij} refer to the expected value for the cell in the ith row and the jth column. RT_i refers to the row total for the ith row and CT_j is the column total of the jth column. n is the total sample size. $Model_{13}$, for example, is the expected value of people who are married or cohabiting in class III

$$Model_{13} = \frac{668 \times 197}{1000} = 131.6$$

We can also refer to the observed values and the residuals with the same subscripts. In fact, we can refer to any characteristic of the cells using these subscripts.

The fit of this model can be calculated in the same way as before. The equations are the same as before but it is worth stressing that the values are summed over all the cells.[1] For this example, either χ^2 formula will do:

$$\chi^2 = \sum \frac{(Observed_{ij} - Model_{ij})^2}{Model_{ij}}$$

$$\chi^2 = \frac{(215 - 192.4)^2}{192.4} + \frac{(156 - 154.3)^2}{154.3} + \ldots + \frac{(19 - 16.5)^2}{16.5} = 30.09$$

If we had used the $L\chi^2$ we would have found $L\chi^2 = 30.57$. When the sample size is as large as it is here the two statistics produce very similar results.

---

1   In this equation a single summation sign ($\sum$) is used to stand for summing over all the cells. In some books this would be written as

$$\chi^2 = \sum_{i=1}^{i=r} \sum_{j=1}^{j=c} \frac{(Observed_{ij} - Model_{ij})^2}{Model_{ij}}$$

where r and c are the number of rows and columns, respectively. This is simply saying 'sum all the cells in each of the columns for each of the rows and then sum these for all the rows'. Sometimes this notation is necessary but for these cases it can be avoided without loss of understanding.

The next step is calculating the degrees of freedom of the residuals. The information we use in the model is the total sample size, the row totals and column totals. However, when we know the total sample size, and three of the row totals, we can calculate the fourth. The same goes for the column totals. Therefore the row totals and the column totals contribute only an additional three pieces of information each. Once we know the sample size, a variable with k categories adds only $k - 1$ more pieces of information (if this seems similar to the arguments about the number of dummy variables in regressions, it should be and it is $k - 1$ for the same reasons). Thus, in this example we have one degree of freedom for the total sample size, three for the row totals and three more for the column total making a total of seven degrees of freedom for the model. Because there are 16 cells in total, this leaves nine for the residuals. Thus, we can look up the critical χ^2 values for nine degrees of freedom and we see they are 16.92 and 21.67 for α equal to 0.05 and 0.01, respectively. Because our observed value is higher than these, we can reject the model that the two variables are not related and conclude that there is an association between marital status and social class.

This type of example, where there are two variables and you are interested in whether they are related, is very common. It is often referred to as *the* χ^2 test. Because of its popularity, textbooks often present an equation for this situation. The most applicable for present purposes is an equation for calculating the degrees of freedom for the residuals. If there are r rows and c columns, then the degrees of freedom of the residuals is $(r - 1)(c - 1)$. In this example, $(4 - 1)(4 - 1) = 3 \times 3 = 9$.

Personally, I find little hints like this sometimes troublesome. I often worry whether my memory for a particular formula or hint is correct, and also whether it applies in whichever situation I am in. I usually find it easier to calculate the numbers from their conceptual basis. Still, I recognise handy hints can sometimes make calculations easier, but make sure you know why these hints work (see Exercise 7 of this chapter).

Another Example: What Is Science?

There is much concern about how people understand the word 'science' and whether people's answers to questions about this are reliable. Gaskell *et al.* (1993: 43) asked 2099 respondents in five different conditions what 'comes to mind when *science* is mentioned' (*italics* in original). The conditions depended on whether respondents were asked a series of knowledge questions before this question and if so, whether the questions were (a) easy or difficult and (b) about physical or life sciences. They wanted to see if people's responses depended on which experimental condition they were in. The respondents were given five options: physical sciences, life sciences, technology, environmental sciences and social sciences. They were also allowed to answer don't know or something else. Table 7.5 shows the observed frequencies. There are in total 30 different cells, or

Table 7.5 *The observed frequencies for what science means to people in different experimental conditions (data calculated from Gaskell et al., 1993)*

Condition	Physical	Life sciences	What comes to mind? Technology	Environmental	Social	Other/DK	Row totals
No questions	373	345	179	122	36	47	1102
Easy physical	137	60	30	31	12	17	287
Hard physical	86	46	21	9	9	10	181
Easy life	85	99	36	39	11	12	282
Hard life	93	75	36	21	12	10	247
Column totals	774	625	302	222	80	96	2099

degrees of freedom: this is obtained by multiplying the number of rows (5) by the number of columns (6) (this point may be useful for Exercise 7).

There are several different models we could explore. One is that all the cells are equally likely. This model uses only one piece of information, the sample size. The prediction is that each cell will have 2099/30 = 70 people in it. The likelihood ratio statistic for the residuals of this model is $L\chi^2 = 2352.81$. Because we have used only one degree of freedom (the sample size), this leaves 29 degrees of freedom for the residual. The observed value exceeds the critical value for $\alpha = 0.01$. Therefore, not surprisingly, we can reject this model.

Looking at the row totals, the numbers of people in each condition are not the same. About half the people were asked no questions beforehand. Because this breakdown was decided by the researchers, it is not of any scientific interest. Therefore, we would want to include the row totals in the model. This model predicts that the percentage of people responding with each of the options will be the same in each group, but that the group sizes can differ. To calculate this for each cell we divide the row total by the number of column categories. The prediction for all the cells in the 'no questions' condition will be 1102/6 which is approximately 184. The fit of this model is $L\chi^2 = 1234.96$. The additional information we used here was the row totals. Because there are five rows, this equates with four additional degrees of freedom being used. Thus, there are five degrees of freedom in the model, leaving 25 in the residuals. This value also exceeds the critical value for $\alpha = 0.01$. Therefore we can also reject this model.

The next set of information we could use is the differences in numbers of people, overall, choosing the different alternatives. This would leave only the association between the conditions and choice of alternatives. The predicted value for each cell is the row total multiplied by the column total divided by the sample size. For example, the prediction for cell$_{12}$ is $Model_{12} = RT_1CT_2/n$. So, $Model_{12} = 1102 \times 625/2099 = 328.13$. The observed value for this cell was 345, thus $Residual_{12} = 16.87$. For this model we have $L\chi^2 = 55.38$. With six alternatives, there are five additional degrees of freedom used in the model. Thus, there are 10 degrees of freedom in the model, leaving 20 degrees of freedom in the residuals. This value also exceeds the critical value at $\alpha = 0.01$ and therefore the model can be rejected.

The only remaining set of information is the association between the two variables. Thus, by rejecting the model that includes information about the sample size, the row totals and the column totals, we can conclude that a person's experimental condition is associated with different responses. If we used the model with all the information, what is called the *saturated* model, the predicted cell values would be the same as the observed cell values. The residuals would all be zero and the χ^2 value would be zero. There would also be zero degrees of freedom for the residuals. Although it seems pointless to test the saturated model, in some circumstances it is useful.

There is a problem with analysing large tables like Table 7.5: there are many possible ways in which the association model can be rejected. With 20 degrees of freedom in the residual, there are 20 pieces of information that could be producing the statistical significance. Ideally researchers should identify which of these are responsible. One method for identifying these is *collapsing* some of the row and/or column values, thereby reducing the number of degrees of freedom in the residuals. This is described in the next section. Another approach is to graph the data. Procedures for this are described towards the end of this chapter. Finally, there are some sophisticated methods for modelling data when particular relationships are expected (see Clogg and Shihadeh, 1994, for details).

In the science example, everything seemed to be highly significant. This often occurs when the sample size is large. As is true for all statistics, as the sample size goes up, even small differences can become highly significant. The simplest solution to this is to think also about the size of the observed effect. The most common effect size for the association is called Cramér's V:

$$V = \sqrt{\frac{\chi^2}{n \min(r-1, c-1)}}$$

where $\min(r-1, c-1)$ is the smaller of $r-1$ and $c-1$ (where r is the number of rows and c is the number of columns). In the case of the original science data, there are five rows and six columns. This value is therefore $\min(5-1, 6-1)$ which is $\min(4, 5)$ or 4. Cramér's V ranges from 0 to 1, higher values representing stronger associations. This will give a better indication of the size of any effect. For the science data, χ^2 was 54.26 and $V = 0.08$. The χ^2 value is large even though V is fairly small because of the large sample size. Another example, described shortly, compares people's societal concerns with the affluence of their neighbourhoods. In that example (using the collapsed data) $\chi^2 = 3.01$ and $V = 0.25$. Here, the test statistic χ^2 is smaller even though the observed size of the effect is larger. This is because in that example the sample size is only 52. There are many other measures of association. Readers interested in calculating these can use the CROSSTABS command with the /STATISTICS option to produce other measures of effect size when there are two variables to compare.

Collapsing

As discussed in relation to the number example (Table 7.3), as the number of cases per cell decreases, it becomes more difficult to achieve a statistically significant result. There is even a problem that the p values become fairly inaccurate when several of the cells have low expected frequencies. In order to achieve a better understanding of the data it is often useful to collapse certain cells. Consider the (fictitious) data in Table 7.6, in which 52 people living in a large city were presented with six topics (poverty, crime, drugs, foreign policy, unemployment, the economy) and asked with which they were most concerned. People's neighbourhoods were classified as being affluent, medium affluent or poor.

The researchers were probably interested in how the patterns of responses varied across the neighbourhoods: do people in wealthy areas have similar concerns to those in poor areas? To test this they would use the model including the total sample size, the row totals and the column totals. This takes into account everything except for how the responses vary across neighbourhoods. The calculation for the expected value for each cell is RT_iCT_j/n. Therefore, the model predicts that there should be about $12 \times 16/52 = 3.69$ people in cell 11 (the wealthy reporting crime), about $12 \times 23/52 = 5.31$ people in cell 12 (the medium affluence people reporting crime), and so on.

The calculations produce $\chi^2(10) = 13.19$ and $L\chi^2(10) = 15.89$. Remember these are measures of deviance. The larger they are the worse the model fits. There are 10 degrees of freedom for the residual because with 18 total cells in total, 8 degrees of freedom are used in the model (1 for the sample size, an additional 2 for neighbourhood and 5 for concern). The critical values for χ^2 with 10 degrees of freedom are 18.31 and 23.21 for $\alpha = 0.05$ and $\alpha = 0.01$ respectively. The observed values are less than these. Therefore we cannot reject the model of no association between neighbourhood and what people think are the biggest problems.

Table 7.6 *Comparing neighbourhood affluence with the responses people gave for their greatest concern. The numbers in the parentheses refer to the observed frequencies after the variable concern is collapsed into two categories*

Value		Affluent	Medium	Poor	Row totals
		Neighbourhood affluence			
1	Crime	3	6	3	12
2	Drugs	4 (7)	8 (14)	7 (10)	19 (31)
3	Poverty	1	2	2	5
4	Foreign policy	3	2	0	5
5	Unemployment	0	3	1	4
6	The economy	5 (9)	2 (9)	0 (3)	7 (21)
	Column totals	16	23	13	52

However, there are some difficulties. First, the χ^2 table assumes the distribution is continuous. This is fine when the sample size is large and the number of cells is small, but in this case several of the cells have small values. The resulting p values will not be very accurate. A general rule of thumb is that if more than 20% of the *expected* cell values are less than 5, then some of the cells should be collapsed. In this example almost all the cells have expected frequency less than 5 (15 of the 18). Another rule of thumb is that all the cells should have an expected cell frequency above 1. There has been some movement away from strict adherence to these rules on purely statistical grounds. However, on practical grounds it is still worth adhering to them. If the expected cell frequency is small then either the row of that cell or its column, or usually both, are quite small. In these circumstances it is always worth questioning whether the characteristic defined by that row and/or by that column might be similar enough to others so that they may be combined. Otherwise, a small row or column total is unlikely to yield reliable results.

In this study, the two lowest row totals are pollution and poverty. Looking at the other options, these seem related to environment and unemployment, respectively. Yes, of course there are differences, but separating these out without ample data dilutes the information either of them can convey. The code for this new analysis and some of the output are shown below.

```
RECODE concern (1,2=1) (3,4,5,6=2).
LOGLINEAR /DESIGN concern (1,2) neigh (1,3).
```

```
Goodness-of-Fit test statistics
  Likelihood Ratio Chi Square =   3.38775     DF = 2    P =    .184
             Pearson Chi Square =   3.30535     DF = 2    P =    .192
```

The new table would still have three columns but now would have only two rows. Therefore there would be only six pieces of information, or degrees of freedom, in total. The model uses one for the sample size, two for the neighbourhoods and only an additional one for the concerns, making a total of four. This leaves two for the residuals. Another way of calculating this is using the formula described earlier $(r - 1)(c - 1)$ or $(2 - 1)(3 - 1) = 2$. The critical χ^2 values for two degrees of freedom are 5.99 and 9.21 for $\alpha = 0.05$ and $\alpha = 0.01$. Although the observed values are still not statistically significant, this is a more valuable test of the model.

There are various rules of thumb for when and how to collapse:

- Collapsing is advisable if 20% or more of expected cell frequencies are less than 5 or if any are less than 1
- Collapse the categories that have small observed values, since these are the ones creating the statistical problem
- Only combine categories that are similar
- Do not combine categories just because the response patterns are similar
- Collapse categories to increase statistical power.

Box 7.1   Special Considerations for 2 × 2 Tables

Collapsing can continue until there are only two rows and only two columns, a 2 × 2 table. If the expected cell sizes are still too small then it is advisable to use what is called *Fisher's exact probability test*. In the days before computers it was necessary to calculate this by hand or you had to look up the values in a table. I will not go into detail about this test because the SPSS CROSSTABS will print the *p* value for Fisher's exact test when appropriate. As this situation is fairly rare, I leave it to interested readers to explore this procedure.

Even when the 2 × 2 table has ample expected cell frequencies, there is much controversy about how to analyse it. The original formula, Pearson's χ^2, has been shown to produce *p* values that are sometimes too small. Yates proposed what is often called the *continuity correction* for this. He proposed subtracting 1/2 from the absolute value of each cell residual before squaring it (see equation below). This will always lower the χ^2 and therefore will always raise the *p* value. The corrected χ^2 tends to give *p* values that are too high. These are the two most common procedures; controversy still exists on which to use and several others have been proposed (see Richardson, 1990, for a comparison of some of these). Because it is usually considered more harmful to reject the null hypothesis incorrectly, Yates's correction for continuity is usually preferred.

Special computational formulae are available for these 2 × 2 tests. As I said earlier, you should be careful with helpful hints and special formulae, but these are used enough to be worth presenting. Suppose the data are in the following form:

	Column 1	Column 2	Row totals
Row 1	*A*	*B*	*A + B*
Row 2	*C*	*D*	*C + D*
Column totals	*A + C*	*B + D*	*n = A + B + C + D*

The following formulae are for Pearson's and Yates's χ^2 values:

$$Pearson's\,\chi^2 = \frac{n(AD - BC)^2}{(A + B)(C + D)(A + C)(B + D)}$$

$$Yates's\,\chi^2 = \frac{n(|AD - BC| - n/2)^2}{(A + B)(C + D)(A + C)(B + D)}$$

As an example, consider a study on the effects of persuasive questioning on memory. Loftus and Palmer (1974: 587) showed people a film of a car crash. Afterwards, some of the people were asked how fast the cars were

162   *Understanding statistics*

going when they 'smashed' into each other, while some had the same
question except the word 'hit' was used. They were then asked if there was
broken glass at the scene of the accident, which there was not. Table 7.7
shows the responses to this question. The two χ^2 values are calculated as
follows.

$$Pearson's \chi^2 = \frac{100(16(43) - 7(34))^2}{(23)(77)(50)(50)} = 4.57$$

$$Yates's \chi^2 = \frac{100(|16(43) - 7(34)| - 100/2)^2}{(23)(77)(50)(50)} = 3.61$$

Table 7.7   *A 2 × 2 table based on Loftus and Palmer (1974) with
calculations for Pearson's and Yates's χ^2.*

	Smashed	Hit	Row totals
Broken glass	16	7	23
No broken glass	34	43	77
Column totals	50	50	$n = 100$

The value for Pearson's is significant at $\alpha = 0.05$, while the value for
Yates's is not. In most cases you would say you have failed to reject the
null hypothesis. However, as urged throughout this book, you should not
worry extensively about whether the *p* value is on one side or the other of
0.05. Here the precise *p* value is 0.057 for the value from Yates's formula,
and this value should be reported.

χ^2: the Equation Approach

As I said earlier, the word 'loglinear' sounds a bit frightening. Here I will
explain why it is used. Table 7.8 shows the collapsed data for the neighbourhood
affluence and concern example along with the observed values; the natural
logarithms, or logs, of these values are given.[2] In loglinear modelling, we are
trying to predict these logs. That is where the 'log' in 'log-linear' comes from.
    The basic equation of statistics is

Observations = Model + Residuals

2   The natural log of a number is the power to which you have to raise the number e
(approximately 2.718) to get this number. Thus, ln(7) = 1.945, because $e^{1.945} = 7$. Don't worry if
you don't understand this; it is useful, but not necessary for understanding loglinear modelling. Most
calculators have a natural logarithm button, denoted by either ln or by $\log_e$.

Table 7.8 *The observed values and their natural logarithms for the neighbourhood and concerns data*

	Affluent	Medium	Poor	Row total
	Neighbourhood affluence			
Crime	7	14	10	31
	1.946	2.639	2.03	3.434
Economic	9	9	3	21
	2.197	2.197	1.099	3.045
Column Total	16	23	13	52
	2.773	3.136	2.565	3.951

In this case we can write this equation as

$$People_{ij} = Model_{ij} + Residuals_{ij}$$

where $People_{ij}$, sometimes denoted O_{ij} for the observed cell frequencies, refers to the observed number of people in the ith row and the jth column.

When we were calculating the expected values for the model of no association, we included information about the row totals, RT_i, and the column totals, CT_j. The formula was

$$E_{ij} = Model_{ij} = \frac{RT_i CT_j}{n}$$

We had to *multiply* the row and column totals. For many reasons it is often better to think of the effects as *adding* together, as they were in the linear regression and ANOVA models discussed in Chapters 5 and 6. Natural logarithms have several useful mathematical properties including that once we take the log of each side of this equation, it becomes additive, or 'linear'. Thus the second part of 'log-linear'. Suppose a multiplied by b is equal to c (in symbol form $ab = c$). Then $\ln(ab) = \ln(c)$ *and* $\ln(a) + \ln(b) = \ln(c)$. Consider the following example:

$$12 = 4 \times 3$$
$$\ln(12) = \ln(4) + \ln(3)$$
$$2.485 = 1.386 + 1.099$$

Further, $\ln(a/b)$ is equal to $\ln(a) - \ln(b)$. We can use these properties to separate the variables RT_i and CT_j from the numbers that are known and create a model similar to regressions we have already encountered.

$$\ln(Model_{ij}) = \ln\left(\frac{RT_i CT_j}{n}\right) = \ln(RT_i) + \ln(CT_j) - \ln(n)$$

164 *Understanding statistics*

If we consider the first cell in Table 7.8, the people in wealthy neighbourhoods choosing crime, the log of the predicted value would be

$$\ln(Model_{11}) = 3.434 + 2.773 - 3.951 = 2.256$$

To find the predicted frequency you take the number e (which is approximately 2.718) and raise it to the power of 2.256. You find the predicted value is 9.54, which is also $31 \times 16/52$, the value found using the traditional method.

In a manner that is similar to using dummy variables in the ANOVA models of Chapter 6, we could construct dummy variables for the different categories and solve this model. As with the discussion in Chapter 6, for a variable with k categories, only $k - 1$ dummy variables (or contrasts) are necessary.

For neighbourhoods, we have three values and therefore two dummy variables are required. Let us use the medium affluent neighbourhood as the base or reference category. We create one dummy variable called *affluent$_j$* which has the value 1 for people in the wealthy areas, and 0 for all others. Similarly let *poor$_j$* have the value 1 for people in the poor areas, and 0 for everyone else. Since the collapsed variable *concern$_i$* has only two values, only one dummy variable is needed. We will let *crime$_i$* have the value 1 for people who thought crime was the most important concern and 0 for people who thought that financial issues were more important. The base category, the cell with a 0 for all the dummy variables, corresponds to the people in medium neighbourhoods who felt economic matters were of most concern. The model is

$$\ln(O_{ij}) = \ln(Model_{ij}) + \ln(e_{ij})$$
$$= \beta_1 crime_i + \beta_2 affluent_j + \beta_3 poor_j + \beta_0 + \ln(e_{ij})$$

The parameter β_1 refers to the difference in the logs of row marginals for these models. I will keep with the βs to avoid confusion. Since $\ln(31) - \ln(21) = 3.434 - 3.045 = 0.389$, this is the value for β_1. Similarly the value for β_2 is $\ln(16) - \ln(23) = 2.773 - 3.136 = -0.363$. β_3 is $2.565 - 3.136 = -0.571$. β_0 is the natural log of the predicted value for cell$_{22}$: $\ln(23(21)/52) = \ln(9.29) = 2.23$. Using this model, we can calculate the predicted values for the other cells. Consider cell$_{11}$:

$$\ln(Model_{11}) = 0.389 - 0.363 + 2.229 = 2.255$$

and

$$e^{2.255} = 9.54$$

which is the value calculated before.

Fortunately, the LOGLINEAR program in SPSS does all the hard work for you. The following command solves this model. Here I have specified the contrasts corresponding to the above dummy variables and told the computer to print the estimates. The relevant output is shown below. Notice that β_0 is not printed with this procedure.

```
LOGLINEAR concern (1,2) neigh (1,3)
    /CONTRAST (neigh) SIMPLE (2)                The reference or base
    /CONTRAST (concern) SIMPLE (2)              category has the value
    /PRINT ESTIM                               2 for neigh and concern.
    /DESIGN concern neigh.

Goodness-of-Fit test statistics

    Likelihood Ratio Chi Square =   3.38775    DF = 2    P =   .184
                Pearson Chi Square =   3.30535    DF = 2    P =   .192

Estimates for Parameters

CONCERN
Parameter       Coeff. Std. Err.    Z-Value Lower 95 CI Upper 95 CI
      1    .3894647635    .28263    1.37802    -.16448      .94341

NEIGH
Parameter       Coeff. Std. Err.    Z-Value Lower 95 CI Upper 95 CI
      2   -.3629053409    .32554   -1.11477   -1.00097      .27516
      3   -.5705447708    .34699   -1.64427   -1.25064      .10955
```

If the value of a parameter is close to zero, this means the contrast or the effect is not large. For each of the parameters, the computer also gives a *z* value. This can be looked up in the same way as the *z* values back in Chapter 2 to see how unlikely we would be to observe an effect of this size if there was no effect in the whole population. It also gives the 95% confidence intervals for the parameters. If the interval includes zero, then we can say it is non-significant at the $\alpha = 0.05$ level. If it does not include zero then the effect is significant at $\alpha = 0.05$. I urge some caution when using normal hypothesis testing methods with these parameters, because when problems grow more complicated many effects are being tested and often these effects will not be independent. This creates problems in deciding on the appropriate α levels.

In the above example, the contrasts were specified. SPSS has a default method that compares each of the first $k - 1$ values with the mean of the logs for all the values of the variable. Because the variable $crime_i$ has only two values, the effect for concern requires only one dummy variable. The computer compares the log of the row total for crime (3.434) with the mean of the logs of the two row totals:

$$\beta_1 = 3.434 - \left(\frac{3.434 + 3.045}{2}\right) = 0.194$$

Understanding statistics

which is within rounding error of the estimate printed below. This compares the crime response with the mean of all responses. Here are the commands and edited output.

```
LOGLINEAR concern (1,2) neigh (1,3)
  /PRINT ESTIM
  /DESIGN concern neigh.
```

```
Goodness-of-Fit test statistics
  Likelihood Ratio Chi Square =   3.38775    DF = 2    P =    .184
             Pearson Chi Square =   3.30535    DF = 2    P =    .192
```

```
Estimates for Parameters
```

```
CONCERN
Parameter       Coeff.  Std. Err.   Z-Value  Lower 95 CI  Upper 95 CI
      1   .1947323818    .14131    1.37802    -.08224       .47171
```

```
NEIGH
Parameter       Coeff.  Std. Err.   Z-Value  Lower 95 CI  Upper 95 CI
      2  -.0517553037    .20287    -.25512    -.44938       .34587
      3   .3111500372    .18659    1.66758    -.05456       .67686
```

An important point to stress is that the χ^2 values are the same. As with the choice of dummy variables in the ANOVAs, so long as they contain the relevant information, the fit of the model will be the same. It is often useful to look at these to gauge the size of any effects and to focus on particular effects.

Graphing Techniques (Optional)[3]

There has been much recent advancement in graphical analysis of categorical data. Much of this has arisen from research in France and the Netherlands and goes under the name of *correspondence analysis*. These techniques can be used for a wide variety of purposes (for details, see van de Geer, 1993a; 1993b). Here I am simply going to describe how to use a computer to produce a useful graph as a purely exploratory tool. There are a few computer programs that can be used for this analysis. The most accessible was developed by GIFI (a collective name used by members of Data Theory Department at Leiden) and is incorporated in recent versions of SPSS. There has been much interest in combining the traditional modelling approach, as discussed earlier, with these graphical approaches (see Goodman, 1991; Van der Heijden *et al.*, 1989).

In a nutshell, this procedure works by rearranging the numerical values given to categories and trying to maximise the correlation between the variables,

---

3   The reason why this material is optional is that the relevant procedures are not included on all implementations of SPSS and on many other statistics programs. Therefore you might not have them on your system.

treating them as if they were continuous. The program creates a map of the values of each of the variables. If there are r rows and c columns, the program can use up to either $(r - 1)$ or $(c - 1)$ dimensions, whichever is smaller. Maps that have just two dimensions are the most useful because they can easily be represented on a piece of paper, but others are also possible.

This procedure essentially is partitioning the residuals of the no association χ^2 model. Therefore, if the χ^2 value is non-significant or not substantially large, this technique should not be used because the residuals are not large enough to partition. This is important because the computer will proceed even when the χ^2 value is too small.

Consider the meaning of science example. The significant χ^2 value only allowed us to conclude that there was a difference among the experimental conditions for 'what came to mind' when science was mentioned. It did not show how the conditions and the responses were associated. The name of the SPSS procedure for exploring this association is ANACOR, which stands for ANAlysis of CORrespondences (actually, it stands for *ANAlyse des CORrespondances*, being based in part on the French work of Benzécri, 1973). The command[4]

```
ANACOR /TABLES condit (1,5) BY mind (1,6) /PLOT JOINT.
```

produces, among other things, a list of coordinates for the row and column values. There is some discussion about the appropriateness of graphing both variables in the same plot (Clogg and Shihadeh, 1994), but it is common practice.

The next step is to decide how many dimensions are necessary. The column showing the proportion of the residuals (that is, of the χ^2 value) accounted for provides a useful guide. If a dimension is accounting for only a small

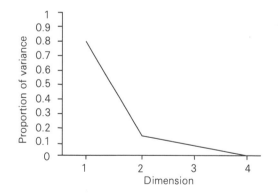

Figure 7.2   *Deciding on the number of dimensions for a correspondence analysis*

---

4   This command will vary in different implementations. If it does not work, look at the CATEGORIES option or use the help facility. With some SPSS for Windows implementations, it is necessary to 'paste' the commands into a syntax box.

percentage, then it is best not to use that dimension. If you graph these proportions by the number of dimensions (called a *scree plot*),[5] you should look for what is called the 'elbow' in the graph, where the dimensions stop accounting for very much. This is shown in Figure 7.2. Here there could be one or two dimensions. The decision how many dimensions to choose is subjective. The purpose of this procedure is to help you understand the association, so choose however many is most helpful. (Note: you must draw this diagram yourself.)

The two-dimensional solution is shown in Figure 7.3. Because the first dimension is by far the most important, as shown in Figure 7.2, it is best to concentrate on this. It shows the people given the easy physics (EP) and hard physics (HP) quizzes on the left with the response of 'physics' (phy) for what comes to mind. To the right are the people given the life sciences quizzes and the responses 'life' and 'environmental' (envir) for what comes to mind. Of interest to Gaskell *et al.* (1993) was that people given no quiz (NQ) gave responses similar to people given the life science quizzes (EL and HL). This means people's responses were not greatly affected by answering life science questions. This, they argued, showed that people's natural view of 'what comes to mind' is more in tune with the life sciences. This is also shown by the proximity of NQ (no questions) to the response 'life'.

This technique is more complex than the way I have presented it and it can be used for many other situations. There are also several related techniques beyond the scope of this book. Interested readers should consult van de Geer (1993a; 1993b) and/or the appropriate SPSS manuals.

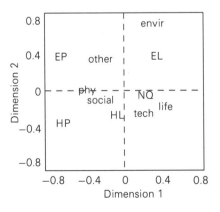

Figure 7.3   *The two-dimensional plot for 'what comes to mind when science is mentioned'*

---

5   A *scree* is the bottom part of a cliff or mountain, where it slopes into the ground. Scree plots are often used with other procedures (such as factor analysis and multidimensional scaling) to help determine the optimal solution.

Summary

Many of the variables encountered in the social and behavioural sciences are categorical. In this chapter I described how to construct and test models for categorical data. While the actual equations are different from the other tests, the basic logic is the same: construct a model and see how well the observations fit it. The statistical tests are based on the size of the residuals. In some textbooks these techniques are described as being quite distinct from the regression and ANOVA families. I have tried to stress the similarities rather than the differences.

We looked at the situation for one variable and for two variables. To test whether the data fit the model, we used a χ^2 test. The approach I took here was to use a format that can be easily extended to more complex examples. I will briefly touch upon these in the next chapter. I encourage you to practise the techniques described in this chapter.

Assignment

1 When a die is thrown, it is assumed that each of the six sides has an equal chance of coming up. Suppose a die was thrown 45 times.
   (a) For the model of equal cell values, what is the expected frequency for each of the six cells (that is, the six sides)?
   (b) Suppose this particular die had been used the previous night and that it seemed as if the number 6 had come up a lot and you wanted to test if 6 had a different chance than the other sides. How would you test this more specific hypothesis?
2 Seventy students were asked what day of the week they felt most anxious. The data are below. Do this problem by hand.
   (a) Test the hypothesis that students are equally likely to feel anxious on all the days.
   (b) Test the hypothesis that weekends are different from weekdays. Discuss why you might want to do this.

M	Tu	W	Th	F	Sa	Su	Total
9	11	15	15	8	5	7	70

3 The table below shows the party of the governor of each US state by region. This is in the states.sps data file in Appendix A. Use either this data set, or create your own using the WEIGHT function.

(a)   With only two states with 'independent' governors, what should be done? Do something with these states for the following analysis.[6]

(b)   Find the fit of the model where the `region` variable (and the total number of states) is taken into account.

(c)   Find the fit of the model where the `region` variable, the number of states, and the `govparty` variable are taken into account.

(d)   Describe in words what is being tested in (c).

(e)   Describe in words what can be inferred from the result of (c).

		region			
		East	Central	Mount/West	Total
govparty	Democratic	6	10	4	20
	Republican	10	10	8	28
	Independent	1	0	1	2
	Total	17	20	13	50

4   The table below, based on Nightingale (1993), shows the number of guilty and not guilty verdicts from 179 university students who read a trial summary about a case in which a young girl was hit by a truck. The victim was 6, 9 or 12 years old. Is there any evidence that the victim's age influenced the verdict about whether the truck driver was negligent?

	Victim's age in years		
	6	9	12
Negligent	42	39	34
Not negligent	20	22	22

5   In the run up to, and during, the Gulf War, those trying to persuade public opinion tended to be suggesting one of two analogies for the West's role: either the Hitler analogy or the Vietnam analogy. Acceptance of each of these obviously implies a different attitude towards the war. Schuman and Rieger (1992) conducted six surveys in which US respondents were asked, among other things, which analogy was better. The months (in 1990–1991) of their surveys and the frequency of respondents' choices are shown below (this constitutes only about a tenth of the total data). The war began on 16 January. Was there a difference in responses before and during the war?

---

6   I will help with this one. There are several options. The simplest is just to exclude these states; treat them as missing values. Another method would be to combine these with the other groups in some sensible way. The two states are Alaska and Connecticut. At the time these data were accumulated, each had more Democratic than Republican representatives in Congress. Thus, if they were going to be combined with one of the other groups, the Democrats would probably be better.

	Oct.	Nov.	Dec.	Early Jan.	Late Jan.	Feb.
Hitler analogy	16	14	12	12	5	22
Vietnam analogy	12	11	12	7	2	5
Totals	28	25	24	19	7	27

6 Schuman and Scott (1989: Table 3) were interested in age effects (by the way, there were large age effects in the study on which Exercise 5 is based and these are discussed in the next chapter) in what people thought were the most important events in the last 50 years. The following shows some of the choices and how old the respondents were.

	Age					
	18–29	30–39	40–49	50–59	60–69	70+
World War II	55	70	58	69	73	37
JFK assassination	19	45	30	8	8	0
Vietnam	81	109	50	16	13	5
Space exploration	36	38	28	25	17	14

Use the ANACOR procedure to graph the relationship between age and choice of major event. Comment on the results. [You might want to draw a line between the age values to show their order.]

7 The degrees of freedom of the residuals for the no association model can be found by $(r - 1)(c - 1)$ where r is the number of rows and c is the number of columns. Show that this works. Begin with the total number of degrees of freedom, subtract the degrees of freedom of the model, and then use a little algebra to obtain $(r - 1)(c - 1)$.

8
Advanced Techniques

In Chapters 5–7, regression models, ANOVA models and loglinear models were described. As noted, these have similar conceptual bases, but differ in other ways. If you have understood the conceptual aspects of these approaches then you have become a competent social statistician. The next step is applying these concepts to more complex problems. Mathematically, the increase in complexity can make computation more difficult and more time-consuming. Instead of describing the mathematics underlying these approaches in detail, I will briefly illustrate the models and then show how they can be implemented by computer using SPSS. You should think of this more as an invitation to learn about many of the techniques that are available, rather than as a survey of all statistical techniques.

The techniques discussed throughout this chapter all have a similar structure and are related. One critical aspect is that they allow more than two variables to be examined simultaneously. This creates various interpretational difficulties. In the next section *collinearity*, which is essentially where many of the variables are related, is discussed. The interpretational difficulties arise when researchers try to make causal attributions from the data because many of the observed associations may be *spurious*, in that they are due to a third variable (see Simon, 1954, or Cook and Campbell, 1979, for detailed treatment).

Figure 8.1 shows an example. With children of school age, shoe size is known to be correlated with intelligence test scores. This correlation is depicted by the dotted line. Of course, there is another variable, age, which influences both of these. The solid arrows from age to these two variables are meant to show that as age increases these tend to increase. We say the correlation between shoe size and intelligence is spurious because it does not represent a direct causal

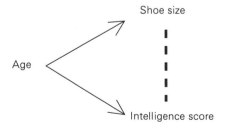

Figure 8.1 *The correlation between shoe size and intelligence does not mean that either of these influences the other. Age is seen as influencing both*

relationship. If we could somehow increase the size of someone's feet without changing anything else, it is doubtful that this would increase the person's intelligence score.

Multiple Regression

In Chapter 5 you met the concepts of regression and correlation when used to investigate relationships between two variables. Here I describe how to investigate relationships when there are more than two variables. The assumption here is that we are trying to predict one of the variables. We call this the *response variable*.

Other techniques (called, among other things, multivariate regressions) can be used when there is more than one response variable. The within-subject ANOVA (Chapter 6 and later in this chapter) can be considered a special case of multivariate regression, but most of these techniques are beyond the scope of this book.

The first steps in doing a simple regression are making a scatterplot, looking for outliers, and observing if there are any patterns in the scatterplot. If the pattern looks fairly linear (that is, it appears to be adequately described by a straight line), then the next step is to perform a simple linear regression. The correlation coefficient is a measure of how good the fit of the regression model is. In this section the regression is extended to when there are multiple variables used in the model to predict the response variable. The form of these is similar to the regression format for the ANOVA models presented in Chapter 6.

I begin with an example where the multiple regression has several predictor variables and the researcher is interested in exploring how all of these, in some way, can be used to predict the response variable. The next example uses multiple regression to investigate more specific hypotheses. Finally, multiple regression is used to perform what is called an analysis of covariance (ANCOVA).

Collinearity and the Partial Correlation

Much of the discussion in this chapter will concern *collinearity*. This is where the predictor variables are correlated among themselves. This did not occur with the simple linear regressions because there was only one predictor variable. It also did not happen with the ANOVAs when run as regressions with dummy variables because the dummy variables were designed either so as to be uncorrelated or in such a way that their relationships were well understood. Collinearity is what makes many regression problems conceptually difficult. A related concept is *partial correlation*. This measures the amount of the response variable accounted for by one variable when the effects of other predictor variables have been accounted for.

A few examples will help to illustrate these concepts. Consider the hypothetical shoe size, intelligence and age example depicted in Figure 8.1. We can represent the proportion of variance that each of these variables shares with the others in the same way as we did for two variables in Figure 5.4. In Figure 8.2, each variable has a circle, of the same size, representing its variance. These circles overlap and each letter in the figure represents either shared or unshared proportions of variance. Each letter refers to just the area that it is in (except for E, which represents the tiny region indicated). A, B and C are the variances of shoe size, age and intelligence, respectively, that are *not* accounted for by either of the other variables. G represents the variance shared by all three variables. D is the variance shared between shoe size and age that is not shared by the intelligence score. E is the same for shoe size and intelligence, *partialling out* age. F is the same for intelligence and age, partialling out shoe size.

For this example, the *partial correlation* of shoe size and intelligence, partialling out age, is based on the amount of variation in intelligence not accounted for by age $(C + E)$ that is accounted for by shoe size (E). The square of the partial correlation is $E/(C + E)$. In multiple regression, the size of the partial correlation is an important factor in determining whether a variable should be included in the model.

Predicting Crime from Several Variables

Much of the time when multiple regression is used, it involves using a large number of predictor variables to try to account for the variation of one response variable. Using multiple regression in this manner is exploratory. The reason is that with a large number of predictor variables, there is an increased likelihood that some of their observed effects will be large by chance and that other effects, which in the population are large, might be too small in the sample to detect.

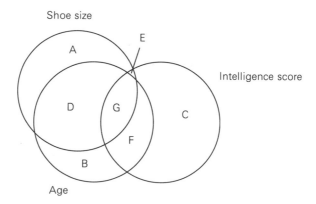

Figure 8.2 *Representing the variances for the shoe size, intelligence and age example*

Using the states data in Appendix A, suppose we wanted to use the dropout rate, the governor's party (using a dummy variable for whether the governor was a Republican or not, see Exercise 3 of Chapter 7) and the natural logarithms[1] of population (lnpop), 1989 prison population (ln89) and 1990 prison population (ln90) to predict the per capita crime rate (crime). For this regression, only the 50 states were used. Washington, DC was excluded because it is the only all-urban area and therefore has a much higher crime rate than any of the others (it is an outlier that can be excluded on substantive grounds). The following is the syntax for this problem. It is basically the same as was used for the regressions discussed in Chapter 5. Comments are to the right.

```
COMPUTE ln89 = LN(prison89).                   Transforming the
COMPUTE ln90 = LN(prison90).                    skewed variables
COMPUTE govrep = 0.                             Creating the dummy
IF (govparty EQ 0) govrep = 1.                  variable

SELECT IF (state NE "Wash_DC").                 Selecting if Not
REGRESSION /VARIABLES crime ln89 ln90 dropout   Equal Washington
  lnpop govrep                                  DC
  /DEPENDENT crime /METHOD ENTER.
```

The output has the same format as with the earlier regressions. The first information output is the R, R^2 and adjusted R^2 values.

```
Multiple R              .84161
R Square                .70830
Adjusted R Square       .67515
```

Multiple R is analogous to Pearson's correlation when there is more than one predictor variable. R square is the proportion of variation in the response variable accounted for by all the predictor variables. It is important to understand what the adjusted value is, because this is the most important of these figures for multiple regressions. Whenever you add a predictor variable into a regression, it will increase the variance accounted for and therefore increase the R^2 value. This is true even if the variable has no real predictive value. The algorithm for the regression capitalises on chance associations in the sample. The R^2 value therefore is an inappropriately high estimate of the variance accounted for in the population. The equation for adjusted R^2 value is

$$Adj.R^2 = 1 - \frac{(n-1)}{(n-k-1)}(1 - R^2)$$

---

1 This transformation was used since the original variables are highly positively skewed. There are a number of different transformations that could have been used for these and some alternatives are discussed later in this section.

where n is the number of cases and k is the number of predictor variables. For this model, with five predictors and 50 cases,

$$Adj.R^2 = 1 - \frac{(50-1)}{(50-5-1)}(1 - 0.70830)$$
$$= 1 - \frac{49}{44}(0.29170) = 0.67515$$

which is the value reported by SPSS. As the number of predictor variables increases, the difference between R^2 and adjusted R^2 also increases. However, as the number of cases increases, the adjustment for each additional predictor variable is less. For most purposes, you should be more concerned with the adjusted R^2 than the actual R^2. It is worth saying that there are other techniques for adjusting R^2, and various arguments as to which is best, but because this measure is what several of the main packages report it has become the most popular.

The analysis of variance table is the next information that is output. Here it simply says that the R^2 value is significantly different than what would be expected if none of the predictor variables had any real value in predicting the crime rate. In later problems the value of this part of the output will become more evident.

Analysis of Variance

	DF	Sum of Squares	Mean Square
Regression	5	2799325.29841	559865.05968
Residual	44	1152839.48979	26200.89750

| F = | 21.36816 | Signif F = | .0000 |

The next part of the output is the parameter estimates and their significance levels. Interpreting these estimates is more difficult than it was with the simple linear regressions when there was only one predictor variable. Taking the variable dropout as an example, we would say that, holding all the other variables constant, for each percentage increase in the dropout rate, we would predict that the crime rate would be 8.17 crimes higher per 100,000 people. The phrase 'holding all the other variables constant' is important. We are saying that if two states had exactly the same values on all the other predictor variables, but one state had a higher dropout rate, we would expect this state to have 8.17 more crimes per 100,000 people for each unit higher its dropout rate is. In reality, this 'holding constant' is seldom possible because of the interrelationships among the predictor variables. However, it is still a useful way of thinking about the relationship.

——————————— Variables in the Equation ———————————

Variable	B	SE B	Beta	T	Sig T
DROPOUT	8.17300	3.76712	.22451	2.170	.0355
GOVREP	-9.31687	46.67916	-.01645	-.200	.8427
LNPOP	-103.79744	74.03666	-.37203	-1.402	.1679
LN89	17.47552	112.63168	.07581	.155	.8774
LN90	216.86641	128.09657	.96104	1.693	.0975
(Constant)	-180.85492	629.92886		-.287	.7754

One way of examining this is comparing what SPSS calls the Beta values. These are standardised parameter estimates. When the dropout rate goes up one standard deviation, the crime rate goes up 0.22 standard deviations. This is useful for comparing the influence of different variables. Another way to examine influence is by looking at the *t* values and their probabilities. These test whether the amount accounted for by each variable, after all the others in the model have been taken into account, is sufficiently different from zero to reject the hypothesis that it is zero in the population. The value for the dropout rate is the only one that is significant at $\alpha = 0.05$, and the natural logarithm of the 1990 prison population (ln90) is almost significant at this level. Something should seem odd. First, you would think that a measure of the prison population would be a highly significant predictor of crime, after all it has a high standardised value and it makes intuitive sense. Also, why should ln89 have such a small value? The answer to these questions is that there is much collinearity among the predictor variables. Below is the *correlation matrix* of these variables.[2]

	CRIME	LN89	LN90	DROPOUT	LNPOP	GOVREP
CRIME	1.0000					
LN89	.7838	1.0000				
LN90	.7940	.9857	1.0000			
DROPOUT	.6013	.4659	.4762	1.0000		
LNPOP	.6719	.9254	.9394	.3132	1.0000	
GOVREP	-.0509	-.0214	-.0468	-.0161	-.0425	1.0000

All of these variables, except for the govrep, have high correlations with crime. The predictor variables are also very highly correlated among themselves, particularly ln89, ln90 and lnpop. This makes interpretation more difficult. When collinearity occurs there is often nothing that can be done. Scientists have to accept that in the real world variables are often highly correlated and therefore they must tread carefully in their interpretations. In a sense, the role of much science is to expose nature's collinearity.[3] However, in

---

2 Some researchers would disapprove of using Pearson's product-moment correlation with a dichotomous variable like govrep. However, here it is simply being used as a rough indicator of collinearity and therefore it is all right here.

3 This is a fairly philosophical point and when fully expanded is the matter of some debate. In addition to explaining existing collinearity in nature, scientists also investigate causal properties of various aspects of nature. There is much controversy about the role of these different quests in science.

this case it is possible to separate some aspects of these variables. In particular, ln89, ln90 and lnpop all are going to be dependent on the size of the population. If we divide prison89 by the population, we get a measure of the proportion of the population in prison in 1989. We can also alter the prison90 variable to be the percentage change in the prison population. Doing this reduces the collinearity among the predictors.

```
COMPUTE p89rat = prison89/popula.
COMPUTE pdiff = (prison90 - prison89) / popula.
```

	CRIME	P89RAT	PDIFF	DROPOUT	LNPOP	GOVREP
CRIME	1.0000					
P89RAT	.4895	1.0000				
PDIFF	.2191	-.4329	1.0000			
DROPOUT	.6013	.4719	.1723	1.0000		
LNPOP	.6719	.1515	.2266	.3132	1.0000	
GOVREP	-.0509	.0234	-.1463	-.0161	-.0425	1.0000

If we rerun the regression with these variables we get an adjusted R^2 of 0.68 (about the same as before) with the following parameter estimates:

```
———————————— Variables in the Equation ————————————
```

Variable	B	SE B	Beta	T	Sig T
GOVREP	.82079	46.08899	1.4492E-03	.018	.9859
DROPOUT	7.19251	3.81203	.19758	1.887	.0658
PDIFF	107767.74412	42770.24299	.26515	2.520	.0155
LNPOP	134.96099	24.26231	.48373	5.563	.0000
P89RAT	114765.14810	30017.85214	.43766	3.823	.0004
(Constant)	-1940.79268	347.61492		-5.583	.0000

NOTE: The 1.4492E-03 in column marked Beta is in scientific notation. It can be read as 1.4492×10^{-3} or 0.0014492.

Now we do get strong effects for both prison measures. Both a large proportion of the population in prison (p89rat) and an increasing proportion (pdiff) are associated with higher crime rates. Population (lnpop) on its own also has a positive association.

The next step in multiple regressions of this type is to select a more parsimonious model by removing the variables that appear to have little effect (the opposite procedure, starting with no variables in the model and adding in predictors, can also be done: see Box 8.1). In this case, the party of the governor would probably be removed from the model. This only slightly changes the other estimates for the variables which you would probably want to keep in the model. You would then explore some of the assumptions of the regression. One of the simplest diagnostic techniques is to plot the residuals with the predicted values. This can be done either using the scatterplot command within the regression procedure or saving the residuals and the predicted values and using the PLOT command. I have taken the latter approach below so that I could include the first letter of each state (see Figure 8.3).

With the exception of the N up at the top (which is for New Mexico), this plot shows marked heteroscedascity. Recall that heteroscedascity is when the variance in the residuals differs depending on the value predicted by the model. This particular pattern, with the predicted values becoming less accurate as they get larger, is fairly common in all sciences. It can indicate missing explanatory variables or that an interaction among the predictor variables (discussed shortly) should be included. The techniques for modelling this variance are beyond the scope of this book. Here, I simply stress that the heteroscedascity should be observed. Discussion of additional techniques for checking the validity of a model are described in most textbooks that focus on regression (see Lewis-Beck, 1993).

Whenever discussing multiple regression, it is always worth reiterating the cliché that correlation does not imply causation. In this example, it is tempting to say that each of the predictor variables *causes* a change in the crime rate. If we

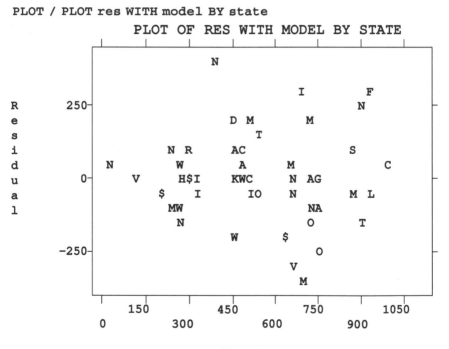

Figure 8.3 *The plot of residuals with the predicted values for the multiple regression with crime rate. The letters are the first letter of each state ($ stands for more than one state). There is marked heteroscedascity in these data.*

look at the prison variables, for example, it is difficult to see how, at least in the short term, increasing the prison population can increase the crime rate. The causal relationship, in the short term, is more likely to be in the opposite direction: as more people commit crimes, more people go to prison. The regression procedures do not tell us what is causing what. Your theories should be suggesting causal relationships and the statistics allow you to measure the hypothesised effects of these causes (this is described more completely in Holland, 1988). There exist some more advanced techniques, called path analysis and structural equation modelling, which provide frameworks within which more complex causal theories can be evaluated (see Box 8.2). However, to demonstrate causality unequivocally, an experimental design is necessary (see Chapter 1).

Low Temperatures and the Dropout Rate

Multiple regressions can also be used to investigate more specific research questions. In Chapter 5 we examined the relationship in the United States between the record low temperature in a state and the high school dropout rate. It seemed a bit silly that the record low temperature should have a strong relationship with dropout rate. What you should have been thinking at that point was that there are likely to be other characteristics that are better statistical predictors and ones that make more sense. Two likely candidates are the per capita crime rate and the money spent on pupils. The crime rate is considered here, while the expenditure variable is explored in the assignment at the end of this chapter.

The percentage of variance of the dropout rate, accounted for by `lowtemp`, was approximately 13% (from the regression including the outliers Hawaii and Alaska). This was statistically significant, but not large in substantive terms. The crime rate has a correlation of 0.62 with the dropout rate, which corresponds to about a third of the variance being accounted for. Two of the questions that can be answered with a multiple regression are how well these two variables together predict the dropout rate and whether the record low temperature has any predictive value once the crime rate has been accounted for.

The model that we are examining is

$$dropout_i = \beta_0 + \beta_1 crime_i + \beta_2 lowtemp_i + e_i$$

We are interested in how much of an improvement it is over the model without `lowtemp`:

$$dropout_i = \beta_0 + \beta_1 crime_i + e_i$$

The difference between these models gives us a measure of the predictive value of `lowtemp` after `crime` has been taken into account. The syntax for these

Box 8.1   Computer Selection of Models

When running regressions, most of the main computer packages have options that allow the computer to choose the 'best' set of predictor variables. As a group these are described as stepwise methods. They either begin with no variables in the model, and add variables, or begin with all the variables in the model and remove variables. The first type are called 'forward' methods, the second 'backward' methods.

For the forward methods, the computer adds in the variable with the highest predictive value into the model. Then, it checks all the other variables that are not in the model and adds the one that has the highest predictive value, accounting for the predictive value of the others that are already in the model. It does this until the variables not in the equation do not have much additional value (that is, their additional contribution is not statistically significant). The backward methods begin with all the variables and remove, one at a time, those that have little impact. It does this until only those with predictive value are left. There are also methods which combine these two techniques, beginning by adding variables into the model, but at each step also checking to see if any variables should be removed. In SPSS this is referred to as *the* 'stepwise' method.

There are problems with these techniques. One problem is that the computer will often not find the best combination of variables. When high levels of collinearity exist, the computer algorithm will often get stuck in what is called a local minimum. It cannot find any single variable to add or to remove that will help the model, but there do exist better models. To find these the computer would have to add and/or remove several variables simultaneously. In other words, the end solution from any of these stepwise procedures may not be the optimal (statistical) model. Some packages have procedures that check all possible models and therefore guarantee the optimal model. However, these are more time-consuming and for reasons outlined below may not be that worthwhile anyway.

There are two (additional) reasons why these procedures tend to be disliked by most methodologists. The first is that the computer is making all the decisions. It decides which variable to put in at each point and which to remove. This is often because one variable has a slightly higher partial correlation than another. In most cases there will be more important reasons to choose a particular variable than just a slight difference in the partial correlation. Stepwise methods take too many of the important, methodological decisions out of the hands of the researchers. They distance researchers from their data. This is wrong. I have seen people blame stepwise procedures for coming up with poor models. Remember, it is just a computer program.

Another problem with stepwise procedures is that the *p* values printed both for the overall model and for the individual effects are difficult to interpret. With all of the main packages they assume *you* actually prespecified the final model that the computer found. This is not true. The computer found the best-fitting model it could. It capitalised on all the random sample deviations it could. My best advice is to be extremely cautious with any *p* value from stepwise procedures. Even with all these problems, it is worth saying that stepwise procedures *may* have a purpose in exploratory research where little is known about the variables . . . but be careful.

models and selected output are shown below (Washington, DC has been excluded).

Comparing the adjusted values, the model without `lowtemp` does better than the model with it. This tells us that we should not reject the null hypothesis that `lowtemp` adds no predictive value beyond using just the crime rate. The next part of the output allows a more direct comparison. Under the heading 'Analysis of Variance', the regression for the first model (with two degrees of freedom) accounts for a sum of squared deviations of 1107.81, while the second model (with one degree of freedom) accounts for 1078.19. The difference between these is the additional amount accounted for by `lowtemp`: 29.62. We are partitioning the regression model sum of squares of the first model into the amount accounted for by `crime` and the additional amount accounted for by `lowtemp`. Because this additional amount corresponds to only one degree of freedom, the mean sum of squares for it is also 29.62. If we divide this by the mean sum of squares for the residuals, we get $F(1, 47) = 29.62/39.88 = 0.74$. This is non-significant (see Appendix D) indicating that once crime is taken into account, the amount of variation in the dropout rate that is accounted for by the state's record low temperature is non-significant.

When you are examining the effects of more than one variable, it is necessary to carry out the above procedure of partitioning the sums of squares. When there is just a single variable, the significance of the parameter estimates conveys the same information. In the next section of output, the estimate for the parameter of `lowtemp` is 0.048. The model predicts that for each degree (Fahrenheit) increase in the record low temperature, the dropout rate tends to go up 0.048. In practical terms this is not much. The t value of 0.86, and its associated significance of 0.393, show it is not sufficiently large to reject the hypothesis that low temperature has no predictive value once crime has been taken into account. When there is just one degree of freedom in the numerator of F (that is, there is only one variable), then $F = t^2$. Thus $0.86^2 = 0.74$. This t value conveys the same information as F. Essentially, it tells us we should concentrate on the simpler regression of model 2.

There is still the possibility that the temperature may have some relationship with dropout rate even after taking into account the crime rate. First, it may have a nonlinear relationship. This can be examined by graphing the residuals with the record low temperature (feel free to do this). It may also be that the crime rate and the temperature interact. For example, it might be when the crime rate is low, low temperatures are associated with low dropout rates, but when the crime rate is high, low temperatures are associated with high dropout rates. To test this we set up a variable to stand for the interaction and then rerun the regression with this variable included in the model (as well as both main effects). The syntax and selected output are given below. If we compare either the adjusted R^2 or the sum of squares of this model to model 1 (with only the main effects), we see that the interaction has little if any explanatory value. The sum of squares of the regression model is now 1107.85, which is only 0.04 more than the model without the interaction.

Model 1

SELECT IF (state NE 'Wash_DC').
REGRESSION /VARIABLES dropout crime lowtemp
   /DEPENDENT dropout
   /METHOD ENTER crime lowtemp.

Multiple R	.60949
R Square	.37147
Adjusted R Square	.34473
Standard Error	6.31514

Analysis of Variance

	DF	Sum of Squares	Mean Square
Regression	2	1107.812	553.906
Residual	47	1874.408	39.881

F = 13.889   Signif F = .000

————— Variables in the Equation —————

Variable	B	SE B	Beta	T	Sig T
LOWTEMP	.048	.055	.108	.86	.393
CRIME	.015	3.43E-03	.561	4.49	.000
(Constant)	18.307	3.491		5.24	.000

Model 2

SELECT IF (state NE 'Wash_DC').
REGRESSION /VARIABLES dropout crime
   /DEPENDENT dropout
   /METHOD ENTER crime.

Multiple R	.60128
R Square	.36154
Adjusted R Square	.34824
Standard Error	6.29819

Analysis of Variance

	DF	Sum of Squares	Mean Square
Regression	1	1078.192	1078.192
Residual	48	1904.028	39.667

F = 27.181   Signif F = .000

————— Variables in the Equation —————

Variable	B	SE B	Beta	T	Sig T
CRIME	.017	3.17E-03	.601	5.21	.000
(Constant)	15.792	1.912		8.26	.000

The standard errors for the crime parameter are listed in scientific notation.

```
COMPUTE int = lowtemp * crime.
REGRESSION /VARIABLES dropout crime lowtemp int
  /DEPENDENT dropout
  /METHOD ENTER crime lowtemp int.
```

```
Multiple R          .60950
R Square            .37149
Adjusted R Square   .33050
Standard Error     6.38335
```

Analysis of Variance

	DF	Sum of Squares	Mean Square
Regression	3	1107.85251	369.28417
Residual	46	1874.36769	40.74712
F = 9.06283		Signif F = .0001	

When you have just a few variables in your model it is worth checking for significant interactions. In the first example, with several variables in the model, most researchers would not check for interactions unless they had some specific ones in which they were interested. The reason is twofold. First, when you have several variables, you end up with lots of interactions to test. You would begin by testing each pair of variables, and then each group of three, and so on. With those regressions there is already a serious problem of some effects appearing large by chance (Type I error) and failing to detect the presence of effects that are substantial (Type II error). Adding in the interactions compounds this. The second reason why researchers do not include interactions in those circumstances is that those regressions are exploratory. All that is required of them is a rough feel for how the predictor variables relate to the response variable. Interactions are more complex and usually not of as much interest in exploratory research as main effects. Over the next few pages you will read much more on interactions and when they are of use.

ANCOVA

The analysis of covariance, or ANCOVA, is a technique that can be considered to be based either on multiple regression or on ANOVA. However, it is probably simpler to consider it as a type of multiple regression. An ANCOVA is usually used when the researcher wants to compare the means of a variable for a number of groups but partialling out the influence of another variable (or variables). These other variables are called the *covariates*. Conceptually this is identical to the previous example, where we explored the relationship between record low temperature and dropout rate, partialling out the crime rate.

Consider the following example from Gaskell *et al.* (1995). One hundred and eighty-one respondents were given a difficult quiz on physical science topics and then were asked how interested they were in science. Another group of respondents ($n = 285$) were asked the interest question and then given the science quiz. Gaskell *et al.* were interested in whether the mean interest scores depended on whether the quiz was asked before the interest question. Almost all research into the relationship between scientific knowledge and scientific interest shows high positive correlations. The researchers wanted to take into account the knowledge scores to get a clearer picture of the influence of the question order. If the response variable and a *covariate* have a high positive correlation, then the ANCOVA procedure is usually more powerful than simply using a *t* test or oneway ANOVA.[4]

The equations we are comparing are

$$interest_i = \beta_1 right_i + \beta_0 + e_i$$
$$interest_i = \beta_1 right_i + \beta_2 order_i + \beta_0 + e_i$$
$$interest_i = \beta_1 right_i + \beta_2 order_i + \beta_3 (right_i * order_i) + \beta_0 + e_i$$

The first equation uses only the number of correct responses (the variable *right*) to predict interest. The second additionally uses the question order (0, quiz first; 1, interest question first). The difference between the fit of these two models is the effect of *order*, controlling for, or partialling out, the number of correct answers. The third model adds a variable to measure the difference in the slopes of the regression lines for the groups. The term *right*order* is the two variables multiplied together. Comparing this equation with the second equation tests whether this interaction is significant.[5]

In the first equation, β_0 is the intercept and β_1 is the slope (Figure 8.4a). In the second equation, β_0 is the intercept for the people given the quiz first. β_2 is the difference between this intercept and the intercept for those given the quiz last. It was hypothesised that β_2 would be positive because, having answered a rather difficult quiz, people would become less interested in science. In the second equation, β_1 is the slope for both groups (Figure 8.4b). The assumption is that the regression lines for the two groups are parallel. This is sometimes called a parallel slope ANCOVA. In the third equation, β_1 is the slope for those asked the quiz first and β_3 is the difference between this and the slope for the others (Figure 8.4c). It was hypothesised that β_3 could be negative, indicating a stronger relationship between the number of correct responses for those answering the quiz first (because respondents would have become aware of how knowledgeable they were and could have used this to infer their interest).

The computer code and selected output are below. In this example, both the covariate (`right`) and `order` clearly help to predict the interest. Thus, Gaskell *et al.* concluded that difficult knowledge questions can lower interest ratings.

---

4 The reason is that the significance is based on the amount accounted for as a proportion of what remains unexplained by the covariate(s) (like the partial correlation). If the amount left to explain is smaller, then this ratio will be higher as long as the covariate is not also highly correlated with which group the person is in (that is, as long as collinearity is not a problem).

5 In this example there were only two groups. In general, if there had been *k* groups, then *k* − 1 dummy variables would have been needed for the second equation to represent the *k* groups, and there would have had to be *k* − 1 interaction terms (each dummy variable multiplied by the covariate).

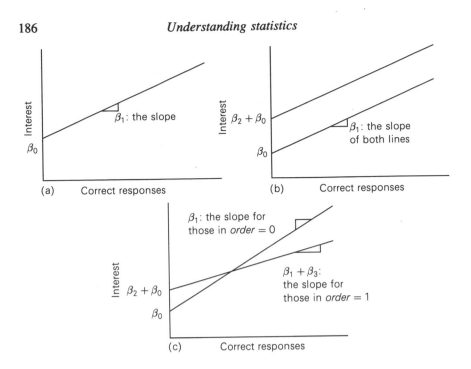

Figure 8.4   *Graphs of the equations for the science data based on Gaskell et al.*
             (1995)

Including the interaction did not greatly increase the adjusted R^2. They concluded that the effect of order was not dependent on the number of correct responses.

```
COMPUTE int = order * right.
REGRESS /VARIABLES interest order right int   /DEPEND interest
   /METHOD ENTER right
   /METHOD ENTER order
   /METHOD ENTER int.
```

Adjusted R Square	.19196	First model

———————————— Variables in the Equation ————————————

Variable	B	SE B	Beta	T	Sig T
RIGHT	.43391	.04110	.44012	10.558	.0000
(Constant)	1.98304	.08641		22.949	.0000

Adjusted R Square	.21920	Second model

———————————— Variables in the Equation ————————————

Variable	B	SE B	Beta	T	Sig T
RIGHT	.43645	.04040	.44269	10.802	.0000
ORDER	.45783	.11044	.16989	4.146	.0000
(Constant)	1.69890	.10914		15.566	.0000

Variable	B	SE B	Beta	T	Sig T
RIGHT	.49339	.06544	.50044	7.540	.0000
ORDER	.60835	.17525	.22575	3.471	.0006
INT	-.09199	.08318	-.09171	-1.106	.2693
(Constant)	1.60484	.13835		11.600	.0000

Adjusted R Square   .21958   Third model
———————————— Variables in the Equation ————————————

This example is fairly simple to interpret because the variable whose effect was investigated, the variable `order`, was experimentally determined. Basically, a random half of the sample were asked the knowledge questions first, and the remainder were asked these questions after the interest question. As discussed in Chapter 1, random allocation is a very important aspect in order to attribute causality.

The ANCOVA design is often used in non-experimental research where the groups that you want to compare occur naturally. Sometimes researchers treat ANCOVA as if it is a replacement for random allocation that somehow gets over the problems encountered when random allocation is impossible. This simply is not true, although ANCOVA does let you focus more specifically on some aspects of the data. This can present various interpretational difficulties.

Consider the hypothetical data in Figure 8.5. Two groups of five children were tested on an arithmetic task (higher scores being better). One group had language difficulties, the other were 'normal'. The researcher also measured general intelligence (higher scores being better). Suppose you were asked which group had higher scores on the arithmetic test. Comparing means would reveal, not surprisingly, that the 'normal' children have *higher* scores. However, the overall intelligence measure is presumably correlated with the arithmetic score and therefore partialling out this variable should give a clearer indication of the group differences. Suppose you were asked which group had the higher scores

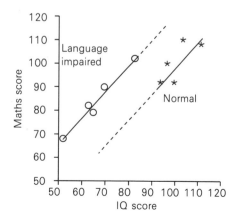

Figure 8.5 *Trying to decide the relationship between aptitude in arithmetic and language deficit*

once the intelligence score was partialled out (here using the parallel slope ANCOVA model like the second equation above). Now you find the children with language difficulties do better. This is indicated by the line for the language-impaired children being higher than the line for normal children. At each IQ level, you would predict a child with language impairment to do better on the arithmetic test than a child without language impairment.

To understand what is going on with these data, it is important to note that in Figure 8.5 I have drawn solid lines for the predicted values within the range of the intelligence scores for each group. I have drawn dotted lines beyond this. This extrapolation assumes that this same linear pattern would continue. Often, if the researcher feels that the intelligence score will be an important predictor of the arithmetic score, s/he will 'match' children on this: choosing pairs of children with similar intelligence scores but where one had language difficulties and one did not. This still leaves problems as the language-impaired children would then probably be older than the other children or be in some way atypical of language-impaired children.

Even if we assume that these problems can be properly addressed, we are still faced with an interpretational problem: which group is better? This really depends on the question that is being asked and on the assumptions made about the measures. There are no easy answers. It is important, if possible, to separate the predictor variables as much as possible. Here, the intelligence variable is probably measuring both language and arithmetic performance. The researcher might wish to be more selective about which abilities should be measured for the covariate. Sometimes in ANCOVA problems researchers use a variable that is measuring something very similar to the predictor variable of interest. Because they partial out the covariate, they are essentially also throwing out part of the variable of interest. The phrase 'throwing the baby out with the bathwater' is sometimes used to describe this, although it is perhaps more macabre than the way I usually like to think of ANCOVA.

Multivariable ANOVA

In Chapter 6, two types of ANOVA were introduced. The first was a between-subjects ANOVA in which the scores of one variable were compared across a number of groups. The second was where the scores of a number of variables were compared, a within-subject design. Here I expand these options. There are a large number of different techniques that fall under the general heading of analysis of variance. The next section describes cases where there are multiple groups and the groups can be described by more than one factor. The concept of interaction is important and is described in some detail. Next, I take a similar step for the within-subject designs. Finally, some designs have both between- and within-subject factors. I describe each of these only briefly; for a more complete treatment you should consult Stevens (1992).

Box 8.2   Path Analysis and Structural Equation Modelling

Path analysis refers to a framework for describing theories. It can be particularly helpful in identifying specific hypotheses to test. Figure 8.6 shows how a criminologist might conceptualise the relationships between population, dropout rate, crime (per capita) and the proportion of the population in prison. Single-headed arrows represent a single direction of causation. Thus, according to this figure, the dropout rate has a causal influence on crime, but not vice versa (this could be argued against, but let us suppose it to be so). Double-headed arrows would indicate that the influence may be in both/either direction.

In Figure 8.6 the researcher has hypothesised only an indirect influence of population on prison population. It influences crime which influences prison rate. Suppose the criminologist was interested in whether the population had an influence on the per capita prison population beyond the influence of the crime rate. It is the dotted line that is being investigated. To examine this s/he would use the crime rate to predict the prison rate, and then see if there was any additional influence of the population. Conceptually this is the same as an ANCOVA. More complex path models can be built up using the same basic logic, examining the influence of a specific part of the framework.

One advance in these models is allowing *latent variables*. The variables we measure are called observed or manifest variables. We often hypothesise that these stand for unobserved or latent variables. Usually we measure lots of different manifest variables in order to estimate a latent variable. In the case of crime, we might measure ten variables about different types of crime that would stand for the latent variable 'crime'. We can then hypothesise causal relationships between these latent variables. This approach has become known as structural equation modelling or the LISREL approach (LISREL is the name of one of the most popular programs for this approach and is often used to describe the method; EQS is the other most popular). These techniques are beyond the scope of this book (see Hoyle, 1995).

A word of warning about these methods. You will probably read or have read papers where they are used. Often the writers say how the results demonstrate causal influences. The equations for structural equation modelling (usually) work just on the correlations (or covariances) between the variables. As I said at the end of Chapter 5, correlation does not imply causation. In reading some papers it seems as if researchers either have forgotten this adage, or believe the great complexity of the mathematics behind this approach means that magically the adage no longer applies. Well, it does still apply.

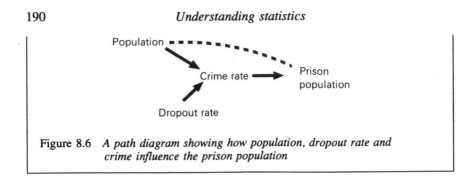

Figure 8.6 *A path diagram showing how population, dropout rate and crime influence the prison population*

Factorial Between-subjects Designs

This procedure is appropriate when you want to compare a single variable for multiple groups. Recall the snooker data from Chapter 6, where the maximum number of shots planned in advance was recorded for expert, intermediate and novice snooker players. Abernethy *et al.* (1994) asked only male snooker players to participate, but suppose that both males and females had been asked. The data might perhaps look like those in Table 8.1. Now there are 46 players, 28 of whom are male and 18 female.

This is referred to as a 3 × 2 between-subjects ANOVA. The 3 means that one of the variables (skill) has three different values or levels. The 2 refers to gender having two possible values. The logic of this is the same as for the oneway ANOVAs. There is an overall measure of error: the sum of squared deviations from the overall or grand mean (here 6.15). We then use these variables (skill and gender) to help predict the scores and account for this error.

In addition to the two variables, researchers usually also look for an interaction between variables. *Interaction* is a strange word. In English it can have lots of different meanings. In statistics it has a very specific meaning. In this problem we would say there is an interaction if the effect of, for example, skill level depended on the gender of the player. In the scientific knowledge/ interest example of the previous section, the interaction occurred if the effect of order was the same at different levels of knowledge.

Figure 8.7 shows the means for each of these six groups. The most noticeable differences are for the skill levels. The novices do not plan as many shots ahead as the more experienced players. The pattern looks a little different for men and women. For men, once they reach intermediate levels, they have reached their

Table 8.1 *Example data for a 3 × 2 between-subjects ANOVA. The scores refer to the maximum number of snooker shots planned ahead for males and females of three different skill levels*

	Skill level		
	Experts	Intermediates	Novices
Males	4, 8, 6, 11, 9, 8	11, 7, 3, 8, 14, 11, 10	4, 3, 7, 4, 6, 2, 3, 2, 7, 4, 3, 5, 4, 4, 4
Females	9, 9, 14, 11, 9	6, 7, 7, 8, 5	2, 3, 2, 5, 3, 5, 4, 2

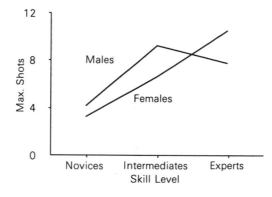

Figure 8.7   *The mean number of shots planned ahead, broken down by gender and skill*

highest point in 'thinking ahead', while expert women appear to think more shots ahead than intermediate women. This difference in pattern reflects an interaction. If there was no interaction, the lines would be parallel. Figures 8.8a–c give some examples of common interactions. Figure 8.8d shows an example where there is no interaction, although both main effects appear fairly large.

In SPSS there are several ways to run an analysis of variance. The ANOVA and MANOVA (which stands for Multivariate ANalysis Of VAriance) procedures have the same basic structure and the MANOVA can be used for the other procedures in this section.[6] Therefore I will use it. It has the same basic structure as the ONEWAY command introduced in Chapter 6. The REGRESSION procedure could also have been used (making two dummy variables for skill and two interaction variables by multiplying these by gender). Below are the syntax and output for this procedure. The variable names are shots (the maximum number of shots planned ahead), gender (0 for males, 1 for females) and skill (0 novices, 1 intermediates and 2 experts).

The first thing to note is that the adjusted R^2 value says that about 60% of the variation in the maximum number of shots planned ahead can be accounted for by these variables. The F value of the model is 13.63, which with five degrees of freedom is statistically significant. The ANOVA table further subdivides the model, giving the significance of the interaction ($F(2,40) = 4.76$, $p = 0.01$), gender ($F(1,40) = 0.12$, $p = 0.73$) and skill ($F(2,40) = 28.92$, $p < 0.001$). From these we can tell that that there is an interaction, that there is no overall main effect for gender (although gender does make a difference as is shown by the interaction) and that the number of planned shots depends on the skill. The effect size measures tell us how important each of these variables is in substantive terms. The main effect of skill is the largest.

---

6   If you are using SPSS for Windows, you need to use the GENERAL FACTORIAL option which activates the MANOVA procedure. The multivariate option, which also uses the MANOVA algorithm, is not appropriate for between-subjects ANOVAs.

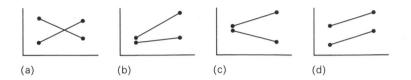

(a)   (b)   (c)   (d)

Figure 8.8   *Types of interaction: (a) a crossover interaction similar to what*
was observed with the snooker data; (b) an interaction that is due
to one condition being different from the others; (c) an interaction
where the groups are the same in one condition but not in the
other; (d) no interaction

MANOVA shots   BY gender(0 1) skill(0 2)
  /PRINT SIGNIF(EFSIZE).

Source of Variation	SS	DF	MS	F	Sig of F
WITHIN+RESIDUAL	173.82	40	4.35		
GENDER	.53	1	.53	.12	.728
SKILL	251.39	2	125.69	28.92	.000
GENDER BY SKILL	41.38	2	20.69	4.76	.014
(Model)	296.11	5	59.22	13.63	.000
(Total)	469.93	45	10.44		

R-Squared =   .630
Adjusted R-Squared =   .584

Effect Size Measures

Source of Variation	Partial ETA Sqd
GENDER	.003
SKILL	.591
GENDER BY SKILL	.192

Within-subject ANOVA

In within-subject designs, each person is measured on several variables. This is a
fairly common procedure in time series studies in economics and in experiments
in psychology. Table 8.2 shows some hypothetical data from a food preference
experiment. Five volunteers were asked to rate the taste of nine different mineral
waters. The water was either normal tap water, non-sparkling mineral water, or
sparkling mineral water. Each of these had no food colouring, a 'touch' of
orange food colouring, or the amount of food colouring that makes it look like
an orange-flavoured soft drink. The researcher was interested in how the food
colouring affected preference and if this differed for the three water types.

    Recall from Chapter 6 that within-subjects ANOVAs work by modelling the
deviation of each score from the overall mean for that person. The interest is not

Table 8.2   *Taste ratings of different waters for five different people*

Water type	Tap water			Non-sparkling			Sparkling			
Colouring	None	Some	Lots	None	Some	Lots	None	Some	Lots	Mean
Subject 1	3	2	1	4	3	2	3	6	2	2.89
Subject 2	5	4	2	3	4	2	4	7	4	3.89
Subject 3	4	5	2	5	2	1	3	6	2	3.33
Subject 4	3	3	3	3	2	1	4	5	5	3.22
Subject 5	2	4	2	4	3	3	5	6	4	3.67
Means	3.4	3.6	2.0	3.8	2.8	1.8	3.8	6.0	3.4	3.40

in differences between people, but how the scores of the different variables differ for each individual. The interest is with deviations 'within' the individual.

Nine different drinks were tasted by each person, so there are nine variables. It is useful to think of these as being based on two *factors*: water type and colouring. Each of these factors has three *levels*. We call this design a 3×3 within-subject design. As with the within-subject ANOVAs in Chapter 6, confidence intervals can also be constructed by subtracting the subject's mean from their responses and then adding the grand mean. The SPSS code for this problem, along with edited output, is shown below (the variable names are in the order printed in Table 8.2). SPSS prints a great deal of information with this. I briefly comment on some of this below, but interested readers are urged to see Stevens (1992). Also, there are many additional features of the MANOVA procedure that can be used, some of which were discussed in Chapter 6.

The significant interaction is due to the colouring having a different effect on the sparkling mineral water than on the other waters: a small amount of colouring helps the sparkling water, but not the other two. The two main effects are also worth noting. The significant effect of water type says that, averaged over the three colour levels, the waters are rated differently; here the sparkling water is rated best. Similarly, averaged over the water types, the colours differ: 'some' has the highest rating. However, it is important to include a qualifying phrase like 'averaged over. . .' so that it is clear that the effects of one factor may depend on the level of another.

Mixed Between-subjects and Within-subject Designs

There are many situations in which both between-subjects and within-subject effects are of interest. In the previous section, the food colouring only seemed to be useful for the sparkling water. The researcher would probably want to investigate this further. In particular, suppose that there was an interest in whether the effect was different for males and females. Suppose a researcher had ten males and ten females taste the sparkling water at the three different colour levels. Suppose also that the means for males were 3.1, 4.2 and 2.4, for none,

```
MANOVA tn ts tl nn ns nl sn ss sl
  /WSFACTORS water (3) colour (3).
```

Tests of Between-Subjects Effects.

Source of Variation	SS	DF	MS	F	Sig of F
WITHIN CELLS	5.47	4	1.37		
CONSTANT	520.20	1	520.20	380.63	.000

Tests involving 'WATER' Within-Subject Effect.
  Mauchly sphericity test, W = .95183
  Chi-square approx. =   .14810 with 2 D. F.
  Significance =   .929

  Greenhouse-Geisser Epsilon = .95404
  Huynh-Feldt Epsilon =   1.00000
  Lower-bound Epsilon =   .50000

Tests involving 'WATER' Within-Subject Effect.

Source of Variation	SS	DF	MS	F	Sig of F
WITHIN CELLS	9.20	8	1.15		
WATER	22.80	2	11.40	9.91	.007

Tests involving 'COLOUR' Within-Subject Effect.

Source of Variation	SS	DF	MS	F	Sig of F
WITHIN CELLS	6.53	8	.82		
COLOUR	24.13	2	12.07	14.78	.002

Tests involving 'WATER BY COLOUR' Within-Subject
Effect.

Source of Variation	SS	DF	MS	F	Sig of F
WITHIN CELLS	11.60	16	.73		
WATER BY COLOUR	13.07	4	3.27	4.51	.013

The output begins with the between-subjects factors. In this example there were none, so this just says that the grand mean is not zero.

As with the within-subject ANOVAs of Chapter 6, the sphericity should be checked. It is applicable for both factors and the interaction. None was significant so the epsilon corrections were not needed.

some and lots, respectively, and were 4.7, 5.8 and 3.4 for females. The syntax and selected output (as with the other within-subject ANOVAs, tests of sphericity and the multivariate statistics are also reported for factors with more than two levels) of this hypothetical study are shown below. This shows that there is a significant main effect for gender $(F(1, 18) = 9.18, p = 0.007)$ indicating that, on average, females liked the mixtures more. There is also a significant main effect for colour $(F(2, 36) = 31.36, p < 0.001)$, but the interaction between these factors is non-significant. In other words, we would not reject the hypothesis that colour has the same effect for males and females. We would reject the other two hypotheses, that males and females, on average, like these drinks equally, and that the colour does not make a difference.

```
MANOVA none  some  lots BY gender (0 1)
  /WSFACTORS colour(3).
```

Tests of Between-Subjects Effects.

Source of Variation	SS	DF	MS	F	Sig of F
WITHIN CELLS	57.67	18	3.20		
GENDER	29.40	1	29.40	9.18	.007

Tests involving 'COLOUR' Within-Subject Effect.

Source of Variation	SS	DF	MS	F	Sig of F
WITHIN CELLS	25.33	36	.70		
COLOUR	44.13	2	22.07	31.36	.000
GENDER BY COLOUR	1.20	2	.60	.85	.435

Summary of ANOVA

While the ANOVAs presented in this section are a step up in complexity from those presented in Chapter 6, it is worth making clear that researchers will often design studies with four or five different factors or grouping variables. This increase in complexity can be easily dealt with by most ANOVA computer procedures. This apparent ease can be problematic. It is important to realise that by increasing the number of factors/variables, the models become more complex, and therefore more difficult to interpret. Suppose you have three between-subjects variables and two within-subject ones. This means your full model (the default in most packages) will test for five main effects, ten pairwise, or two-way, interactions (for the ten possible pairings), ten three-way interactions, five four-way interactions and one five-way interaction: 31 in total. Further, each of these 31 effects could itself be quite complex if there are more than two levels for any of the factors.

The p values quoted by most packages assume that each individual effect is the only one being tested. In most cases this is not true. Therefore it is important to be cautious when interpreting the significance of these (and, as I have stated in several places, do not worry too much about the exact p values). It is usual practice to begin by seeing if the highest-order interactions are significant, and then progressing to the lower-order effects and finally the main effects. This is done because if there is a significant interaction, any lower-order effects would have to be described carefully (since their effects depend on levels of another variable). This said, it is not obviously clear that this approach is always optimal. If you have specific research questions, and translate these into specific codings, then this is preferable. It is the fact that ANOVA models are easy enough to run with modern computer programs that has led many people to forget the important stage of thinking about how the research questions translate into statistical ones.

Analysing Categorical Variables

In the past few decades use of techniques for categorical variables has increased dramatically. Much of this popularity is due to the pioneering work of the sociologist and statistician Leo Goodman (see, for example, Goodman, 1978). Others, for example Agresti, Benzécri, Clogg, the GIFI group (de Leeuw, Van der Meer and others), Greenacre, Haberman, Hagenaars and Kruskal, have also made notable contributions. In much of this work there is a philosophical message about data and theory (this is probably most exemplified by GIFI). There is the notion that all data are categorical or nominal. A single datum either has a value or it does not have this value. The scales, or the metrics, that are often imposed are characteristics of our theories of the world, not the data. Accordingly, data analysts should always begin without any scale assumptions and allow the data to impose these characteristics if empirically justified. This is a radical approach, given that most scientists are engulfed in theories and use data for theory evaluation (and base their statistical tests on their theory-based ideas). This radical approach, however, could prevent many of the mistakes that occur when scientists do not let the data 'speak' for themselves.

This said, I personally am more driven by theory than by data. The techniques I describe do not carry as strong a philosophical message as above. I do recommend, for example, the GIFI system (which includes the ANACOR program discussed in Chapter 7) for exploring and graphing the relationships. It is most valuable when used in conjunction with methods based on the traditional approaches (see Goodman, 1991; Van der Heijden *et al.*, 1989).

Loglinear Modelling with Three Variables

In Exercise 5 of Chapter 7 you were asked to examine the relationship between people's choice of Gulf War analogy (Hitler or Vietnam) by when the survey took place. There was interest in whether the choice of analogy was different before the war compared with during the war. Table 8.3 shows how this broke down by age. I have split the age variable into those born after 1945 and those born in 1945 or earlier (this choice is based more on these people being in a critical stage of their own social and political development during the Vietnam

Table 8.3 *Young and old people's preferences for Gulf War analogy, before and during the war (column percentages are within parentheses)*

| | Before war | | During war | | |
	≤1945	>1945	≤1945	>1945	Row totals
Hitler analogy	249 (65%)	274 (51%)	78 (85%)	190 (80%)	791 (63%)
Vietnam analogy	134 (35%)	264 (49%)	14 (15%)	47 (20%)	459 (37%)
Column Totals	383	538	92	237	1250

War, than being born after World War II). I have estimated these numbers from Schuman and Rieger (1992: Figure 1).

This problem is much like those discussed in Chapter 7, but instead of there being two variables, there are now three: when the survey occurred, when the respondents were born, and which analogy they preferred. The loglinear models like those introduced in Chapter 7 can be used with three or more variables. This generality is why, like the multiple regression, loglinear modelling is very useful.

In this table there are eight separate pieces of information corresponding to the eight cell frequencies: eight degrees of freedom to play with. All the row and column totals can be calculated from these. The first thing to do is decide which bits of information we are *not* interested in. We then include these in our initial model and examine the effects of adding in the information in which we are interested. This gives us a measure of the importance of these pieces of information.

We are usually not interested in the overall number of people who were surveyed. Here, we are also not interested in the fact that more people were interviewed before than during the war. We probably are also not interested in the overall breakdown of respondents' ages, nor whether there is an interaction between age and when the survey took place. We can describe these as the intercept, the main effect of age, the main effect of time, and the interaction of age and time. Because each of these variables has only two categories, they can each be described by a single dummy variable. Therefore, four degrees of freedom are used in this *baseline model*.

The baseline model for this example can be denoted as {age, time, age by time} for the two main effects and the interaction (it is assumed that the overall sample size is included in the models). Sometimes this is denoted as {age*time} and called the *generating class*. Using this notation, generating classes automatically include any main effects mentioned in the highest-order term. In general, the terms denoted in the generating class notation include all lower-order terms. Thus, {age*time*analogy} is the same as {age, time, analogy, age by time, age by analogy, time by analogy, age by time by analogy}. As you can see, the generating class notation is a useful shorthand. In most cases if you are including an interaction you want to include all the lower-order terms in the model.

To find the predicted values for this model we simply put the information included in the model into the table and calculate the predictions in a manner similar to that used in Chapter 7. In this case the four pieces of information are the column totals listed in Table 8.3. Our prediction is simply that these are split equally between the two choices. Table 8.4 shows the predicted values.

We calculate the χ^2 value in the same way as in Chapter 7. It is preferable to use $L\chi^2$ in these situations because it can be decomposed (this will be explained shortly):

$$L\chi^2 = 2 \sum \left(249 \ln \frac{249}{191.5} + 274 \ln \frac{274}{269} + \ldots + 47 \ln \frac{47}{118.5} \right) = 176.80$$

Table 8.4   *The predicted values for the baseline model, {age*time}*

	Before war		During war	
	≤1945	>1945	≤1945	>1945
Hitler analogy	191.5 (50%)	269 (50%)	46 (50%)	118.5 (50%)
Vietnam analogy	191.5 (50%)	269 (50%)	46 (50%)	118.5 (50%)
Totals	383	538	92	237

This is a measure of the residuals. As there are eight degrees of freedom in total, and four in the model, this leaves four in the residual. The value $L\chi^2$ is highly significant (that is, $p < 0.001$). Therefore, the baseline model does not fit the data. We must decide what to add to the baseline model. As with the regression and ANOVA procedures, we could have added all the variables in and worked backwards by removing terms. It is worth trying several approaches. The first piece of information we add is the main effect for analogy. It results in $L\chi^2 = 87.55$, which with three degrees of freedom is significant. To compare this with the previous model we calculate the difference between the two χ^2 values to get 89.25. Because there is only one degree of freedom difference, we compare this with the χ^2 distribution with df $= 1$ and see that it is highly significant. This means that the proportion choosing each analogy is different.

We know from Exercise 5 in Chapter 7 that the choice of analogy varied by when the survey was conducted. We add this information into the model. We could instead have added whether the choice varied by the age of the respondent. These are labelled models 3 and 4, respectively, in Table 8.5. To see if these are significant we subtract their χ^2 values from model 2. Essentially what we are doing is decomposing the original 176.80, the original measure of the residuals, into the amount accounted for by each of the effects. Both of these differences are significant, meaning they should be included in the model. This is a characteristic of $L\chi^2$. The difference between two $L\chi^2$ values can be compared with the χ^2 distribution. The number of degrees of freedom is equal to the difference in degrees of freedom of the two models.

From Table 8.5 we would conclude that both age and when the survey took place are useful for predicting the analogy: older people were more likely to opt

Table 8.5   *Comparing models for data in Table 8.3*

	Generating class	$L\chi^2$ (df)	Change in $L\chi^2$	Effect measured
1	{age*time}	176.80 (4)	–	
2	{age*time, analogy}	87.55 (3)	m1–m2 = 89.25	analogy
3	{age*time, time*analogy}	19.20 (2)	m2–m3 = 68.35	time by analogy
4	{age*time, age*analogy}	77.24 (2)	m2–m4 = 10.31	age by analogy
5	{age*time, age*analogy, time*analogy}	0.52 (1)	m3–m5 = 18.68	age by analogy
6	{age*time*analogy}	0 (0)	m5–m6 = 0.52	age by time by analogy

for the Hitler analogy as were people during the war. The final effect added is age by time by analogy. To test its significance you subtract model 5 from model 6. The difference (0.52) is non-significant with one degree of freedom. Therefore we do not reject the hypothesis that the change from before the war to during the war was different for younger and older people.

Logistic Regression

In the previous example, there was one particular variable that could be considered the response variable: which analogy the person felt was most appropriate. Conceptually, we can think of this as a type of regression in which we use the other variables (age and time) to predict the choice of analogy. If we tried using the multiple linear regression that was introduced earlier in this chapter to predict the proportion of each condition responding with each analogy, we would run into the problem that our predicted values could correspond to values greater than one or less than zero. Because neither of these can actually happen for a proportion (which can only range between zero and one), it is desirable to restrict the predicted values to the potential range of observed values.

In order to constrain the predicted values to within these limits we use the *logit* transformation. If *prop* is the proportion in one cell, then

$$\text{logit}(prop) = \ln\left(\frac{prop}{1 - prop}\right)$$

While *prop* can only range from zero to one, logit(*prop*) can range from $-\infty$ to $+\infty$, which is appropriate for the regressions discussed. For analysing the data in Table 8.5, logistic regressions will produce equivalent results to the loglinear models that include the terms age, time and age by time.

Logistic regressions have some advantages over the basic loglinear framework because they bring out several interesting parallels with the regressions which have already been discussed. One of the main researchers in this field described this as a 'modified multiple regression approach' (Goodman, 1972: 28). One advantage it has over the basic loglinear approach is the ability to include both categorical and continuous predictor variables. In this way it is like the earlier regressions. While the algorithms usually used to solve these are different, conceptually it is worth thinking of logistic regressions as regressions in which the response variable has only two values.[7]

---

7 In actuality, both loglinear modelling and logistic regression are more flexible than I am suggesting. I am focusing on their standard usage and how they can be used within SPSS without much extra effort. Logistic regressions, for example, can be used with response variables that have more than two possible values, but their main use is with binary response variables and this is the only situation that I discuss here.

In Exercise 4 of Chapter 7 you examined data from a study by Nightingale (1993) on verdicts in a civil liability case. A girl was hit by a truck and the mock jurors had to decide whether the driver was negligent. I slightly simplified that example. Half of these jurors read that an eyewitness saw the child 'at the curb by the cross-walk shortly before the accident' (Nightingale, 1993: 683). The data, broken down by the victim's age, whether there was a corroborating witness and whether the juror thought the driver was negligent, are shown in Table 8.6. Nightingale was interested in whether there was an effect by age, by whether there was a witness, and in whether the effects of these depended on the level of the other (that is, the interaction).

The LOGISTIC REGRESSION procedure in SPSS allows both categorical and continuous variables in the model to predict a binary (that is, two-category) response variable. The variable negli is whether the juror thought the driver was negligent. The * in the /METHOD command tells the computer that the age by corrob interaction is included (that is, it means 'by'). The /CONTRAST command tells the computer that these variables are categorical and describes the coding that is desired. Deviation is one of the more popular choices of coding. It compares each of the values of a variable with the final value of the variable. Thus, if a variable has three values, the first contrast would compare the first value with the third value. The second contrast would compare the second with the third. You can use the /CONTRAST command for other coding schemes or create your own.

The first line gives the Wald statistic for the effect of age. Its significance can be looked up in the χ^2 table. In this case it is not significant. The next two lines give the effects for the two age dummy variables (because there are three age categories, it is described by two dummy variables). The first compares age 6 with age 12, the next age 9 with age 12. These are also non-significant, as are the remaining effects, except for the constant (which is significant since there were many more 'negligent' verdicts than 'not negligent' verdicts). Given these results, the researcher would not reject any of the null hypotheses about the effects of age and having a corroborating witness.[8]

Table 8.6   *Whether Nightingale's mock jurors felt the truck driver was negligent (adapted from Nightingale, 1993: Table 1)*

	Age of victim						
	6		9		12		
Witness	No	Yes	No	Yes	No	Yes	Total
Negligence							
Yes	17	25	22	17	14	20	115 (64%)
No	14	6	10	12	13	9	64 (36%)

8   Nightingale (1993) also looked at criminal cases. When all the data were used, some of the effects were significant.

```
LOGISTIC REGRESSION negli
  /METHOD=ENTER age corrob age*corrob
  /CONTRAST (age)=DEVIATION  /CONTRAST (corrob)=DEVIATION.
```

The main part of the resulting output is the estimates of the parameters.

——————————————— Variables in the Equation ———————————————

Variable	B	S.E.	Wald	df	Sig	R	Exp(B)
AGE			.8868	2	.6418	.0000	
AGE(1)	.2055	.2324	.7819	1	.3766	.0000	1.2282
AGE(2)	-.0367	.2234	.0270	1	.8694	.0000	.9639
CORROB(1)	-.2529	.1611	2.4645	1	.1164	-.0446	.7766
AGE * CORROB			4.8163	2	.0900	.0591	
INT_1	-.3636	.2324	2.4473	1	.1177	-.0438	.6952
INT_2	.4729	.2234	4.4813	1	.0343	.1031	1.6047
Constant	.6051	.1611	14.1130	1	.0002		

With the loglinear modelling and with the regressions, it was shown that in many cases it is useful to add and to remove effects to test specific hypotheses. The same can be done with the logistic regression procedure. It produces an overall χ^2 value which can be decomposed in the same way as with the loglinear model.

Graphing Three Variables

In Chapter 7 I showed how graphical analysis was useful in examining Gaskell *et al.*'s (1993) results about what the British public thought science meant. Recall that the previous questions influenced what 'came to mind'. They were also interested in examining differences between males and females, and across age categories. Table 8.7 shows the data for their subjects who were not given any science quiz before the 'comes to mind' question. These responses will not be contaminated by the knowledge questions. The responses are broken down by age and gender.

The standard loglinear approach yields the model {field*age, field*gender, age*gender} with $L\chi^2 = 20.45$ for the residual. The only term not in this is the three-way interaction age by field by gender. The number of degrees of freedom for this term and therefore the residual of the model is 15. The value is not significant. However, with $L\chi^2 = 20.45$, there still is some discrepancy between the model and the observations. It is not significant because of having 15 degrees of freedom (see Figure 7.1 for the effect of degrees of freedom on the necessary $L\chi^2$ for achieving significance). There are some complex statistical procedures that allow this to be decomposed, taking into account, for example, that the variable age is ordinal (see Clogg and Shihadeh, 1994, for a detailed treatment of dealing with ordinal variables with the loglinear approach). Here I simply show how this information can be graphically presented.

Table 8.7   *The responses to 'What comes to mind when science is*
mentioned?' broken down by age and gender (Gaskell et al., 1993)

| | What comes to mind | | | | | | | |
| | Physical science | | Life science | | Technology | | Other | |
	Male	Female	Male	Female	Male	Female	Male	Female
15–24	47	43	25	37	26	9	7	10
25–34	43	44	20	41	35	10	11	20
35–44	29	42	33	34	25	8	14	17
45–54	21	21	19	41	21	8	15	15
55–64	33	16	14	29	16	5	15	31
65+	12	22	11	41	8	8	19	31

In the last chapter I showed how ANACOR (ANAlysis of CORrespondences) could be used to present categorical data graphically for two variables. In this section I show how this can be extended to three variables. There are other techniques within the GIFI system (and SPSS) that are designed for multiple variables: HOMALS (HOMogeneity analysis using Alternating Least Squares) and PRINCALS (PRINCipal components analysis using Alternating Least Squares). These are described in detail in van de Geer (1993b: Chapters 2 and 4). I will stay with the ANACOR procedure but you are encouraged to try these other procedures.

To use ANACOR with three variables, you need to combine two of the variables. To do this, construct a new variable that incorporates both age and gender information with 12 different values. Using the techniques described in Chapter 7 you can create a plot of these data. Because the values for age are ordered, it is often useful to draw a line connecting these. This is shown in Figure 8.9. From this it is clear males are more likely to mention technology while females mention the life sciences. There is also a tendency for younger

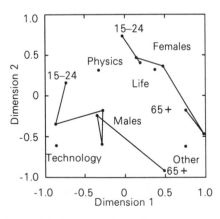

Figure 8.9   *The two-dimensional ANACOR solution for using a 12-category*
variable for gender by age

people to mention the physical sciences while the older people often mentioned other areas such as the environmental and social sciences. That the two lines show the same general pattern indicates that the three-way (age by gender by field) interaction is not large: the effect of age is similar for males and females.

Overall Summary

The techniques described in this chapter all involved simultaneously considering multiple variables. For the multiple regression, several predictor variables were used; for the ANOVA, several factors; and for loglinear modelling, several groupings. These were chosen because they are general frameworks which can be extended to even more complex techniques. These techniques are used in much social science research.

There are some other techniques which could have been presented (for a simple introduction to some other techniques, see Manly, 1994). However, if you feel comfortable with the material up to this point, you should feel comfortable reading more technical books and some of the academic journals (these vary in their readability, but a quick glance should be enough to tell).

Assignment

Questions 1–4 are to be done using the states.sps file.
1 Try to predict the salary of governors from a subset (about four or five) of the other variables. Say why you are choosing the predictor variables you choose and if any have obvious overlaps (like the size of the population and the size of the prison population). Conduct a multiple regression and plot the residuals against the predicted values. Describe what your regression means and discuss any difficulties you may have encountered and how you tried to minimise them.
2 Does the expenditure on pupils predict dropout rate when the crime rate has already been taken into account?
3 Is the crime rate different among the three main regions once the record low temperature has been accounted for? Include tests for interactions between region and low temperature. Exclude Washington, DC from this analysis but include Alaska and Hawaii. Check the residuals (which in this case are very informative).
4 Is there a difference in the change in prison population by the three regions?
5 The following data have been taken from Heath *et al.*'s (1995) analysis of the changing class–party relationship in Britain. Many people believe that the relationship between social class and party identification has become weaker over time. They looked at election surveys over the past 30 years. I have collapsed across many of their categories, and the data are shown below. The social class variable is divided into classes I to IV (class IV, the

petty bourgeoisie, includes self-employed non-professonal, farmers, etc.) and class V (foremen and technicians) to class VII. Is there any evidence of a changing relationship between class and party preference over the years?

Years	Classes I–IV (higher)			Classes V–VII (lower)		
	Tory	Labour	Liberal	Tory	Labour	Liberal
1964–1966	698	293	167	424	1084	106
1970–1974	1272	607	454	685	1546	339
1979–1983	1313	404	547	666	974	384
1987–1992	1672	608	686	659	1008	358
Totals	4955	1912	1854	2434	4612	1187

6 (optional) For the data in Exercise 5, use the ANACOR procedure and draw an appropriate graph. Use this graph to help interpret the changing relationship between class and voting preference in the UK. To do this you should create a new variable combining class and year.

Further Reading

Lewis-Beck, M. S. (ed.) (1993) *Regression analysis*. London: Sage.

Manly, B. F. J. (1994) *Multivariate statistical methods: A primer* (2nd edition). London: Chapman & Hall.

Mills, C. and Wright, D. B. (in press) *Introducing loglinear modelling*. London: Sage.

Stevens, J. (1992) *Applied multivariate statistics for the social sciences*. London: Lawrence Erlbaum Associates.

Answers to Selected Exercises

This section is included to help you to check some of your calculations. The answers you obtain should be approximately the same as these, although there may be small differences due to rounding.

Chapter 1

2   The median is 43.5 (the mean of 42 and 45).

3   The mean is 15.33, the median 16 and the mode 20.

4   The mode is the only one which makes sense.

5   The values for the equation are 5.0 for β_1 and -0.5 for β_0. The means are -0.5 for the control group and 4.5 for the experimental group.

7   The mean is 4.2, the median 4.5 and the mode 1.

Chapter 2

1   (a)   The standard deviation is 4.24.

     (b)   The resulting $z = 3.16$, which has a p value of less than 0.001.

2   (a)   The z score is 0.67 (two-thirds, so rounded up). The percentage less than this is about 25%.

     (b)   The percentage greater is about 75%.

3   (a)   The z score is 0.8, so approximately 20% of the lunch periods have this many or more.

     (c)   The new z is 2.0. This is high enough to reject the null hypothesis if you are using the conventional $\alpha = 0.05$.

4   The z value is 4 so is highly significant no matter which test is used.

8   The z scores are 2.50 and 1.67 which produce upper tails of 0.006 (that is, less than 1%) and 0.047 (about 5%).

Chapter 3

1   The statistic is non-significant, so we would not reject the hypothesis that the number of people waiting is the same in the afternoon and morning. However, regardless of whether the statistic is significant, having observed longer waits in the afternoon means you should go in the morning unless further research shows otherwise. In other words, step back from the statistics and use some common sense.

2   The difference is significant.
4   If you do a normal *t* test on these variables there are several extreme outliers (California, Hawaii, . . .). Therefore you might want to use one of the tests that do not make distributional assumptions (such as the Wilcoxon or sign test). All three tests yield significant results.
6, 7 The tests of a shift in central tendency (that is, *t* test, Wilcoxon and sign tests) all produce non-significant results. However, plotting the data shows an interesting pattern. In particular, you might have tried plotting the difference by the type of teaching method (creating a new variable with the COMPUTE command) by formal.

Chapter 4

1   The result is $t(18) = 2.84$, $p < 0.05$.
2   The politician's conclusion is not valid.
7   Yes it should influence your choice. While the mean temperatures are about the same, the standard deviations are very different. The greater standard deviation in Deserta means that you may get extremely hot or cold weather, while Tropica stays around 80 °F.

Chapter 5

1   (i) c; (ii) d; (iii) b; (iv) a.
3   The regression equation is

$$y_i = -6.80x_i + 63.55 + e_i$$

R^2 is approximately 0.58.
5, 6 Do not conclude any causal relationships from these data.
7   Note that the distribution-free correlations are the same for the untransformed and the transformed variables. This is because the distribution-free correlations are based on the ranks of the data, and the ln transformation does not change the ranks.
9   (i)   c. $\beta_0 = f$.
     (ii)   a. $\beta_0 = g$, $\beta_1 = f$.
     (ii)   d. $\beta_0 = f$, $\beta_1 = g$.
     (iv)   b. $\beta_0 = h$, $\beta_1 = f$, $\beta_2 = g$.

Chapter 6

1   The *F* value is approximately 3.43, which is significant at $p < 0.05$. *SST* is 1212.78, *SSR* is 1143.89 and by subtraction *SSM* is 68.90 (though if you find this directly you get a slightly different number due to rounding).

Chapter 7

2   (a) $L\chi^2(6) = 9.03$, $p = 0.17$ (remember to include a constant as a covariate).

(b) $L\chi^2(1) = 4.96$, $p = 0.03$ (remember to collapse the variable, include the constant as a covariate, and a cell weight, whose value is 5/2 bigger for the weekdays than for the weekend days).

4    $L\chi^2(2) = 0.64$, $p = 0.73$.

5   If the test is done without collapsing the time variable, you obtain $L\chi^2(5) = 7.19$, $p = 0.21$. However, if you collapse so that the first four codes are given the value 0 and the second two the value 1, you obtain $L\chi^2(1) = 6.10$, $p = 0.01$.

6   Depending on your release, you may get a warning message because one of the cells has a zero weight (no one over 70 thought the JFK assassination was the most important event). The computer still should run the test and give you $L\chi^2(15) = 146.91$, $p < 0.001$. If it does not, put the value 1 into the empty cell. The ANACOR should show JFK and Vietnam with the under 50s and World War II with the over 50s.

Chapter 8

3   This is a fairly tricky question. There is an apparent interaction between the covariate and region. Graph in particular the western region, as the outliers will be very apparent.

5, 6 $L\chi^2(6) = 19.35$, $p = 0.004$. Looking at the ANACOR solution, the shift appears to be due to both classes moving towards the Liberal party.

References

Abernethy, B., Neal, R. J. and Koning, P. (1994) Visual-perceptual and cognitive differences between expert, intermediate, and novice snooker players. *Applied Cognitive Psychology*, 8, 185–211.

Benzécri, J.-P. (1973) *L'Analyse des Données*. Paris: Dunod.

Blair, R. C. and Higgins, J. J. (1985) Comparison of the power of the paired samples *t*-test to that of Wilcoxon's signed-rank test under various population shapes. *Psychological Bulletin*, 97, 119–128.

Bornstein, B. H. (1994) David, Goliath, and Reverend Bayes: Prior beliefs about defendants' status in personal injury cases. *Applied Cognitive Psychology*, 8, 233–258.

Breakwell, G. M., Hammond, S. and Fife-Schaw, C. (eds) (1995) *Research Methods in Psychology*. London: Sage.

Cliff, N. (1993) Dominance statistics: Ordinal analyses to answer ordinal questions. *Psychological Bulletin*, 114, 494–509.

Clogg, C. C. and Shihadeh, E. S. (1994) *Statistical Models for Ordinal Variables*. London: Sage.

Cohen, J. (1968) Multiple regression as a general data-analytic system. *Psychological Bulletin*, 70, 426–443.

Cohen, J. (1988) *Statistical Power Analysis for the Behavioural Sciences* (2nd edn). Hillsdale, NJ: Academic Press.

Cohen, J. (1990) Things I have learned (so far). *American Psychologist*, 45, 1304–1312.

Cohen, J. (1992) A power primer. *Psychological Bulletin*, 112, 155–159.

Cohen, J. (1994) The Earth is round ($p < 0.05$). *American Psychologist*, 49, 997–1003.

Cook, T. D. and Campbell, D. T. (1979) *Quasi-experimentation: Design and Analysis Issues for Field Settings*. London: Houghton Mifflin Company.

Gaskell, G. D., Wright, D. B. and O'Muircheartaigh, C. A. (1993) Measuring scientific interest: The effect of knowledge questions on interest ratings. *Journal for the Public Understanding of Science*, 2, 39–57.

Gaskell, G. D., Wright, D. B. and O'Muircheartaigh, C. A. (1995) Context effects in the measurement of attitudes: A comparison of the consistency and framing explanations. *British Journal of Social Psychology*, 34, 383–393.

Gigerenzer, G. (1993) The superego, the ego and the id in statistical reasoning. In G. Keren and C. Lewis (eds), *A Handbook for Data Analysis in the Behavioural Sciences: Methodological issues*. Hillsdale, NJ: Lawrence Erlbaum Associates, pp. 311–339.

Goldstein, H. (1995) *Multilevel Statistical Methods* (2nd edn). London: Edward Arnold.

Goodman, L. A. (1972) A modified multiple regression approach to the analysis of dichotomous variables. *American Sociological Review*, 37, 28–46.

Goodman, L. A. (1978) *Analyzing Qualitative/Categorical Data: Log-linear Models and Latent-structure Analysis*. London: Addison-Wesley Publishing Company.

Goodman, L. A. (1991) Models, measures, and graphical displays in the analysis of contingency tables (with discussion). *Journal of the American Statistical Association*, 86, 1085–1138.

Greaney, V. and Kellaghan, T. (1984) *Equality of Opportunity in Irish Schools*. Dublin: Educational Company.

Harrison, D. and Rubinfeld, D. L. (1978) Hedonic prices and the demand for clean air. *Journal of Environmental Economics & Management*, 5, 81–102.

Heath, A., Evans, G. and Payne, C. (1995) Modelling the class–party relationship in Britain, 1964–92, *Journal of the Royal Statistical Society, A*, 158, 563–574.

Holland, P. W. (1988) Causal mechanism or causal effect: Which is best for statistical science? *Statistical Science*, 3, 186–188.

Hoyle, R. H. (ed.) (1995) *Structural Equation Modelling: Concepts, Issues and Applications*. London: Sage.

Kinnear, P. R. and Gray, C. D. (1992) *SPSS/PC+ Made Simple*. Hove: Lawrence Erlbaum Associates.

Kinnear, P. R. and Gray, C. D. (1994) *SPSS for Windows Made Simple*. Hove: Lawrence Erlbaum Associates.

Kreft, I. G. G. and de Leeuw, J. (forthcoming) *Random coefficient linear regression models* (provisional title). London: Sage.

Kubovy, M. and Psotka, J. (1976) The predominance of seven and the apparent spontaneity of numerical choices. *Journal of Experimental Psychology: Human Perception and Performance*, 2, 291–294.

Lehmann, E. L. (1993) The Fisher, Neyman–Pearson theories of testing hypotheses: One theory or two? *Journal of the American Statistical Association*, 88, 1242–1249.

Lewis-Beck, M. S. (ed.) (1993) *Regression Analysis*. London: Sage.

Loftus, E. F. and Palmer, J. C. (1974) Reconstruction of automobile destruction: An example of the interaction between language and memory. *Journal of Verbal Learning and Verbal Behavior*, 13, 585–589.

Loftus, G. R. and Masson, M. E. J. (1994) Using confidence intervals in within-subject designs. *Psychonomic Bulletin & Review*, 1, 476–490.

Lovie, A. D. (1981) On the early history of ANOVA in the analysis of repeated measure designs in psychology. *British Journal of Mathematical and Statistical Psychology*, 34, 1–15.

Manly, B. F. J. (1994) *Multivariate Statistical Methods: A Primer* (2nd edn). London: Chapman & Hall.

Mills, C. and Wright, D. B. (forthcoming) *Introducing Loglinear Modelling*. London: Sage.

Nightingale, N. N. (1993) Juror reactions to child victim witnesses: Factors affecting trial outcome. *Law and Human Behavior*, 17, 679–694.

O'Muircheartaigh, C. A., Gaskell., G. D. and Wright, D. B. (1993) Intensifiers in behavioral frequency questions. *Public Opinion Quarterly*, 57, 552–565.

Oppenheim, A. N. (1992) *Questionnaire Design, Interviewing and Attitude Measurement*. London: Pinter Publishers.

Richardson, J. T. E. (1990) Variants on chi-square for 2×2 contingency tables. *British Journal of Mathematical and Statistical Psychology*, 43, 309–327.

Scariano, S. and Davenport, J. (1987) The effects of violations of the independence assumption in the one way ANOVA. *American Statistician*, 41, 123–129.

Schuman, H. and Rieger, C. (1992) Historical analogies, generational effects, and attitudes toward war. *American Sociological Review*, 57, 315–326.

Schuman, H. and Scott, J. (1989) Generations and collective memories. *American Sociological Review*, 54, 351–381.

Serlin, R. C. and Lapsley, D. K. (1993) Rational appraisal of psychological research and the good-enough principle. In G. Keren and C. Lewis (eds), *A Handbook for Data Analysis in the Behavioral Sciences: Methodological issues*. Hillsdale, NJ: Lawrence Erlbaum Associates.

Siegel, S. and Castellan, N. J. Jr (1988) *Nonparametric Statistics for the Behavioral Sciences* (2nd edn). London: McGraw-Hill.

Simon, H. A. (1954) Spurious correlation: A causal interpretation. *Journal of the American Statistical Association*, 49, 467–479.

Stevens, J. (1992) *Applied Multivariate Statistics for the Social Sciences*. London: Lawrence Erlbaum Associates.

Stevens, S. S. (1946) On the theory of scales of measurement. *Science*, 103, 677–680.

Stevens, S. S. (1951) Mathematics, measurement and psychophysics. In S. S. Stevens (ed.), *Handbook of Experimental Psychology*. New York: Wiley, pp. 1–49.

Stewart, I. (1995) Statistical sampling. *New Scientist: Inside Science*, No. 82.

van de Geer, J. P. (1993a) *Multivariate Analysis of Categorical Data: Applications*. London: Sage.

van de Geer, J. P. (1993b) *Multivariate Analysis of Categorical Data: Theory*. London: Sage.

Van der Heijden, P. G. M., de Falguerolles, A. and de Leeuw, J. (1989) A combined approach to contingency table analysis using correspondence analysis and log-linear analysis (with discussion). *Applied Statistics*, 2, 249–292.

Wainer, H. (1984) How to display data badly. *American Statistician*, 38, 137–147.

Wilcox, R. R. (1995) ANOVA: A paradigm for low power and misleading measures of effect size? *Review of Educational Research*, 65, 51–77.

Wolter, K. M. (1991) Accounting for America's uncounted and miscounted. *Science*, 253, 12–15.

Wright, D. B. (forthcoming) *Ten Steps for Learning Statistics*. London: Sage.

Wright, D. B. and McDaid, A. T. (1996) Comparing system and estimator variables using data from real line-ups. *Applied Cognitive Psychology*, 10, 75–84.

Wright, D. B., Gaskell, G. D. and O'Muircheartaigh, C. A. (1994) How much is 'Quite a bit'? Mapping absolute values onto vague quantifiers. *Applied Cognitive Psychology*, 8, 479–496.

Zwick, R. (1993) Pairwise comparison procedures for one-way analysis of variance designs. In G. Keren and C. Lewis (eds), *A Handbook for Data Analysis in the Behavioral Sciences: Statistical issues*. Hillsdale, NJ: Lawrence Erlbaum Associates, pp. 43–71.

Appendix A
The US States Data Set

These data were gathered from *The World Almanac and Book of Facts 1992* (New York: Pharos Books). The page numbers in the value labels refer to where the data are from in the book.

```
DATA LIST FREE /state (A) dropout expend crime lowtemp mental
   popula govparty revenue area prison90 prison89 region.
VARIABLE LABELS
   dropout 'high school dropout rate p. 219'/
   expend 'expenditure per pupil p. 214'/
   crime 'violent crimes per 100,000 p. 953'/
   lowtemp 'recode low temp degrees F pp. 210-211'/
   mental 'spending per capita mental health p. 948'/
   popula 'population in 1990 p. 75'/
   govparty 'party of governor pp. 600-601'/
   revenue 'revenue 1990 in millions p. 154'/
   area 'enclosed inland area p. 386'/
   prison89 'sentence to 1 year + p. 955'/
   prison90 'sentence to 1 year + p. 955'/
   region 'region of state, from p. 939'.
VALUE LABELS govparty 0 'republican' 1 'democrat' 2
   'independent'/
         region 0 'east' 1 'central' 2 'west/mount'.
MISSING VALUE govparty revenue (-9).
BEGIN DATA

Alabama   22.3 3197  708.6 -27  29  4040587  1  9041  51705 15365 13575 1
Alaska    35.8 7716  524.5 -80  53   550043  2  5500 591004  1851  1908 2
Arizona   31.2 3902  652.4 -40  20  3665228  1  8598 114000 13781 12726 2
Arkansas  11.5 3273  532.2 -29  27  2350725  0  4511  53187  6718  6306 1
Californ  32.7 4121 1045.2 -45  37 29760021  1 88704 158706 94122 84338 2
Colorado  24.1 4408  526.4 -61  36  3294394  0  7527 104091  7018  6908 2
Connecti  16.8 6857  553.7 -32  68  3287116  2  9591   5018  7771  6309 0
Delaware  28.5 5422  655.2 -17  57   666168  1  2316   2045  2231  2284 0
Wash_DC   42.3 7850 2458.2 -15 129   606900 -9    -9     69  6660  6735 0
Florida   38.5 4563 1244.3  -2  34 12937926  0 23868  58664 44387 39966 0
Georgia   27.9 3852  756.3 -17  36  6478216  0 13108  58910 21605 19619 0
Hawaii    18.3 4121  280.9  12  25  1108229  0  4326   6471  1708  6908 2
Idaho     21.8 2838  275.7 -60  17  1006749  0  2417  83564  2074  1850 2
Illinois  21.5 4906  967.4 -35  24 11430602  1 24313  56345 27516 24712 1
Indiana   13.8 4284  473.9 -35  44  5544159  0 11456  36185 12615 12220 1
Iowa      13.6 4285  299.7 -47  32  2776755  1  6728  56275  3967  3584 1
Kansas    17.9 4443  447.7 -40  44  2477574  0  5136  82277  5777  5616 1
Kentucky  32.7 3347  390.4 -34  23  3685296  0  8593  40410  9023  8289 1
Louisian  43.1 3317  898.4 -16  25  4219973  1 10096  47752 18599 17257 1
Maine     22.5 4744  143.2 -48  63  1227928  1  3246  33265  1480  1432 0
```

Maryland	26.0	5758	919.0	-40	64	4781468	0	12195	10460 16684 15378	0
Massachu	28.0	5979	736.3	-35	62	6016425	1	17034	8284 7899 7268	0
Michigan	29.3	5116	790.4	-51	67	9295297	1	23405	58527 34267 31639	1
Minnesot	11.4	4755	306.1	-59	54	4375099	1	13162	84402 3176 3103	1
Mississi	39.9	2874	340.4	-19	22	2573216	0	5344	47689 8179 7700	1
Missouri	26.5	4263	715.3	-40	31	5117073	1	9343	69697 14919 13921	1
Montana	15.0	4293	159.3	-70	36	799065	1	2225	147046 1409 1328	2
Nebraska	13.9	4360	330.0	-47	28	1578385	0	3073	77355 2286 2278	1
Nevada	28.1	3791	600.9	-50	28	1201833	0	3266	110561 5322 5112	2
N_Hampsh	25.9	4807	131.5	-46	51	1109252	1	1922	9279 1342 1166	0
N_Jersey	20.4	7549	647.6	-34	51	7730188	0	22624	7787 21128 19439	0
N_Mexico	28.5	3473	780.2	-50	24	1515069	0	4731	121593 2879 2759	2
New_York	35.0	7663	1180.9	-52	140	17990455	0	64253	49108 54895 51227	0
N_Caroli	31.2	3874	623.5	-34	40	6628637	1	14485	52669 17713 16628	0
N_Dakota	12.1	3952	73.9	-60	42	638800	0	1810	70702 435 404	1
Ohio	24.4	4649	506.2	-39	45	10847115	1	28516	41330 31855 30538	1
Oklahoma	25.6	3379	547.5	-27	31	3145585	0	7201	69956 12322 11608	1
Oregon	29.2	5182	506.8	-54	34	2842321	0	7001	97073 6436 6744	2
Pennsylv	20.8	5609	431.0	-42	68	11881643	0	27223	45308 22281 20458	0
Rhode_Is	28.1	5976	431.9	-23	52	1003464	0	3034	1212 1585 1469	0
S_Caroli	35.0	3736	976.6	-19	44	3486703	1	8750	31113 16208 14808	0
S_Dakota	13.8	3581	162.8	-58	31	696004	1	1494	77116 1345 1252	1
Tennesse	21.3	3491	670.4	-32	36	4877185	0	9110	42144 10388 10630	1
Texas	35.8	3877	761.4	-23	21	16986510	0	30975	266807 50042 44022	1
Utah	17.9	2579	283.9	-69	33	1722850	1	4302	84899 2482 2368	2
Vermont	19.2	5481	127.2	-50	52	562758	0	1592	9614 681 626	0
Virginia	25.3	4539	350.6	-30	39	6187358	0	13607	40767 17124 16273	0
Washingt	23.6	4352	501.6	-48	36	4866692	0	14999	68139 7995 6928	2
W_Virgin	23.3	3883	169.3	-37	23	1793477	0	4435	24232 1565 1536	0
Wisconsi	18.2	5266	264.7	-54	31	4891769	1	13388	56153 7335 6775	1
Wyoming	23.5	5375	301.4	-63	30	453588	0	1900	97809 1110 1016	2

END DATA.
COMPUTE lnpop = LN (popula).
VARIABLE LABEL lnpop 'natural log of population'.

Appendix B
The Normal (z) Distribution

z	Two-tailed	One-tailed	z	Two-tailed	One-tailed	z	Two-tailed	One-tailed
0.00	1.000	0.500	1.25	0.211	0.106	1.70	0.089	0.045
0.05	0.960	0.480	1.26	0.208	0.104	1.71	0.087	0.044
0.10	0.920	0.460	1.27	0.204	0.102	1.72	0.085	0.043
0.15	0.881	0.440	1.28	0.201	0.100	1.73	0.084	0.042
0.20	0.841	0.421	1.29	0.197	0.099	1.74	0.082	0.041
0.25	0.803	0.401	1.30	0.194	0.097	1.75	0.080	0.040
0.30	0.764	0.382	1.31	0.190	0.095	1.76	0.078	0.039
0.35	0.726	0.363	1.32	0.187	0.093	1.77	0.077	0.038
0.40	0.689	0.345	1.33	0.184	0.092	1.78	0.075	0.038
0.45	0.653	0.326	1.34	0.180	0.090	1.79	0.073	0.037
0.50	0.617	0.309	1.35	0.177	0.089	1.80	0.072	0.036
0.55	0.582	0.291	1.36	0.174	0.087	1.81	0.070	0.035
0.60	0.549	0.274	1.37	0.171	0.085	1.82	0.069	0.034
0.65	0.516	0.258	1.38	0.168	0.084	1.83	0.067	0.034
0.70	0.484	0.242	1.39	0.165	0.082	1.84	0.066	0.033
0.75	0.453	0.227	1.40	0.162	0.081	1.85	0.064	0.032
0.80	0.424	0.212	1.41	0.159	0.079	1.86	0.063	0.031
0.85	0.395	0.198	1.42	0.156	0.078	1.87	0.061	0.031
0.90	0.368	0.184	1.43	0.153	0.076	1.88	0.060	0.030
0.95	0.342	0.171	1.44	0.150	0.075	1.89	0.059	0.029
1.00	0.317	0.159	1.45	0.147	0.074	1.90	0.057	0.029
1.01	0.312	0.156	1.46	0.144	0.072	1.91	0.056	0.028
1.02	0.308	0.154	1.47	0.142	0.071	1.92	0.055	0.027
1.03	0.303	0.152	1.48	0.139	0.069	1.93	0.054	0.027
1.04	0.298	0.149	1.49	0.136	0.068	1.94	0.052	0.026
1.05	0.294	0.147	1.50	0.134	0.067	1.95	0.051	0.026
1.06	0.289	0.145	1.51	0.131	0.066	1.96	0.050	0.025
1.07	0.285	0.142	1.52	0.129	0.064	1.97	0.049	0.024
1.08	0.280	0.140	1.53	0.126	0.063	1.98	0.048	0.024
1.09	0.276	0.138	1.54	0.124	0.062	1.99	0.047	0.023
1.10	0.271	0.136	1.55	0.121	0.061	2.00	0.046	0.023
1.11	0.267	0.133	1.56	0.119	0.059	2.01	0.044	0.022
1.12	0.263	0.131	1.57	0.116	0.058	2.02	0.043	0.022
1.13	0.258	0.129	1.58	0.114	0.057	2.03	0.042	0.021
1.14	0.254	0.127	1.59	0.112	0.056	2.04	0.041	0.021
1.15	0.250	0.125	1.60	0.110	0.055	2.05	0.040	0.020
1.16	0.246	0.123	1.61	0.107	0.054	2.06	0.039	0.020
1.17	0.242	0.121	1.62	0.105	0.053	2.07	0.038	0.019
1.18	0.238	0.119	1.63	0.103	0.052	2.08	0.038	0.019
1.19	0.234	0.117	1.64	0.101	0.051	2.09	0.037	0.018
1.20	0.230	0.115	1.65	0.099	0.049	2.10	0.036	0.018
1.21	0.226	0.113	1.66	0.097	0.048	2.11	0.035	0.017
1.22	0.222	0.111	1.67	0.095	0.047	2.12	0.034	0.017
1.23	0.219	0.109	1.68	0.093	0.046	2.13	0.033	0.017
1.24	0.215	0.107	1.69	0.091	0.046	2.14	0.032	0.016

z	Two-tailed	One-tailed	z	Two-tailed	One-tailed	z	Two-tailed	One-tailed
2.15	0.032	0.016	2.33	0.020	0.010	2.51	0.012	0.006
2.16	0.031	0.015	2.34	0.020	0.010	2.52	0.012	0.006
2.17	0.030	0.015	2.35	0.019	0.009	2.53	0.011	0.006
2.18	0.029	0.015	2.36	0.018	0.009	2.54	0.011	0.006
2.19	0.029	0.014	2.37	0.017	0.009	2.55	0.011	0.005
2.20	0.028	0.014	2.38	0.016	0.009	2.56	0.010	0.005
2.21	0.027	0.014	2.39	0.016	0.008	2.57	0.010	0.005
2.22	0.026	0.013	2.40	0.016	0.008	2.58	0.010	0.005
2.23	0.026	0.013	2.41	0.015	0.008	2.59	0.010	0.005
2.24	0.025	0.013	2.42	0.015	0.008	2.60	0.009	0.005
2.25	0.024	0.012	2.43	0.014	0.008	2.70	0.007	0.003
2.26	0.024	0.012	2.44	0.014	0.007	2.80	0.005	0.003
2.27	0.023	0.012	2.45	0.014	0.007	2.90	0.004	0.002
2.28	0.023	0.011	2.46	0.013	0.007	3.00	0.003	0.001
2.29	0.022	0.011	2.47	0.013	0.007	3.50	<.001	<.001
2.30	0.021	0.011	2.48	0.012	0.007	4.00	<.001	<.001
2.31	0.021	0.010	2.49	0.012	0.006	4.50	<.001	<.001
2.32	0.020	0.010	2.50	0.012	0.006	5.00	<.001	<.001

[This table was produced by the author using SYSTAT's Data Basic.]

Both the two-tailed and one-tailed probabilities are shown. Suppose we were adopting an α level of 0.05 or 5%. This is the conventional level adopted by many researchers, but there is nothing particularly special about it (except that it has become a convention). If we were doing a two-tailed test we would need to find a z either greater than 1.96 or less than -1.96 to reject the hypothesis. Only the positive values are shown in the table. The 5% is based on there being 2.5% of the area under the curve greater than $z = 1.96$ *and* 2.5% less than $z = -1.96$. For the one-tailed tests only z values in the predicted direction can be used to reject the hypothesis. In the text I describe why two-tailed tests are generally discouraged.

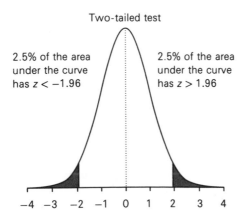

Two-tailed test

2.5% of the area under the curve has $z < -1.96$

2.5% of the area under the curve has $z > 1.96$

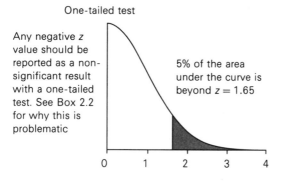

One-tailed test

Any negative *z* value should be reported as a non-significant result with a one-tailed test. See Box 2.2 for why this is problematic

5% of the area under the curve is beyond $z = 1.65$

Appendix C
Student's *t* distribution

	Two-tailed α level						One-tailed α level				
df	0.001	0.010	0.050	0.100	0.200	0.500	0.001	0.010	0.050	0.100	0.200
2	31.60	9.92	4.30	2.92	1.89	0.82	22.33	6.96	2.92	1.89	1.06
3	12.92	5.84	3.18	2.35	1.64	0.76	10.21	4.54	2.35	1.64	0.98
4	8.61	4.60	2.78	2.13	1.53	0.74	7.17	3.75	2.13	1.53	0.94
5	6.87	4.03	2.57	2.02	1.48	0.73	5.89	3.36	2.02	1.48	0.92
6	5.96	3.71	2.45	1.94	1.44	0.72	5.21	3.14	1.94	1.44	0.91
7	5.41	3.50	2.36	1.89	1.41	0.71	4.79	3.00	1.89	1.41	0.90
8	5.04	3.36	2.31	1.86	1.40	0.71	4.50	2.90	1.86	1.40	0.89
9	4.78	3.25	2.26	1.83	1.38	0.70	4.30	2.82	1.83	1.38	0.88
10	4.59	3.17	2.23	1.81	1.37	0.70	4.14	2.76	1.81	1.37	0.88
11	4.44	3.11	2.20	1.80	1.36	0.70	4.02	2.72	1.80	1.36	0.88
12	4.32	3.05	2.18	1.78	1.36	0.70	3.93	2.68	1.78	1.36	0.87
13	4.22	3.01	2.16	1.77	1.35	0.69	3.85	2.65	1.77	1.35	0.87
14	4.14	2.98	2.14	1.76	1.35	0.69	3.79	2.62	1.76	1.35	0.87
15	4.07	2.95	2.13	1.75	1.34	0.69	3.73	2.60	1.75	1.34	0.87
16	4.01	2.92	2.12	1.75	1.34	0.69	3.69	2.58	1.75	1.34	0.86
17	3.97	2.90	2.11	1.74	1.33	0.69	3.65	2.57	1.74	1.33	0.86
18	3.92	2.88	2.10	1.73	1.33	0.69	3.61	2.55	1.73	1.33	0.86
19	3.88	2.86	2.09	1.73	1.33	0.69	3.58	2.54	1.73	1.33	0.86
20	3.85	2.85	2.09	1.72	1.33	0.69	3.55	2.53	1.72	1.33	0.86
21	3.82	2.83	2.08	1.72	1.32	0.69	3.53	2.52	1.72	1.32	0.86
22	3.79	2.82	2.07	1.72	1.32	0.69	3.50	2.51	1.72	1.32	0.86
23	3.77	2.81	2.07	1.71	1.32	0.69	3.48	2.50	1.71	1.32	0.86
24	3.75	2.80	2.06	1.71	1.32	0.68	3.47	2.49	1.71	1.32	0.86
25	3.73	2.79	2.06	1.71	1.32	0.68	3.45	2.49	1.71	1.32	0.86
30	3.65	2.75	2.04	1.70	1.31	0.68	3.39	2.46	1.70	1.31	0.85
35	3.59	2.72	2.03	1.69	1.31	0.68	3.34	2.44	1.69	1.31	0.85
40	3.55	2.70	2.02	1.68	1.30	0.68	3.31	2.42	1.68	1.30	0.85
45	3.52	2.69	2.01	1.68	1.30	0.68	3.28	2.41	1.68	1.30	0.85
50	3.50	2.68	2.01	1.68	1.30	0.68	3.26	2.40	1.68	1.30	0.85
60	3.46	2.66	2.00	1.67	1.30	0.68	3.23	2.39	1.67	1.30	0.85
70	3.44	2.65	1.99	1.67	1.29	0.68	3.21	2.38	1.67	1.29	0.85
80	3.42	2.64	1.99	1.66	1.29	0.68	3.20	2.37	1.66	1.29	0.85
90	3.40	2.63	1.99	1.66	1.29	0.68	3.18	2.37	1.66	1.29	0.85
100	3.39	2.63	1.98	1.66	1.29	0.68	3.17	2.36	1.66	1.29	0.85
$\infty(z)$	3.29	2.58	1.96	1.64	1.15	0.67	3.09	2.33	1.64	1.28	0.67

[This table was produced by the author using SYSTAT's Data Basic].

Suppose you were comparing the means of two groups of people and did not know the population standard deviations. The usual test in this circumstance is the group *t* test (Chapter 4). Suppose one group had 28 people in it and the other group had 24. The number of degrees of freedom is $20 + 24 - 2$, which is 42. If you were doing a two-tailed test and were using $\alpha = 0.05$ for rejecting hypotheses then you would need a t value greater than 2.02. When the exact number of degrees of freedom is not listed, as in this case, most researchers recommend using the higher critical t value. This lessens the chances of a Type I error (rejecting a true hypothesis), but it does increase the chances of a Type II error (failing to reject a false hypothesis).

Appendix D
The F Distribution

The top value in each row is the necessary F value to reject the hypothesis at $\alpha = 0.05$. The second value is for $\alpha = 0.01$.

df	Numerator degrees of freedom												
	1	2	3	4	5	6	7	8	9	10	20	50	1000
1	161.45	199.50	215.71	224.58	230.16	233.99	236.77	238.88	240.54	241.88	248.01	251.77	254.19
	4052.18	4999.50	5403.35	5624.58	5763.65	5858.99	5928.36	5981.07	6022.47	6055.85	6208.73	6302.52	6362.68
2	18.51	19.00	19.16	19.25	19.30	19.33	19.35	19.37	19.38	19.40	19.45	19.48	19.49
	98.50	99.00	99.17	99.25	99.30	99.33	99.36	99.37	99.39	99.40	99.45	99.48	99.50
3	10.13	9.55	9.28	9.12	9.01	8.94	8.89	8.85	8.81	8.79	8.66	8.58	8.53
	34.12	30.82	29.46	28.71	28.24	27.91	27.67	27.49	27.35	27.23	26.69	26.35	26.14
4	7.71	6.94	6.59	6.39	6.26	6.16	6.09	6.04	6.00	5.96	5.80	5.70	5.63
	21.20	18.00	16.69	15.98	15.52	15.21	14.98	14.80	14.66	14.55	14.02	13.69	13.47
5	6.61	5.79	5.41	5.19	5.05	4.95	4.88	4.82	4.77	4.74	4.56	4.44	4.37
	16.26	13.27	12.06	11.39	10.97	10.67	10.46	10.29	10.16	10.05	9.55	9.24	9.03
6	5.99	5.14	4.76	4.53	4.39	4.28	4.21	4.15	4.10	4.06	3.87	3.75	3.67
	13.75	10.92	9.78	9.15	8.75	8.47	8.26	8.10	7.98	7.87	7.40	7.09	6.89
7	5.59	4.74	4.35	4.12	3.97	3.87	3.79	3.73	3.68	3.64	3.44	3.32	3.23
	12.25	9.55	8.45	7.85	7.46	7.19	6.99	6.84	6.72	6.62	6.16	5.86	5.66
8	5.32	4.46	4.07	3.84	3.69	3.58	3.50	3.44	3.39	3.35	3.15	3.02	2.93
	11.26	8.65	7.59	7.01	6.63	6.37	6.18	6.03	5.91	5.81	5.36	5.07	4.87
9	5.12	4.26	3.86	3.63	3.48	3.37	3.29	3.23	3.18	3.14	2.94	2.80	2.71
	10.56	8.02	6.99	6.42	6.06	5.80	5.61	5.47	5.35	5.26	4.81	4.52	4.32
10	4.96	4.10	3.71	3.48	3.33	3.22	3.14	3.07	3.02	2.98	2.77	2.64	2.54
	10.04	7.56	6.55	5.99	5.64	5.39	5.20	5.06	4.94	4.85	4.41	4.12	3.92
11	4.84	3.98	3.59	3.36	3.20	3.09	3.01	2.95	2.90	2.85	2.65	2.51	2.41
	9.65	7.21	6.22	5.67	5.32	5.07	4.89	4.74	4.63	4.54	4.10	3.81	3.61
12	4.75	3.89	3.49	3.26	3.11	3.00	2.91	2.85	2.80	2.75	2.54	2.40	2.30
	9.33	6.93	5.95	5.41	5.06	4.82	4.64	4.50	4.39	4.30	3.86	3.57	3.37
13	4.67	3.81	3.41	3.18	3.03	2.92	2.83	2.77	2.71	2.67	2.46	2.31	2.21
	9.07	6.70	5.74	5.21	4.86	4.62	4.44	4.30	4.19	4.10	3.66	3.38	3.18
14	4.60	3.74	3.34	3.11	2.96	2.85	2.76	2.70	2.65	2.60	2.39	2.24	2.14
	8.86	6.51	5.56	5.04	4.69	4.46	4.28	4.14	4.03	3.94	3.51	3.22	3.02
15	4.54	3.68	3.29	3.06	2.90	2.79	2.71	2.64	2.59	2.54	2.33	2.18	2.07
	8.68	6.36	5.42	4.89	4.56	4.32	4.14	4.00	3.89	3.80	3.37	3.08	2.88
16	4.49	3.63	3.24	3.01	2.85	2.74	2.66	2.59	2.54	2.49	2.28	2.12	2.02
	8.53	6.23	5.29	4.77	4.44	4.20	4.03	3.89	3.78	3.69	3.26	2.97	2.76
17	4.45	3.59	3.20	2.96	2.81	2.70	2.61	2.55	2.49	2.45	2.23	2.08	1.97
	8.40	6.11	5.18	4.67	4.34	4.10	3.93	3.79	3.68	3.59	3.16	2.87	2.66
18	4.41	3.55	3.16	2.93	2.77	2.66	2.58	2.51	2.46	2.41	2.19	2.04	1.92
	8.29	6.01	5.09	4.58	4.25	4.01	3.84	3.71	3.60	3.51	3.08	2.78	2.58
19	4.38	3.52	3.13	2.90	2.74	2.63	2.54	2.48	2.42	2.38	2.16	2.00	1.88
	8.18	5.93	5.01	4.50	4.17	3.94	3.77	3.63	3.52	3.43	3.00	2.71	2.50
20	4.35	3.49	3.10	2.87	2.71	2.60	2.51	2.45	2.39	2.35	2.12	1.97	1.85
	8.10	5.85	4.94	4.43	4.10	3.87	3.70	3.56	3.46	3.37	2.94	2.64	2.43

df	1	2	3	4	5	6	7	8	9	10	20	50	1000
				Numerator degrees of freedom									
25	4.24	3.39	2.99	2.76	2.60	2.49	2.40	2.34	2.28	2.24	2.01	1.84	1.72
	7.77	5.57	4.68	4.18	3.85	3.63	3.46	3.32	3.22	3.13	2.70	2.40	2.18
30	4.17	3.32	2.92	2.69	2.53	2.42	2.33	2.27	2.21	2.16	1.93	1.76	1.63
	7.56	5.39	4.51	4.02	3.70	3.47	3.30	3.17	3.07	2.98	2.55	2.25	2.02
40	4.08	3.23	2.84	2.61	2.45	2.34	2.25	2.18	2.12	2.08	1.84	1.66	1.52
	7.31	5.18	4.31	3.83	3.51	3.29	3.12	2.99	2.89	2.80	2.37	2.06	1.82
50	4.03	3.18	2.79	2.56	2.40	2.29	2.20	2.13	2.07	2.03	1.78	1.60	1.45
	7.17	5.06	4.20	3.72	3.41	3.19	3.02	2.89	2.78	2.70	2.27	1.95	1.70
75	3.97	3.12	2.73	2.49	2.34	2.22	2.13	2.06	2.01	1.96	1.71	1.52	1.35
	6.99	4.90	4.05	3.58	3.27	3.05	2.89	2.76	2.65	2.57	2.13	1.81	1.53
100	3.94	3.09	2.70	2.46	2.31	2.19	2.10	2.03	1.97	1.93	1.68	1.48	1.30
	6.90	4.82	3.98	3.51	3.21	2.99	2.82	2.69	2.59	2.50	2.07	1.74	1.45
1000	3.85	3.00	2.61	2.38	2.22	2.11	2.02	1.95	1.89	1.84	1.58	1.36	1.11
	6.66	4.63	3.80	3.34	3.04	2.82	2.66	2.53	2.43	2.34	1.90	1.54	1.16

To find whether an F value is significant you need to know both the degrees of freedom of the numerator and the degrees of freedom of the denominator. Usually these are the degrees of freedom of the model and of the residuals, respectively, but for certain hypotheses this need not be the case. Suppose for 45 subjects that we had divided them into five groups. Our model would therefore have four degrees of freedom (four dummy variables to represent the five values). The residuals would have 40 degrees of freedom. The critical values are 2.61 and 3.83 for $\alpha = 0.05$ and $\alpha = 0.01$, respectively.

Appendix E
The χ^2 Distribution

	α level				α level		
df	0.10	0.05	0.01	df	0.10	0.05	0.01
1	2.71	3.84	6.63	23	32.01	35.17	41.64
2	4.61	5.99	9.21	24	33.20	36.42	42.98
3	6.25	7.81	11.34	25	34.38	37.65	44.31
4	7.78	9.49	13.28	30	40.26	43.77	50.89
5	9.24	11.07	15.09	35	46.06	49.80	57.34
6	10.64	12.59	16.81	40	51.81	55.76	63.69
7	12.02	14.07	18.48	45	57.51	61.66	69.96
8	13.36	15.51	20.09	50	63.17	67.50	76.15
9	14.68	16.92	21.67	60	74.40	79.08	88.38
10	15.99	18.31	23.21	70	85.53	90.53	100.43
11	17.28	19.68	24.72	80	96.58	101.88	112.33
12	18.55	21.03	26.22	90	107.51	113.15	124.12
13	19.81	22.36	27.69	100	118.50	124.34	135.81
14	21.06	23.68	29.14	200	226.02	233.99	249.45
15	22.31	25.00	30.58	300	331.79	341.39	359.91
16	23.54	26.30	32.00	400	436.65	447.63	468.73
17	24.77	27.59	33.41	500	540.93	553.13	576.50
18	25.99	28.87	34.81	600	644.80	658.09	683.52
19	27.20	30.14	36.19	700	748.36	762.66	789.98
20	28.41	31.41	37.57	800	851.67	866.91	895.99
21	29.62	32.67	38.93	900	954.78	970.90	1001.63
22	30.81	33.92	40.29	1000	1057.72	1074.68	1106.97

[This table was produced by the author using SYSTAT's Data Basic.]

All probabilities in this table refer to the extreme tail (see figure). Suppose you were analysing some categorical data and that there were five degrees of freedom in the residuals. This might happen if you were looking to see if there was an association in a 2 × 5 contingency table (one variable has two possible values, the other five). If you were using the $\alpha = 0.05$ level then you would need a χ^2 value of 11.07. The area beyond this point on the graph is 5% of the total area under the curve. Only 5% of the time would you expect a value this high (or higher) if there is no association in the population (providing proper sampling and procedures are used).

χ^2 distribution with five degrees of freedom

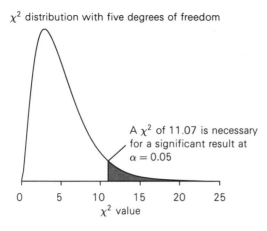

A χ^2 of 11.07 is necessary
for a significant result at
$\alpha = 0.05$

χ^2 value

Index

Compiled by Caroline Eley